GERMANY

LUXEMBOURG

BATTLE OF THE BULGE

BATTLE OF THE BULGE

STEVEN J. ZALOGA

First published in Great Britain in 2010 by Osprey Publishing,
Midland House, West Way, Botley, Oxford OX2 0PH, United Kingdom.
44-02 23rd St, Suite 219, Long Island City, NY 11101, USA.

Email: info@ospreypublishing.com

Previously published as CAM 115, *The Battle of the Ardennes (1)* and CAM 145,
The Battle of the Bulge (2) by Steven Zaloga.

A CIP catalog record for this book is available from the British Library.

ISBN: 978 1 84908 165 8

Page layout by Myriam Bell Design, France
Battlescene artwork by Howard Gerrard and Peter Dennis
Index by Alison Worthington
Typeset in Sabon and Myriad Pro
Originated by PPS Grasmere Ltd
Printed in China through Worldprint

10 11 12 13 14   10 9 8 7 6 5 4 3 2 1

Front Cover: A patrol of armored infantry of the 2nd Armored Division passes a burned out
Panther of the 9th Panzer Division in Immendorf on November 16, 1945 at the start of
Operation *Queen*. (NARA)
Back Cover: American infantrymen of 290th Regiment fight in fresh snowfall near Amonines,
Belgium on 4 January, 1945. (Topfoto)

For a catalog of all books published by Osprey please contact:

NORTH AMERICA
Osprey Direct, c/o Random House Distribution Center
400 Hahn Road, Westminster, MD 21157, USA
E-mail: uscustomerservice@ospreypublishing.com

ALL OTHER REGIONS
Osprey Direct, The Book Service Ltd., Distribution Centre,
Colchester Road, Frating Green, Colchester, Essex, CO7 7DW
E-mail: customerservice@ospreypublishing.com

Osprey Publishing is supporting the Woodland Trust, the UK's leading
woodland conservation charity, by funding the dedication of trees.

www.ospreypublishing.com

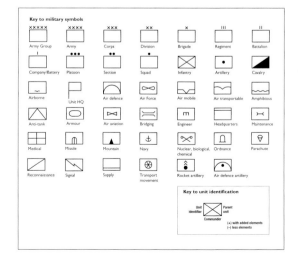

Key to military symbols

CONTENTS

INTRODUCTION: ORIGINS OF THE CAMPAIGN

On December 16, 1945, the Wehrmacht launched an offensive in the Ardennes region of Belgium, catching the First US Army by surprise. The ensuing "Battle of the Bulge" was the decisive campaign in western Europe during World War II and sealed the fate of the Wehrmacht in the west.

The aim of the German attack was to punch through the overextended American defenses in the Ardennes and race to Antwerp. Not only would the capture of this vital port decisively impair Allied operations, but Hitler hoped that it might precipitate a catastrophic rout of Allied forces. It might cut off Montgomery's 21st Army Group and force another Dunkirk-style evacuation of the British Army from the Continent. By any rational calculation, the operation had no chance of success. The badly weakened Wehrmacht was incapable of carrying out such an ambitious scheme. But Germany's military prospects were so dire that Hitler was willing to take a last, desperate gamble. The attack failed in the first two weeks, but it took another month for the US Army to push the Wehrmacht back to its original starting positions.

The center of gravity of the German attack was heavily weighted towards its right wing, the attack by Sepp Dietrich's 6th Panzer Army towards the Meuse River near Liège. This attack contained the best-equipped Waffen-SS Panzer divisions and was the shortest and best route to accomplish the mission. On its right flank, the attack by the 12th SS-Panzer Division was stymied by determined US opposition in the villages of Krinkelt-Rocherath and Dom Bütgenbach and failed to secure a penetration of American lines. The neighboring 1st SS-Panzer Division succeeded in pushing through a weak spot in American lines near the Losheim Gap and reached as far as La Gleize before being surrounded. In the process, its spearhead batttlegroup perpetrated the Malmédy massacre against captured US prisoners, an incident that only served to stiffen US morale. The failure of the Panzer spearheads of the 6th Panzer Army doomed the Ardennes offensive since the best routes to Antwerp were effectively shut tight by the US Army's defense.

While this assault failed to win a breakthrough, its smaller neighbor, Manteuffel's 5th Panzer Army, overran the green 106th Division, finally opening up a gap in the American lines. The Panzer formations in this army raced forward to the intermediate objective, the Meuse River, encircling the critical road junction at Bastogne in the process. During the second week of the fighting, Hitler attempted to redeem his failing offensive by exploiting the success of the 5th Panzer Army. Panzer divisions formerly assigned to 6th Panzer Army were shifted towards the rupture in the center. Although the Panzer spearheads managed to penetrate deep behind the American lines and reach the Meuse River, precious time had been lost and American armored reinforcements arrived in the days around Christmas. "Lightning Joe" Collins' VII Corps rushed two heavy armored divisions from the north which crashed into the onrushing Panzer divisions in a series of violent tank battles around Christmas in the snow-covered fields north of Bastogne. From the south, Patton's Third Army sent two corps on a headlong dash, with the spearheads entering the besieged city of Bastogne a day after Christmas. In the final days of December, the Panzer divisions were decimated and the attack decisively halted. By January 3, 1945, even Hitler acknowledged that the offensive had failed. With the onset of harsh winter weather, it would take three weeks of hard fighting to finally erase the bulge.

CHRONOLOGY

September 1944	Hitler first mentions plans for Ardennes offensive.
October 11	Jodl submits first draft of Ardennes plan, codenamed *Wacht am Rhein* (Watch on the Rhine), to Hitler. The operation is later renamed *Herbstnebel* (Autumn Mist).
October 22	Senior German commanders are briefed on the Ardennes plan.
Early November	First German units begin moving into the Eifel for the offensive.
Mid-November	US 99th Division arrives in Ardennes, takes over Monschau sector.
December 9–10	US Army G-2 intelligence report sees no immediate threat of German offensive operations.
December 10	US Army begins another offensive against Roer dams with first objectives near Wahlerscheid.
December 11	US 106th Division arrives near St. Vith and takes over Schnee Eifel defense from 2nd Infantry Division.
December 16	
0400hrs:	Infantry in 5th Panzer Army sector begins infiltration past Schnee Eifel over Our River.
0530hrs:	Operation *Herbstnebel* (Autumn Mist) begins with opening barrages against forward US positions in Ardennes.
0600hrs:	German preparatory artillery ends.
0600–0700hrs:	German infantry begins advancing.

Afternoon:	Major General Robertson begins moving 2nd Infantry Division units back towards Krinkelt to reinforce flank. 3rd Fallschirmjäger Division takes Lanzerath; Krewinkel–Losheim Gap open.
Afternoon–evening:	Major General Middleton commits CCB/9th Armored Division to 106th Division; Bradley orders 10th Armored Division to Bastogne; allots 7th Armored Division to VIII Corps. Eisenhower agrees to shift XVIII Airborne Corps to Ardennes.
Evening:	After 277th Volksgrenadier Division fails to penetrate Krinkelt woods, Gruppenführer Hermann Preiss orders 12th SS-Panzer Division "Hitlerjugend" to commit armor to make breakthrough.
December 17	110th Infantry Regiment HQ overwhelmed in Clerf; gap in American lines is open after nightfall.
0330hrs:	Kampfgruppe Peiper begins drive at Buchholz.
0900hrs:	106th Division encircled as 18th Volksgrenadier Division reaches Schönberg.
1500hrs:	12th Volksgrenadier Division finally takes Losheimergraben. Massacre of US POWs by Kampfgruppe Peiper at Baugnez crossroads.
1800hrs:	Kampfgruppe Peiper halts on approaches to Stavelot.
Midnight:	Middleton deploys CCR, 9th Armored Division, to block approaches to Bastogne. 12th Volksgrenadier Division takes Mürringen.
December 18	
0700hrs:	Kampfgruppe Peiper begins attack on Stavelot.
1000hrs:	Kampfgruppe Peiper passes through Stavelot by this time.
1200hrs:	Bridges blown at Trois Ponts, forcing Kampfgruppe Peiper to La Gleize.
Afternoon:	Kampfgruppe Peiper reaches La Gleize, probes sent west to find route to Werbomont.
Evening:	12th SS-Panzer Division "Hitlerjugend" fails to take Krinkelt-Rocherath, Gruppenführer Preiss orders division to move west instead. Major General Robertson decides to pull back from Krinkelt-Rocherath to Elsenborn Ridge.
Nightfall:	First elements of 101st Airborne arrive in Bastogne.

December 19	Eisenhower meets with senior US commanders in Paris to plan further responses to German attack.
0230hrs:	First major attack by 12th SS-Panzer Division "Hitlerjugend" against 1st Infantry Division at Dom Bütgenbach crossroads.
0800hrs:	First probes by German reconnaissance units into US defenses on outskirts of Bastogne.
1200hrs:	US troops retake control of Stavelot, cutting off Kampfgruppe Peiper.
Afternoon:	CCB/7th Armored Division begins deploying near St. Vith.
Nightfall:	US defenses in Wiltz overwhelmed by end of day; another road to Bastogne is open.
December 20	Eisenhower shifts control of US First and Ninth Army units, except for Middleton's VIII Corps, from Bradley's 12th Army Group to Montgomery's 21st Army Group.
Noon:	Model redeploys the 2nd SS-Panzer Corps from the failed 6th Panzer Army attack to the center.
December 21	12th SS-Panzer Division "Hitlerjugend" abandons attacks on Dom Bütgenbach.
Morning:	III Corps of Patton's Third Army begins attack to relieve Bastogne.
Afternoon:	116th Panzer Division reaches Hotton but cannot secure town. Battles for the road junctions on the Tailles plateau begin.
By evening:	12th SS-Panzer Division "Hitlerjugend" abandons attacks on Dom Bütgenbach.
December 22	Montgomery takes command of US units in northern shoulder of the Ardennes.
1130hrs:	German emissaries demand Bastogne's surrender; General McAuliffe replies "Nuts."
0800hrs:	Obersturmbannführer Skorzeny's 150th Panzer Brigade launches attack on Malmédy but fails.
Evening:	Bastogne is surrounded when Panzer Lehr Division begins moving towards the Ourthe River.
Night December 22/23:	High-pressure front moves into Ardennes bringing clear skies and freezing temperatures.

December 23

0600hrs: US forces begin withdrawal from St. Vith salient.

Late morning: 2nd SS-Panzer Corps begins moving towards Tailles plateau with 2nd SS-Panzer Division in the lead.

Evening: 2nd Panzer Division reports it has reached within 6 miles (9km) of Meuse River near Dinant.

Late evening: 2nd SS-Panzer Division "Das Reich" overruns US defenses and seizes Manhay road junction.

December 24, 0200hrs: Kampfgruppe Peiper begins escape from La Gleize.

December 25   Clear weather permits intense Allied air activity.

Morning: US 2nd Armored Division begins surrounding and destroying advance guard of the 2nd Panzer Division on the approaches to Dinant.

December 26

Late afternoon: Task force from 4th Armored Division punches through German defenses, beginning the relief of Bastogne.

December 27

Dawn: 2nd SS-Panzer Division pushed out of Grandmenil and Manhay; 6th Panzer Army ordered over to the defensive.

December 30   Germans and Americans plan attacks in Bastogne area; German attacks fail to make headway.

January 1, 0930hrs: Operation *Bodenplatte* is launched.

January 4   Manteuffel attempts a final attack on Bastogne that fails; last major German attack of the Ardennes campaign. US First Army begins attack towards Houfallize to meet up with Patton's Third Army.

January 16   US First Army and US Third Army link up at Houfallize.

January 28   The last of the territory lost to the German attack is retaken by US troops.

THE STRATEGIC SITUATION

SETTING THE STAGE: THE ALLIES' STRATEGIC FRUSTRATIONS IN SEPTEMBER

The Ardennes offensive was shaped by the autumn campaigns along the German frontier. Following the defeat of Army Group B in Normandy, the retreating German units were decimated in a series of encirclement operations starting with the Roncey pocket and Falaise pocket in Normandy during July and early August 1944, the deeper encirclement on the Seine in late August, and the Mons pocket in Belgium in early September. The disasters of the late summer were called "the Void" by German commanders. Complete annihilation of the German Army in the west was avoided by Allied logistical problems.

The spectacular Allied advances in the latter half of August and early September far outstripped their logistical abilities. Allied pre-D-Day planning had not anticipated such a rapid advance, and the devastation of the French railroad network further constrained Allied supply efforts. The pre-invasion planning had anticipated that the Allies would reach the Belgian border shortly before Christmas 1944 and the German border north of Aachen in May 1945; these objectives had already been reached. In September 1944, the Allies in northwest Europe had two potential operational opportunities, a thrust towards the lower Rhine by Montgomery's 21st Army Group or a thrust towards Frankfurt and the Saar by Patton's Third Army. Eisenhower chose Montgomery's bold plan for a combined airborne and ground assault to seize the lower Rhine bridge at Arnhem. This was seen as a means to gain quick access to Germany's

Opposite:
American troops advancing through the ruins of Nijmegen after failure of Operation *Market Garden*, September 29, 1944. This failure meant the Allied troops were overextended across a wide front. (Getty Images)

vital Ruhr industrial area, a major strategic objective of the campaign, which might bring a speedy conclusion to the war. The operational planning for Operation *Market Garden* presumed that the chaos of early September would continue and that the Wehrmacht in the Netherlands would remain ineffective; instead the German Army rallied and displayed its usual defensive vigor. No foothold on the Rhine was gained and the British and Canadian forces ended up holding an extended corridor into the Netherlands.

The failure of Operation *Market Garden* had two consequences for the later Ardennes campaign. On the one hand, it distorted the operational direction of the Allied armies to a more northerly avenue than originally planned, placing Montgomery's Anglo-Canadian forces further into the Netherlands and stretching Bradley's 12th Army Group along a wider front. During planning sessions in late September 1944, Eisenhower warned that this extension might lead to "a nasty little 'Kasserine' if the enemy chooses at any point to concentrate a bit of strength." Kasserine was a reference to the battle in Tunisia in February 1943 where a US Army corps received a bloody nose after it was badly overextended. In the event, Eisenhower was not overly worried about this threat due to the German weaknesses in forces and supplies in September 1944. When the Germans failed to take advantage of the Allied overextension in October and November, this threat began to fade from the minds of Allied senior planners.

The more substantial problem caused by Operation *Market Garden* was that it distracted Montgomery's forces from securing the vital port of Antwerp, one of the main blunders of the late summer campaign. Operations along the German frontier needed a substantial port nearer than the available ports at Cherbourg, Le Havre, and Marseilles. Although the British Army had captured Antwerp's port intact in September, they had not pursued the German Army up the Scheldt estuary. The port was useless until German forces could be routed from the Scheldt defenses. Canadian and

STRATEGIC SITUATION: THE GERMAN PLAN

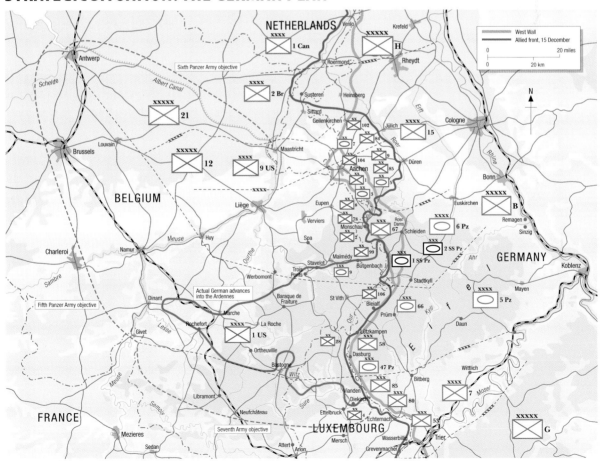

Among the frustrations of the autumn 1944 campaign was Operation *Queen*, an attack by the US 12th Army Group starting on November 16, 1944 that was intended to break through the German border area and reach the Roer River. The operation ended in stalemate. In this photograph, a patrol of armored infantry of the 2nd Armored Division passes a burned out Panther of the 9th Panzer Division in Immendorf on November 16 at the start of Operation *Queen*. (NARA)

British forces spent most of October and November on this difficult task, and in the meantime the Allied armies were constrained in their offensive operations until the supply situation was restored. Antwerp became a major strategic objective for Hitler since the Allied 1945 offensives into Germany depended on the port for their logistical lifeblood.

Logistical constraints during October and November 1944 presented Eisenhower with two principal options. On the one hand, the three army groups under his command could wait out the autumn and build up their forces for an offensive into Germany in the early spring of 1945 as originally planned. The downside of this option was that it would permit the Germans to reinforce their defenses along the German frontier and rebuild their shattered army. The second option was to continue to conduct military operations along the German frontier, even if they had little hope of a decisive outcome, to prevent a stabilization of German defenses and to weaken the crippled German Army through attrition. Eisenhower chose the second option.

With the basic strategic posture selected, the actual conduct of the autumn campaign came under intense debate. Montgomery continued to advocate a narrow front scheme on the northern flank using his 21st Army Group and elements of Bradley's 12th Army Group, primarily the Ninth US Army and First US Army which were mostly north of the Ardennes. This would leave Patton's Third US Army in Lorraine and Devers' Franco-American 6th Army Group in Alsace largely inactive. Montgomery's option was most strongly resisted by Bradley who viewed it as simply another attempt by Montgomery to favor the British Army with resources regardless of the actual merits of the operation. The Montgomery option was unlikely for several reasons. The British 21st Army Group's performance in the ground phase of Operation *Market Garden* had not inspired American confidence in its ability to conduct such a thrust, and led to considerable skepticism over whether it would be the ideal vehicle for such an operation rather than another Allied force such as Patton's Third Army. By the autumn of 1944, the British Army in North West Europe (NWE) was a wasting asset,

No battle better symbolized the grim attritional battles of the autumn of 1944 than the fighting in the Hürtgen forest. Here, a squad from Co. E, 2/110th Infantry, 28th Division begins moving into the "Death Factory" on the opening day of the attack, November 2, 1944. (NARA)

barely able to keep its order-of-battle at current levels. In contrast, the US Army in the European Theater of Operations (ETO) was substantially larger and would continue to grow through 1945 as more and more divisions arrived. Since 1943 and early 1944, the center of gravity of Allied decision-making had shifted from London to Washington.

However, the issue was not British versus American narrow thrusts, since Eisenhower did not favor the narrow thrust option regardless of which army conducted the campaign. The problem with a narrow thrust option was that it would allow the Wehrmacht to concentrate its diminished resources against a small fraction of Allied ground power. Eisenhower favored a broad front approach since it would place the greatest stress on the Wehrmacht and would force its overextension. Under such circumstances, the Wehrmacht might suffer local defeats that could be exploited by the greater Allied mobility. Eisenhower viewed the broad front strategy as the best use of the Allied advantages in manpower, mobility, and firepower.

As a result of this decision, all three Allied army groups had a demanding scheme of operations for October–November 1944. Montgomery's Anglo-Canadian 21st Army Group in the Netherlands was primarily focused on clearing the Scheldt estuary in Holland to open up Antwerp. Operations towards the Rhineland began, but were circumscribed by the commitment of forces in the Scheldt campaign. Bradley's 12th Army Group had multiple operational directions due to geography. The primary focus of the First US Army was the penetration of the Siegfried Line beyond Aachen. This campaign proved enormously frustrating and by November had become bogged down on its right flank in the Hürtgen forest and on its left flank in the industrialized German towns in the Stolberg corridor. The Siegfried Line campaign was largely distinct from Patton's Third Army campaigns due to the geographic interruption posed by the Ardennes region of Belgium. This hilly and forested area was not viewed as particularly suitable for offensive operations, and so was lightly screened but not otherwise the focus of military operations. Patton's Third Army to the south of the Ardennes in Lorraine was directed to push through one of the traditional invasion routes into Germany via Nancy. Since it was a traditional invasion route, Lorraine had been heavily fortified over the years by both France and Germany with the Metz fortified area being a particularly difficult objective.

THE STRATEGIC SITUATION   19

The southern wing of the Allied advance was Devers' 6th Army Group in Alsace with the Seventh US Army assigned the forbidding task of reaching the Alsatian plains along the Rhine by overcoming the High Vosges mountains, a military operation never accomplished in modern times. The First French Army was ordered to gain access to the Rhine by penetrating the Belfort Gap, another heavily fortified zone.

The autumn campaign had its share of disappointments and successes. The weather was a major hindrance to the Allied operations along the German frontier as it was the wettest and rainiest in several decades. The rain constrained one of the main Allied advantages, its tactical air power. In addition, the wet ground conditions hampered mobile operations since the soggy ground forced Allied mechanized units to use roads, creating a front "one tank wide" in many operations which facilitated German defenses. Montgomery's 21st Army Group managed to clear the Scheldt estuary and the first inbound convoy arrived in Antwerp on November 28. Although the First US Army had managed to push through the Siegfried Line around Aachen, it was held up in the Hürtgen forest until early December, and had not yet captured the dams controlling the Roer River.

Patton's Third Army spent much of November engaged in bitter fighting in the Metz fortified zone in Lorraine. Fort Jeanne d'Arc did not surrender until December 13, 1944, as seen here with its garrison being led away. (NARA)

Patton's Third Army had finally overcome the Metz fortifications in mid-November, and had proceeded towards the Saar. Devers' 6th Army Group had enjoyed considerable success, with the Seventh US Army penetrating the High Vosges in November and taking the Saverne Gap and some of the Low Vosges in December. The neighboring First French Army penetrated the Belfort Gap, and much of the German 19th Army was trapped in the Colmar pocket between the French and American forces.

SETTING THE STAGE: GERMANY ON THE BRINK OF DEFEAT

The stunning Wehrmacht losses in the summer of 1944 had put Germany on the brink of defeat. In the east, the Red Army had crushed Army Group Center during Operation *Bagration* in June 1944 and followed this victory with a rampage into central Europe, pushing into the Reich in East Prussia and to Germany's eastern border via Poland. As catastrophic as these defeats may have been, the loss of Romania in August signaled the death knell of the Wehrmacht. Modern war demands plentiful supplies of fuel, and the loss of Romania's oil production as well as smaller oil fields in Polish/Ukrainian Galicia meant that the Wehrmacht would inevitably grind to a halt when it ran out of gasoline. Germany's synthetic fuel plants had been heavily

The Red Army's summer offensive of 1944 crushed Army Group Center and propelled Soviet forces into Poland and East Prussia. The Soviet attacks on the central front were halted by late summer when Stalin decided to exploit the political opportunities of an advance into the Balkans. Seen here are some of the summer casualties, a pair of StuG III assault guns. (Author)

damaged by the May 1944 US Army Air Force (USAAF) bombing raids and could not make up for the Romanian loss.

Germany received a modest respite from the Allied onslaught in the early fall when the Red Army deliberately shifted its center of gravity away from Berlin and into the Balkans. Stalin decided to harvest his political spoils when the opportunity presented itself, and so the Red Army temporarily halted its advance on Berlin until early 1945 and turned its attention to Bulgaria, Hungary, and Yugoslavia through the autumn and early winter of 1944.

The situation in the west was grim. Both western army groups, Army Group B in Normandy and Army Group G in central and southern France, had been decisively routed in August 1944 and their units decimated. The larger of the two forces, Rundstedt's Army Group B, had been decisively defeated in Normandy; it was the severity of this devastation that had led German commanders to call the last weeks of August and early September "the Void." The situation had been no better in southern and central France

The Wehrmacht's Army Group B was decimated in a series of encirclement battles in the summer of 1944 of which the most famous was the Falaise pocket. Seen here is a wrecked PzKpfw IV and half-track in the ruins of Chambois near the spot where Canadian, Polish, and American units joined to finally seal off the pocket. (NARA)

The first of the encirclement battles in Normandy in the summer of 1944 occurred in the wake of Operation *Cobra* in late July when the First US Army finally broke out of the hedgerow country near St Lô. In the process, a number of German units were trapped; these PzJg 38(t) Ausf. M Marder tank destroyers of the 2nd SS-Panzerjäger Battalion were among the elements of the 2nd SS-Panzer Division trapped in the Roncey pocket in late July 1944. (NARA)

after the Operation *Dragoon* amphibious landings on the Mediterranean coast. Army Group G had been badly weakened to reinforce the Normandy front, and proved completely unable to resist the onrush of American and French divisions. In a pell-mell retreat up the Rhone valley, Army Group G lost half of its forces before Devers' 6th Army Group ended the chase on the gates to Alsace in mid-September. As in Belgium, the advance would have continued but for the Allied fuel and supply problems.

The scale of the disaster can be seen from German Army casualty figures; losses in 1944 were almost double those of 1943, 2.9 million casualties versus 1.5 million. Casualties in 1944 alone amounted to 40 percent of total German casualties since the start of the war.

German equipment losses present much the same picture. German armored vehicle losses on the Russian front up to the end of 1943 had totaled 18,800; losses in 1944 were 14,537 on the Russian front plus a further 4,513 in western Europe for a total of 19,050. In other words, German armored vehicle losses in 1944 alone exceeded the entire previous four years of war.

GERMAN FIELD ARMY CASUALTIES, 1944

	Dead	Wounded	Missing	Sub-total
Russian front	241,700	1,050,757	687,096	1,979,553
Polar front	5,173	1,954	4,825	11,952
Balkans	11,103	34,445	13,124	58,672
Western front	57,125	188,382	388,947	634,454
Italy	30,492	106,420	79,841	216,753
Total	*345,593*	*1,381,958*	*1,173,833*	*2,901,384*

In addition to its substantial manpower and equipment losses in the summer of 1944, the Wehrmacht lost its qualitative edge over the Allied armies. The Wehrmacht had frequently been able to fight and win when outnumbered in past campaigns, but the 1944 battles were so destructive that Germany's tactical excellence was forfeited. Fighting power depended on the quality of its combat leadership, especially small unit officers and NCOs. The summer 1944 losses completely exhausted this most precious resource, and the Wehrmacht did not have the time to recreate this fighting force in the autumn of 1944.

The breathing space provided by the lull in Anglo-American attacks in late September and early October, and by the Red Army's swing towards the Balkans, gave the Wehrmacht a short respite to rebuild. The fuel crisis caused by the loss of Romania provided an unexpected though short-lived bonus. The lack of fuel led to a profound curtailment of normal Wehrmacht activities, but it struck the Luftwaffe and Kriegsmarine most strongly. The Kriegsmarine was obliged to halt virtually all of its naval operations with the exception of some selected U-boat operations. The Luftwaffe curtailed much of its training, and was forced to retire large segments of its combat squadrons except for fighter units committed to the defense of the Reich. This substantial demobilization of the Kriegsmarine and Luftwaffe created a large pool of manpower that was exploited to rebuild the decimated army divisions.

German army divisions seldom were totally destroyed unless completely surrounded. Usually it was only the close-combat troops such as the infantry, Panzer, and pioneer forces that were lost. In many cases, the organizational skeleton of the division including the headquarters, supply elements, signals troops, and field artillery would escape total annihilation and leave a "shadow division" that could be rebuilt. This process was repeated many times in the summer of 1944. Divisions that were rendered completely ineffective in combat would be resurrected and reappear on the front a few months later. The reconstructed divisions in late 1944 seldom had the combat effectiveness of the adequately trained divisions in early 1944, but they were better than nothing.

The equipment situation was bad but not hopeless. German military industrial production in many key categories of weapons such as tanks actually increased in 1944. Some of this was due to diversions from the civilian economy. However, much of it was made possible by diversions from other sectors of the military industries which would eventually have pernicious consequences for Wehrmacht combat performance. For example, German tank production reached new peaks in 1944 by diverting military truck production as well as the production of spare parts for tanks. On paper, the industry could boast of more new tanks. But in the field, fewer trucks meant that the tanks could not be supplied with fuel and parts, and the severe cutback in the production of spare parts meant that once tanks broke down, they could not be repaired. The increase in German weapons production was a bit of an illusion and the production numbers did not translate into increased combat power.

To add to these woes, the focus of Allied air attacks shifted in the autumn of 1944 to include elements of the military industries that had previously escaped bombing. During Operation *Pointblank* from the autumn of 1943 to the early summer of 1944, USAAF heavy bombers had concentrated on Luftwaffe fighter factories. Many other prime weapons plants were spared for the time being. This changed in the summer and autumn of 1944 as bomber missions began to strike a broader range of targets. The German tank industry is a good example of the increasing German predicament.

The German tank industry had been spared from major strategic bomber attacks through 1943. Due to a focus on German fighter plants, the Allies attempted to locate a bottle-neck in German tank production rather than attack each tank plant individually. Recognizing that Panthers and Tigers were powered by Maybach engines, the Royal Air Force (RAF) struck this plant on the night of April 27/28, 1944, which essentially stopped production for five months through September 1944. This would have halted

Panther production but for armament minister Albert Speer's prescient decision to disperse production, and the second source, the Auto-Union plant at Siegmar, came on-line in May 1944, narrowly averting a disaster in the Panzer industry. In August 1944, the RAF and USAAF began a systematic air campaign against the German tank and vehicle industry. The main Panther tank plant, MAN at Nuremberg, was hit hard on September 10, 1944, which cost the Wehrmacht the equivalent of over four months' production or about 645 tanks. Daimler-Benz was hit as well, but the second most important plant, the MNH (Maschinenfabrik Niedersachsen) in Hanover, was ignored until March 1945. The Henschel plant in Kassel suffered some of the most extensive damage, and planned production of 940 Kingtiger tanks in the September 1944–March 1945 period was substantially curbed to only 234 tanks, for a production loss of 706 tanks. The Allies were unhappy with the results of the tank plant raids and they petered out in October, only to be resumed in the wake of the Battle of the Bulge.

A post-war assessment concluded that the short-lived bombing campaign against the tank industry cost the Wehrmacht 2,250 tanks and assault guns in the latter half of 1944. This of course had an immediate effect on re-equipping units earmarked for the Ardennes offensive which had priority for new equipment. While the raids may not have had the immediate results expected by Allied bomber chiefs, they had insidious effects on the Panzer force. Speer was able to keep tank production at adequate levels through the end of 1944 by shifting plant resources away from other products such as trucks and focusing on tanks. For example, truck production at the Henschel plant in Kassel completely ended in September 1943 to provide resources to tank production. More critically, the Panther plants dramatically cut production of spares parts, which in 1943 had constituted as much as 25 to 30 percent of the tank contracts. By the summer of 1944, only about 15 percent of Maybach engines were put aside as spares, and by the autumn of 1944, this had been halved again to only about 8 percent. This hidden cost of the air campaign would have dire consequences for tank regiments during the Battle of the Bulge due to the continuing unreliability of some Panzers and the growing decline in spare parts. Panzers that suffered mechanical breakdowns in the field were often too difficult to repair in field conditions and so had to be abandoned.

The Allied strategic bombing campaign in the late summer and early autumn of 1944 was the first serious effort to cripple the Panzer industry. It was halted in October 1944 due to other priorities, but resumed after the Ardennes campaign. The last Panther plant, the MNH plant in Hanover, was hit in early 1945 but its production was more seriously impeded by the general collapse of German industry brought about by cut-offs of fuel and the collapse of the rail network under bombing attack. (NARA)

When replacement Panther tanks were sent to the Ardennes in December 1944 they were cannibalized for parts rather than being issued intact in order to repair the numerous broken-down Panthers already with front-line units. Another source of loss was deliberate sabotage of tanks by the disaffected slave labor force; for example there is some evidence from recent museum restorations of deliberate sabotage of Panther fuel and lubrication lines. The Allied bombing attacks not only interfered with production, they also badly disrupted delivery from the factory to the troops in the field. For example, production of the 88mm PaK 43 antitank gun increased in mid-1944, but acceptances by the army fell by 55 percent in October 1944 simply because the guns couldn't be shipped from the plant.

The most pernicious effect of the autumn 1944 fuel crisis was the collapse in German training. Pilot training suffered the most, but it also had a detrimental effect on other branches of the Wehrmacht including the Panzer force. There was not enough fuel to train Panzer drivers adequately, and small unit training came to an abrupt end. While a certain amount of book training could be conducted, modern combat requires a high level of proficiency in the use and maintenance of sophisticated weapons that needs hands-on experience. The fuel shortage was a major contributor to the rapid decline in German combat effectiveness in late 1944.

Allied bombing attacks progressively crippled German industry in the final months of 1944. The peak of German industrial production was July 1944 and it declined continually afterwards. Attacks on railroad centers and industrial canals compromised the supply of raw materials. Coal was the lifeblood of the German war industries as gasoline was the lifeblood of the Wehrmacht. About 90 percent of Germany's energy resources came from coal. It took 6 tons (5.5 tonnes) of coal to smelt a ton of iron; 115 tons (105 tonnes) of coal were needed to produce a tank. In October 1944, the Allied strategic bomber force unleashed Operation *Hurricane I*, a focused air campaign to paralyze the Ruhr industrial basin by cutting its railways and waterways, strangling its supplies of materials from the regions outside, and preventing the shipment of coal from the Ruhr. The Rhine River was cut as a supply route on October 14, 1944, when the Cologne bridge collapsed during a bombing attack; ironically it wasn't the Allied bombs that downed the bridge, but an accidental detonation of bridge demolition charges. Albert Speer reported to Hitler on November 11, 1944 that the Ruhr had been effectively sealed off from the Reich, leading to shortages both of hard coal from the Ruhr and of steel supply to the Ruhr. The paralysis of the rail and canal lines and the disruption of coal supplies were the death knell of German armament production, which would catastrophically collapse in early 1945.

From a strategic perspective, Germany's prospects in the autumn of 1944 looked grim: the enemy on Germany's doorstep; the armed forces gravely weakened and unlikely to recover; the military industries collapsing under bombing attack. Unfortunately for Germany, strategic decision-making had been completely taken over by Hitler, and he was in no mood for any talk of surrender or compromise. Hitler and other members of Germany's Great War generation had had their strategic perspective profoundly warped by one of the great myths of World War I, that Germany's defeat had been a "stab in the back" by spineless politicians and that the army had not been defeated in the field. This myth had been one of the propelling forces of the early Nazi movement. For Hitler, it was inconceivable that Germany would accept unconditional surrender while there was a chance that victory could be wrested from the jaws of defeat. Hitler grasped at illusive miracles to justify the last-ditch defense of the Reich. The most preposterous was that new weapons would turn the tide.

Hitler had an amateur's appreciation of weapons technology and grossly exaggerated the potential of the new weapons. Germany's new jet aircraft were on the bleeding edge of technology, powered by engines that had a life span of barely a dozen hours. The V-2 ballistic missile depended on liquid oxygen for its rocket engine, but production of this precious substance was barely enough to fuel ten missile launches a day. The V-1 cruise missile was far more practical, but its basic unreliability and lack of accuracy made it useless for anything other than terror bombing large cities such as London and Antwerp, and even then in quantities insufficient to create anything more than a bloody nuisance.

If technological miracles could not turn the tide, then perhaps some earth-shaking battlefield victory could be won. Hitler seems to have given up hope of any miracles on the Russian front and opportunities there seemed very slim in the autumn of 1944. The Red Army was massing its forces in Poland for the inevitable final push on Berlin in the near future. In mid-September 1944, Hitler first fastened on to the idea of an offensive in the Ardennes. During his recuperation from the July 20, 1944 bomb plot, Alfred Jodl, the chief of the Wehrmacht operations staff, made a casual mention that the Ardennes was the most weakly held sector of the Allied front. Hitler immediately connected this remark with the bold Panzer drive across the Meuse in 1940 that had led to Germany's stunning victory over France.

The Ardennes offensive was an echo of the last-ditch offensive of the Great War, the German spring offensive of 1918, variously called the Michael offensive, the Ludendorff offensive, or the *Kaiserschlacht*. As in the case of the Ardennes offensive, the German 1918 spring offensive was intended to gain control of the Channel ports supplying the British Army; it was a final attempt to turn the tide of the war before the balance tipped in favor of France and Britain as more and more American troops arrived in 1918. The most critical difference between the 1918 offensive and its 1944 echo in the Ardennes was the matter of the eastern front; this alone helps explain its poor chances for success. In 1918, Russia had been knocked out of the war; the German Army in the west experienced a sudden surge in power as units were transferred from east to west. In spite of this sudden influx of resources, the 1918 offensive did not succeed. In 1944, there was no such influx of reinforcements. Furthermore, there was an overwhelming threat that the Red Army's main front in the east would become active again and begin its inexorable march on Berlin.

Given Germany's desperate circumstances Hitler convinced himself that a success in the west could change the course of the war. In his fevered mind, the alliance between Britain and the United States was fragile, and if their forces could be separated by an assault to the North Sea, the Allied front would collapse. Hitler dreamed that a third to a half of the Allied divisions on the western front could be destroyed. The Ardennes offensive was a final gamble concocted out of desperation.

OPPOSING PLANS

GERMAN PLANS

Jodl was assigned the task of elaborating Hitler's plans and he submitted the first draft on October 11, 1944. The Ardennes offensive was shaped by earlier German counteroffensives. Two previous Panzer operations against the advancing US Army – near Mortain in early August and in Lorraine in September – had failed. Although the attacking German forces had modest numerical superiority in both battles, this was not enough when faced by American artillery and air power. Hitler concluded that the Ardennes operation would require substantial superiority in men and materiel. Since only four American divisions were holding the Ardennes, Hitler calculated that a total of about 30 German divisions would be needed. Given the weakened state of the Wehrmacht after the summer disasters, such a force could not be assembled until late November 1944, but the poor weather in the late autumn would hobble Allied air power. An essential element of the plan, first dubbed *Wacht am Rhein* (Watch on the Rhine), was total secrecy. Since the attempted military coup of July 1944, Hitler had a pathological distrust of the commanders of the regular army. Details of the plan were kept to an absolute minimum of planners, and the movement of troops and materiel to the German frontier in the late autumn was explained as an effort to prepare for Allied offensives over the Rhine that were expected in the New Year.

The offensive was aimed at the Ardennes sector most weakly held by the US Army from Monschau in the north to Echternach in the south, a distance of about 40 miles (60km). The neighboring German sector in the Eifel was

Opposite:
Hitler (center) and members of his General Staff review plans for Operation *Bodenplatte* (also known as "the Great Blow"), an airstrike in support of the Ardennes offensive, scheduled for January 1, 1945, pictured here in late 1944. (Getty Images)

Hitler recognized the strategic importance of Antwerp and planned counteractions even before the Ardennes campaign. The city was subjected to V-weapon attacks on a scale greater even than London. This is a view inside the city on November 27, 1944, with US troops assisting in cleaning up after a V-2 ballistic missile has devastated a neighborhood. (NARA)

heavily wooded, shielding fresh German units from aerial observation. The offensive would be conducted by three armies: two Panzer armies in the north and center and a relatively weak infantry army on the southern flank to block counterattacks against this shoulder. Hitler would have preferred to use only his trusted Waffen-SS Panzer divisions, but there were not enough. So he settled on an attack by the 6th SS-Panzer Army in the vital northern sector with a parallel assault by the 5th Panzer Army in the center. The 6th Panzer Army sector from Monschau to St. Vith was the most important, since success here would secure the shortest route over the Meuse through Liège to Antwerp. German planners believed that the main logistics network for the First US Army was in this area and its capture would assist the German attack by providing supplies as well as weakening the American response. The weakest of the attacking German armies, the 7th Army, would strike towards Bastogne. Unlike the two Panzer forces to the north, the 7th Army had virtually no armored support. Bastogne had little role in the original Ardennes plan since it was quite distant from any strategic objectives. The Waffen-SS Panzer commanders were fairly confident they could reach the Meuse River in a day or two, and the planners considered that it might be possible to reach Antwerp by the seventh day of the offensive.

In the 6th Panzer Army sector, Hitler wanted two special operations to seize vital bridges over the Meuse before they could be destroyed by retreating American forces. Operation *Greif*, led by Hitler's favorite adventurer, Obersturmbannführer Otto Skorzeny, would consist of a special brigade of English-speaking German troops disguised as Americans which would surreptitiously make its way through the American lines to capture vital objectives ahead of the main Panzer force. Operation *Stösser* was a paratroop drop to seize vital objectives deep behind the American lines while paralyzing any attempts to reinforce the northern sector.

The plan for the 6th Panzer Army was based around the use of two SS-Panzer corps. After the lead infantry divisions had penetrated the American defenses, the first of these corps would secure bridgeheads over the Meuse after which the second Panzer corps would be committed to exploit towards Antwerp. Hitler allotted priority in assault guns and tank destroyer units to

PLANNED ROUTES OF ADVANCE

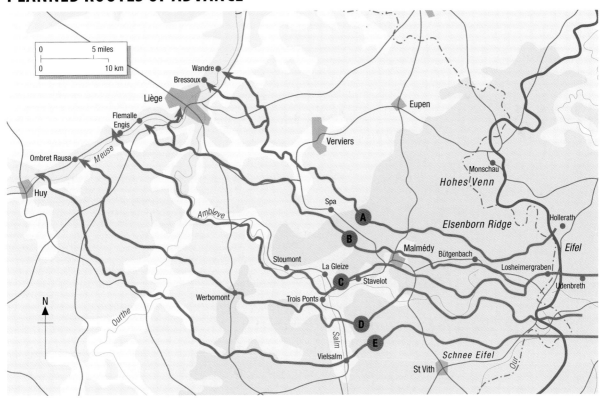

Walter Model (left), commander of
Army Group B, is seen here planning
the Ardennes offensive with the
commander of the Germany Army in
the West, Gerd von Rundstedt (center)
and Hans Krebs, Model's chief of staff.
(Military History Insitute)

this sector, since the American response would be to divert forces from the
Aachen area and move them south against the 6th Panzer Army's right flank.
He directed that this sector receive the best infantry formations including two
Fallschirmjäger (paratrooper) divisions and the 12th Volksgrenadier Division,
which had distinguished itself in the recent Aachen fighting. Hitler stressed
that the lead Panzer corps was to avoid becoming entangled in fighting along
its right flank with counterattacking American units, a mission that should be
left to a blocking force of infantry and separate tank destroyer units.

The senior commanders were brought in for their first briefing on
Wacht am Rhein on October 22, 1944. The western front commander,
Generalfeldmarshall Gerd von Rundstedt, and Army Group B commander,
Generalfeldmarshall Walter Model, were aghast at the details of the plan,
which they viewed as wildly impractical. Knowing that Hitler would not
be amused by their doubts, they approached Jodl with a "small solution":
an alternative offensive aimed at enveloping the US forces around the
recently fallen city of Aachen. Jodl was unwilling even to broach the idea
with Hitler, knowing he was determined to embark on this desperate final
gamble for the fate of Germany.

Wacht am Rhein was foolhardy with few realistic chances for success. The quality of German forces in the late autumn of 1944 had plummeted drastically since the summer, due to the catastrophic losses in France and eastern Europe. The plan could only succeed if the initial American defenses could be rapidly breached and if the US Army dawdled as the Panzers raced for the Meuse. This was pinned on Hitler's exaggerated estimation of German combat power and a dismissive underestimation of American battlefield prowess. Any delays in reaching key objectives would doom the plan, since many key routes through the wooded hill country of the Ardennes could be blocked by relatively small forces at choke points and key river crossings. Delays of only a few days would be fatal since the Americans could use their better mobility to reinforce the Ardennes. The plan's logistical underpinning was suspect. Fuel and ammunition were in short supply and once the offensive began, the rail lines running into the Eifel would be relentlessly bombed regardless of weather, preventing resupply.

At the tactical level, the two principal armies had different approaches to the initial break-in operation. The 5th Panzer Army commander, Hasso von Manteuffel, was an energetic commander who had fought against US forces since the summer. As German commanders put it, he had an intuitive "finger-feel" for the battlefield based on a sharp intellect and experience. Contrary to Hitler's orders, he permitted scouting along his front, and after donning a colonel's uniform he scouted the front lines himself in the days before the offensive. This convinced him that there was a major gap in the American lines in the Losheim area. He also determined that American patrols were very active at night, but that they returned to base before dawn and did not resume patrols until mid-morning. Manteuffel was convinced that the planned artillery preparation would do little good against the forward US trenches and would only serve to alert the Americans. Since Hitler would not agree to an abandonment of the barrage, he won approval for an initial infiltration of American lines by assault groups followed by the artillery. Dietrich paid little attention to the details of his sector, and remained convinced that an initial barrage would soften the American defenses and make them easy to overrun. Unlike Manteuffel, he had no experience of the infernal combat in the Hürtgen forest, and had no appreciation of the challenges posed by the wooded areas that had to be breached on the first day.

AMERICAN PLANS

Allied planning in December 1944 was in a period of transition, since the opening of the port of Antwerp would permit the renewal of major Allied offensive operations within a month. A meeting of the senior leadership on December 7 was inconclusive. Montgomery reiterated his proposal for a single thrust into the Ruhr, under his command of course. Having accepted Montgomery's argument in September, which resulted in the disaster at Arnhem, Eisenhower no longer had much patience and reminded him that their central objective was not territorial but the defeat of the German Army. To the north of the Ardennes, Bradley hoped for a repeat of the July breakout from Normandy, but until the Roer dams were seized, the US forces would have no freedom of maneuver. After attacks by specialized RAF bombers failed to bring down the dams, two corps were assigned to another set of ground attacks which started on December 10. When the second corps joined

The ultimate objective of US Army operations in December 1944 was the control of the Roer River dams. These could be opened by the Wehrmacht to flood the lowlands that the Allies needed to cross to reach the Rhine River beyond. When the US Army failed to secure them in December, the RAF attempted to breach them with heavy bombs, as can be seen from the craters near the Zwischendamm Paulushof dam. (NARA)

the offensive on December 13, it ran into fierce resistance, little realizing that it had encountered the northern shoulder of the German Ardennes attack force. Although the key Wahlerscheid crossroads were taken, the American attacks stalled. To the south of the Ardennes, Patton's Third Army had finally overcome the obstinate German resistance in the fortified city of Metz, and had pushed out of Lorraine and into the Saar. The Third Army was planning an offensive on December 19 through the Westwall towards Frankfurt. In the British 21st Army Group area to the north, Field Marshal Montgomery was planning his Rhine offensive.

There were no immediate plans for operations from the "ghost front" in the Ardennes, as the mountainous Eifel area to the east promised to be every bit as difficult as the Hürtgen forest, with no strategic objectives worth the cost. The First Army used the Ardennes to rest battle-weary infantry divisions and to acquaint green divisions with life at the front. In mid-December, there were four infantry divisions in the Ardennes. In the

The 9th Infantry, 2nd Infantry Division pass though the Krinkelt woods on December 13, 1944, on their way to attack towards the Roer dams. A few days later, the 1/9th Infantry would return to the area, serving as a breakwater against the 12th SS-Panzer Division at the Lausdell crossroads outside Krinkelt. (NARA)

north opposite the 6th Panzer Army were the 99th Division and the 106th Division, both green units recently arrived from the United States. Further south were two veteran divisions, the 4th and 28th divisions that had been badly mauled during the savage fighting in the Hürtgen forest in November. Portions of another green division, 9th Armored Division, were in reserve to the rear of these units.

The senior US commanders, Omar Bradley of 12th Army Group and Courtney Hodges of First Army, both recognized that the divisions in the Ardennes were stretched much too thinly along the frontier. Middleton's VIII Corps was stretched over three times as much as US doctrine considered prudent but there was no expectation of a major attack in the area. This intelligence failure resulted from two major factors: the success of the Germans in strategic deception and the conviction by senior Allied commanders that the Ardennes was unsuitable for a winter offensive.

Until the Ardennes offensive, Allied signals intelligence had provided the high command with such a steady stream of reliable intelligence data that the senior leadership had come to depend upon it. There was no evidence in the top-secret Ultra traffic of a German offensive. This was a testament to the success of the Wehrmacht in maintaining a signals blackout prior to the attack. The 12th Army Group weekly intelligence summary of December 9, 1944 concluded that the Germans were in a situation analogous to late July before the Operation *Cobra* breakout from Normandy. German forces were unable to replace their losses and the reserve 6th Panzer Army would be kept around Cologne to respond eventually to a breakout by either the US First or Third Army. The First Army's G-2 summary of December 10 placed greater emphasis on the possibility of a German counteroffensive but again expected it against after they had crossed the Roer. General K. Strong, Eisenhower's G-2, was so alarmed by the accumulating, if inconclusive, evidence of German reinforcement of the Ardennes that he visited Bradley in early December to express his misgivings. Bradley heard him out but repeated his belief that no strategic objectives were in the path of an attack through the Ardennes.

Colonel Oscar Koch, the Third Army G-2, convinced Patton of the likelihood of a German attack against the First Army's VIII Corps in the Ardennes, with the 6th Panzer Army as its likely spearhead. Koch and Patton did not share the view that the Germans were waiting for a First Army

offensive, arguing that the likely breakthrough of the Westwall in the Third Army sector in mid-December should have caused the Germans to move part of their reserve towards the Saar in response. The fact that they had not moved suggested that they had more immediate plans to the north. On December 13, 1944, Patton sent a message to Eisenhower's headquarters warning of an Ardennes attack, and echoing Strong's concerns.

Bradley didn't think that the Germans were foolhardy enough to launch a winter attack in an area with such a restricted road network with very strong American forces on either flank. Such an assessment was the classic intelligence error of mirror-imaging an enemy's intentions based on one's own inclinations. The senior American commanders like Eisenhower, Bradley, and Hodges were conservative and risk-averse in their operational planning and so could not imagine the perspective of someone as desperate and reckless as

A 9th Infantry squad huddles in a snowy ditch during the fighting on the approaches to "Heartbreak Crossroads" near Wahlerscheid on December 13, 1944. (NARA)

Hitler. Audacious commanders such as Patton made a more astute assessment of German intentions. In the end, Bradley was proven correct that the German attack was a foolish adventure. But the risky deployment of such a thin cover force in the Ardennes should have been accompanied by a more deliberate intelligence effort, especially in view of the accumulating evidence of German activity in the Eifel area in the days prior to the offensive. Bradley's G-2, Brigadier General Edwin Sibert, was later sacked.

An analogous example took place a few weeks later in Alsace. As in the case of the German 1918 spring offensive, Hitler envisioned subsidiary offensives to support the main effort. In this case, Operation *Nordwind* was intended to take advantage of the thinning of American lines opposite the Saar when they reinforced the Ardennes. Preparation for *Nordwind* largely paralleled the Ardennes offensive in terms of security, and there were no discoveries of the offensive in the Ultra signals intelligence. Yet the Seventh US Army G-2 correctly predicted that an offensive was in the works using precisely the sort of tactical intelligence which Bradley's staff had discounted. Not only did this G-2 predict the offensive, they predicted the day it would occur, New Year's Eve. The Seventh US Army was even more badly extended than First US Army in the Ardennes, but due to more perceptive intelligence assessment, the German *Nordwind* attack was blunted almost from the outset. As a result, the *Nordwind* offensive is not as well known as the Ardennes offensive, if for no other reason than its lack of dramatic consequence.

After nearly three months of bloody fighting in the mud and forests along the Westwall, Bradley continued to voice the hope that the Germans would emerge from their Westwall fortifications for an all-out fight. He got far more than he wished.

WEATHER AND TERRAIN

Wacht am Rhein was strongly affected by weather and terrain conditions. Weather would prove a very mixed blessing for the German attack. Early December was overcast; on the one hand, this limited Allied air reconnaissance before the offensive began, and Allied air attacks after the attack started. But it also meant that Luftwaffe attempts to provide air support for the offensive would be frustrated by the weather.

In terms of ground conditions, the weather had generally adverse effects on the initial phase of the German attack. The autumn weather in Belgium had been wetter than usual and the soil was saturated and muddy. Temperatures for the first week of the offensive were slightly above freezing during the day, though often below freezing at night. There was a thaw on December 18, and the temperatures were not cold enough until December 23 to actually freeze the soil to any depth. This severely limited German mobility since vehicles, even tanks, became bogged down after they left the roads. US forces had dubbed the condition "a front one tank wide" since all traffic was road-bound. The muddy fields channeled German attack forces down available roads, and made towns and road junctions especially important. German schemes to bypass centers of resistance were impossible for the Panzer columns and their essential support vehicles. A divisional

The farm roads leading out of the Eifel in the northern sector were churned up by the advancing columns of Panzers and quickly became channels of mud, trapping this captured jeep being used by an officer of the 1st SS-Panzer Corps. (Military History Institute)

commander later recalled that the mud "played a decisive role since even undamaged tracked vehicles stuck fast. This was decisive because, towards the end of the war, our own infantry attacked unwillingly and reluctantly if there was no armored support."

Although the popular image of the Battle of the Bulge is of a snow-covered terrain, in fact, snow cover was not predominant in the first week of the fighting. Snow began to fall in the second week of November, but it did not cling due to frequent daylight thaws. The exception was in the shady forested areas, where the snow often endured. Significant snowfalls did not begin until after Christmas. The weather during the first few days of the fighting was characterized by clinging ground fog especially in the early morning hours with frequent spells of rain or freezing rain, and occasional snow at night.

The northern Ardennes consists of rolling hills with woods interspersed with open farmland. The forests were often cultivated pine stands, harvested for wood. As a result, the spacing of the trees was uniform, with little undergrowth, and a pattern of fire breaks and narrow forest trails for logging. But some of the rougher hill terrain in the river valleys comprised pine barrens, with thick undergrowth. The roads from the German border into Belgium were mostly graveled. While adequate for infantry, the tanks and tracked vehicles churned them into glutinous mud trenches, trapping subsequent vehicle columns.

The initial attack area for the 6th Panzer Army was forested, varying in depth from about 2 to 4 miles (3 to 6km). Beyond this was a band of open farm terrain with better roads. To the north was the Elsenborn Ridge, a shallow plateau, with the upland moors of the Hohes Venn further north. This meant that once the German forces had broken out of the woods, there was a relatively open area to deploy mechanized units. The best roads out of the area towards Liège were on the Elsenborn Ridge and through Malmédy. Access via the Amblève River valley was problematic as the roads were very narrow and winding, with forested slopes on one side, and wooded drops towards the river on the other side. If this could be rapidly traversed, the region beyond was more suitable for advance.

The attack area in the 5th Panzer Army sector was significantly different since the attack was launched from farmlands towards the forested plateau of the Schnee Eifel. However, there were open areas to either side, most notably the Losheim Gap, which was a traditional access route westward. This permitted a relatively quick passage in the initial stages of the offensive, but the terrain became progressively more difficult to the west with wooded ravines and hills nearer the Meuse.

OPPOSING COMMANDERS

GERMAN COMMANDERS

Wacht am Rhein was the brainchild of Adolf Hitler. Most senior Wehrmacht commanders regarded the campaign as foolhardy. However, their influence on strategic issues had declined precipitously since the army bomb plot against Hitler of July 1944. Hitler played a central role in all the planning of *Wacht am Rhein*, and his increasingly delusional views underlay the unrealistic expectations of the campaign. Hitler's main aide in planning the Ardennes offensive was Generaloberst Alfred Jodl, the chief of the Wehrmacht operations staff. Conditioned by his traditional training to value loyalty, Jodl's unassuming manner helped him survive Hitler's irascible temper. He was injured in the bomb explosion in July 1944 and so was one of the few senior German generals to retain the Führer's confidence until the end of the war.

Field command of the German forces in the Ardennes campaign was under Generalfeldmarshall Gerd von Rundstedt who commanded the western theater. Rundstedt was respected by Hitler for his competence, but was outside Hitler's circle of intimates due to his blunt honesty on military matters. Unlike Jodl, Rundstedt was not afraid to tell Hitler his misgivings about his more outlandish schemes, and so he was kept out of the planning until Jodl had completed the essential details. When he was finally handed a copy of the draft, he found that Hitler had personally marked it "Not to be altered." Although the American press often referred to the Ardennes attack as the "Rundstedt offensive," in fact he had little connection to its planning or execution. After studying the plan, he concluded that the Wehrmacht would be very lucky indeed if it even reached the Meuse, never mind Antwerp.

Opposite:
Generalfeldmarshall Gerd von Rundstedt was commander of OB West (High Command West), which directed the Ardennes offensive. Although it was sometimes called the "Rundstedt offensive" at the time, in fact, Rundstedt had little to do with planning the operation and was skeptical of its potential. (NARA)

The senior field commander for the offensive was Generalfeldmarshall Walter Model, commander of Army Group B. By 1944, Model had become Hitler's miracle worker. When all seemed hopeless and defeat inevitable, Hitler called on the energetic and ruthless Model to save the day. After a distinguished career as a Panzer commander during the Russian campaign, in March 1944 he became the Wehrmacht's youngest field marshal when assigned to the key position of leading Army Group North Ukraine. When Army Group Center was shattered by the Red Army's Operation *Bagration* in the summer of 1944, Model was assigned by Hitler the almost hopeless task of restoring order, which he accomplished. In mid-August, after German forces in France had been surrounded in the Falaise Gap, Hitler recalled Model from the eastern front and assigned him command of Army Group B. During the Ardennes offensive Model commanded the assault force: 7th Army, 5th Panzer Army, and 6th Panzer Army. Model was equally skeptical of the plan, calling it "damned fragile," but he understood Germany's desperate situation and set about trying to execute the plan to the best of his ability.

The army commander most central in the attack in the northern sector was SS-Oberstgruppenführer Josef "Sepp" Dietrich. Unlike the other senior German commanders, he had little formal officer training. Senior German commanders regarded him as an uncouth lout and a dim sycophant of the Führer. His military talents were damned with faint praise as those of a "splendid sergeant." He was a jovial, hard-drinking, and down-to-earth commander who was very popular with his troops. Brutal to opponents, Dietrich was maudlin and sentimental with his own soldiers. He had won the Iron Cross in World War I in a storm troop unit, and served in one of the few German tank units during 1918. He fought against the Poles with the Silesian militias in 1921 and returned to Bavaria to serve as a policeman since there were few opportunities in the army. Dietrich joined the Nazi party in 1928 and was promoted to command of the Munich SS (*Schutzstaffeln*), a group of toughs formed as a personal guard for Hitler in the rough and tumble street politics of the fractious Weimar Republic. Hitler's trust in Dietrich as a reliable enforcer led to his appointment as the head of the enlarged SS-*Leibstandarte Adolf Hitler* (Adolf Hitler Bodyguard) after he became Chancellor in 1933. He demonstrated his loyalty to Hitler by rounding up his brown-shirt comrades for summary execution in the "Night of the Long Knives" in 1934 when Hitler ordered the SA (Sturmabteilung) crushed to curry favor with the army. The *Leibstandarte* was committed to combat for the first time during the 1939 Polish campaign, gradually shaking off its reputation as "asphalt soldiers." Dietrich was a charismatic fighter, but unprepared in intellect or training to command a large formation. So the practice began of placing him in a prominent position while at the same time assigning a talented officer as his chief of staff to carry out the actual headquarters and staff functions. Dietrich was Hitler's alter ego – a common soldier of the Great War, a man of the people, a man of action, and a polar opposite to the type of intellectual, aristocratic Prussian staff officer that Hitler so despised. Dietrich

Nicknamed "Obersepp" by his troops, Oberstgruppenführer Josef "Sepp" Dietrich was the commander of the 6th Panzer Army. (NARA)

was awarded the Iron Cross 1st and 2nd Class for the undistinguished performance of the *Leibstandarte* in Poland, and the Knight's Cross for its role in the French campaign. These were the first of many preposterous awards and rank increases which Hitler used as much to rankle the blue-bloods of the German military establishment as to reward Dietrich. In 1943, he was ordered to form the 1st SS-Panzer Corps, with the considerable help of his new right hand man, Colonel Fritz Kraemer, a talented staff officer who would serve with him in the Ardennes. The 1st SS-Panzer Corps was first committed to action in Normandy where it earned a formidable reputation for its obstinate and skilled defense of Caen against British tank assaults. On August 1, 1944, Dietrich was elevated to SS-Oberstgruppenführer, and a few days later Hitler added Diamonds to his Iron Cross, making him one of only 27 soldiers so decorated during the war. On September 14, 1944, Hitler instructed him to begin the formation of the 6th Panzer Army. Dietrich had grown increasingly despondent over the conduct of the war, but he was too inarticulate to convey his views, and too beholden to his Nazi sponsors to press his complaints with any conviction. He vaguely blamed the setbacks at the front on "sabotage," unwilling to recognize that the source of the problem was the regime he so ardently served.

Dietrich's counterpart in command of the 5th Panzer Army was General der Panzertruppen Hasso von Manteuffel. He was the most talented of the army commanders involved in the Ardennes operation, a dynamic, intelligent officer, sometimes nicknamed "Kleiner" by his close friends due to his short stature of only 5ft 2in (1.57m). He was wounded in combat in 1916 while fighting on the western front, and had been a youthful advocate of the Panzer force in the 1930s while serving under Heinz Guderian. He had none of Dietrich's political connections and started the war commanding an infantry battalion in Rommel's 7th Panzer Division in France in 1940. He won the Knight's Cross in Russia in 1941, and while still a colonel led an improvised division in Tunisia so ably that General von Arnim described him as one of his best divisional commanders. Hitler liked

Commander of the 5th Panzer Army, General Hasso von Manteuffel on the left confers with the Army Group B commander General Walter Model (right) and the inspector of the Panzer force on the western front, Generalleutnant Horst Stumpf (center). (Military History Institute)

the brash young officer and assigned him to command the 7th Panzer Division in June 1943, and the elite "Grossdeutschland" Panzergrenadier Division later in the year. Hitler took personal interest in his career and on September 1, 1944 he was given command of 5th Panzer Army, leapfrogging to army commander in a single step, and bypassing the usual stage as a Panzer corps commander. Manteuffel learned the task the hard way during tough fighting against Patton's Third Army in Lorraine through the early autumn. His units were in continual combat with the US Army through December 1944.

Commanding the 7th Army to the south was General der Panzertruppen Erich Brandenberger. He was a highly capable officer, but his leadership style did not earn him the favor of either Hitler or Model. The Army Group B commander preferred the flashy brilliance of Manteuffel to the steady, scholarly approach of Brandenberger whom he derided as "a typical product of the general staff system." Yet Brandenberger had a fine combat record, leading the 8th Panzer Division during the invasion of Russia in 1941. He commanded the 29th Army Corps in Russia for a year before the Ardennes offensive when he was given command of the 7th Army.

General der Panzertruppen Erich Brandenberger, commander of the 7th Army in the Ardennes. (Military History Institute)

Corps Commanders

The 6th Panzer Army contained a preponderance of Waffen-SS Panzer divisions so not surprisingly it included several senior Waffen-SS commanders. All three corps commanders were highly experienced Russian front veterans. The 1st SS-Panzer Corps commander was SS-Gruppenführer Hermann Preiss. He was too young to have served in the Great War, but saw combat in the Freikorps in Latvia in 1919. He joined the Nazi Party and the

Commander of the 1st SS-Panzer Corps was SS-Gruppenführer Hermann Preiss, who previously commanded the 1st and 3rd SS-Panzer divisions. (NARA)

SS in 1933, serving in one of the early armed units and advancing to battalion command by the time of the outbreak of the war. He commanded the "Totenkopf" artillery regiment in Russia and was repeatedly decorated for his combat leadership with the Iron Cross in 1939, the German Cross in Gold in 1942 and the Knight's Cross in 1943. He took over command of the 3rd SS-Panzer Division "Totenkopf" in 1943, and was assigned to command the 1st SS-Panzer Corps in October 1944 in place of Georg Keppler.

The neighboring 2nd SS-Panzer Corps was commanded by SS-Obergruppenführer Willi Bittrich who had served as a fighter pilot in the Great War and trained German pilots at secret air bases in the Soviet Union during the 1920s. He joined the Nazi Party and the SS in 1932, serving in their military arm. He earned the Iron Cross in 1939 in Poland while serving with the *Leibstandarte*, and commanded SS-Regiment "Deutschland" during the invasion of the Soviet Union in 1941. He became the commander of SS-Cavalry Division "Florian Geyer" in 1942, and in 1943 headed the formation of the 9th SS-Panzer Division "Hohenstaufen." He took over command of the 2nd Panzer Corps from Paul Hausser on June 29, 1944, in the midst of the Normandy campaign, and was a central figure in the defeat of British paratroop forces at Arnhem in September 1944.

The 67th Army Corps was commanded by General der Infanterie Otto Hitzfeld. After serving as a young officer in the Great War when he received the Iron Cross, Hitzfeld remained in the army in senior teaching posts. He was an infantry battalion commander at the start of the war, becoming a regimental commander in late 1940 and a divisional commander with the 102nd Infantry Division in January 1943. He was wounded repeatedly in combat in Russia and awarded the German Cross in Gold in 1942, the

Knight's Cross in 1941 and the Knight's Cross with Oak Leaves in 1942.

Manteuffel's 5th Panzer Army corps commanders were also seasoned Russian front veterans. They had all started the war as young battalion or regimental commanders and worked their way up through divisional command in Russia. General der Artillerie Walther Lucht had begun the war in 1939 as an artillery regiment commander in Poland, and by the time of the France campaign in 1940 he had been elevated to corps artillery command. During the Russian campaign, he was first promoted to army artillery commander, then in February 1942 to command of the 87th Infantry Division, and in March to command of the 336th Infantry Division, which took part in the efforts to relieve the encircled forces in Stalingrad. He was the area commander for the Kerch Straits in the summer and autumn of 1943 before being posted to 66th Corps command in November 1943 when the formation was on occupation duty in southern France.

General der Waffen-SS Willi Bittrich, commander of the 2nd SS-Panzer Corps. (NARA)

General der Panzertruppen Walter Krüger began the war as an infantry regimental commander, was a brigade commander in the 1st Panzer Division during the France campaign in 1940, and was promoted to command the division in July 1941 during the invasion of Russia. He served as the 1st Panzer Division commander in Russia for most of the war, until he was appointed to command the 58th Panzer Corps in February 1944, taking part in the 1944 fighting in France.

General der Panzertruppen Heinrich von Lüttwitz resembled the Hollywood caricature of a German general: fat, monocled, and arrogant. Yet he was a seasoned, dynamic Panzer commander. He started the war commanding a motorcycle battalion and became a regimental commander

General der Panzertruppen Heinrich von Lüttwitz, commander of 47th Panzer Corps. (Military History Institute)

after the French campaign. He first assumed divisional command with the 20th Panzer Division in October 1942, seeing heavy fighting in Russia, and was transferred to the 2nd Panzer Division in February 1944, serving as its commander in the summer fighting in France until the end of August when he was promoted to corps command of 47th Panzer Corps. The 2nd Panzer Division was the spearhead of his corps during the Ardennes campaign, and he paid it special attention, on account of both his past connection to the division and also his doubts about the capabilities of its current commander, Oberst Meinrad von Lauchert, who took command only a day before the offensive began.

The corps commanders in Brandenberger's 7th Army were also seasoned eastern front veterans, two of them survivors of the summer 1944 debacles in the east. General der Infanterie Baptist Kneiss began the war as commander of the 215th Infantry Division, leading it through the early campaigns in France and northern Russia. In November 1942 he was promoted to command the 66th Corps, which was on occupation duty in southern France, and in July 1944 he took over the 85th Corps, also in southern France.

General der Infanterie Franz Beyer began the war as an infantry regiment commander, and was promoted to lead the 331st Infantry Division at the end of 1941 during its training in Austria. He remained in command of the division during its assignment to the Russian front. In March 1943 he was transferred to command the 44th Infantry Division, which was being re-formed in Austria after the original division was lost at Stalingrad and subsequently the unit was deployed to Italy. He was given corps command in late April 1944 on the eastern front, serving for short periods with four different corps in the summer battles, finally in the disastrous Crimean campaign in July–August 1944. He was appointed to the 80th Army Corps in early August 1944.

Among the German tactical commanders, the one to emerge with the most notoriety was Joachim Peiper, who headed Kampfgruppe Peiper in its mad dash to La Gleize. Peiper was born in 1915, the son of a Prussian army officer. Believing "Joachim" to sound too Jewish, he preferred to be called "Jochen." He joined the SS in October 1933 and an early meeting with SS-Reichsführer Heinrich Himmler led to his appointment to a junior officers' school. As a result, he spent most of his young adulthood within the expanding SS military organization, including Hitler's bodyguards, the *Leibstandarte*. In July 1938, he was appointed to Himmler's staff and remained there until the autumn of 1941 when he was assigned to a company command in SS-Division "Leibstandarte" during the fighting in Russia. He was appointed to battalion command in September 1942, and returned to the Russian front in early 1943 during the fighting around Kharkov; he received the Knight's Cross with Oak Leaves in January 1943. His Panzergrenadier battalion fought during the battle of Kursk, and he took over the division's Panzer regiment in late November 1943 when the previous commander was killed in action. After recuperating in early 1944, he again led the 1st SS-Panzer Regiment in Normandy and Dietrich personally decorated him with Diamonds to the Knight's Cross for his actions. However, he relinquished command in early August 1944 due to combat fatigue, and he did not return to service until October 1944 during the preparations for the Ardennes offensive. Peiper's infamy stems from the Malmédy massacre at the start of the Ardennes campaign as well as associated massacres of Belgian

Standartenführer Hugo Kraas commanded the 2nd SS-Panzergrenadier Regiment until assigned to command the 12th SS-Panzer Division "Hitlerjugend." (NARA)

Generalleutnant Fritz Bayerlein, Rommel's former aide in North Africa, and the commander of the Panzer Lehr Division in the Ardennes. (Military History Institute)

civilians by his troops. Peiper had become hardened by his service in Russia where atrocities against prisoners-of-war were commonplace. While there was little evidence directly linking Peiper to the Malmédy massacre, his unit's trail of atrocities in the Ardennes reveals either an unwillingness to rein in the brutality of his troops or an encouragement of these excesses. He was sentenced to death in a war crimes trial after the war but his sentence was commuted at the end of 1956. Curiously enough, he decided to live in France and was killed at his home near Traves under mysterious circumstances after his wartime career was publicized in the local French press.

Another notorious commander during the Ardennes campaign was SS-Obersturmbannführer Otto Skorzeny. Unlike Peiper, who served mainly as a conventional small unit commander, Skorzeny's claim to fame came as Hitler's bold adventurer, a leader of German special operations. Skorzeny joined the Austrian Nazi Party in 1931 and after rejection by the Luftwaffe due to age, served as a junior officer in the Waffen-SS in France and Russia. After being wounded in late 1942, Skorzeny prepared a detailed proposal on commando operations while recuperating in Vienna. This attracted the attention of the SD, the intelligence arm of the SS, which set up the Waffen Sonderverband Friedenthal near Berlin under his command to promote these schemes. The first was a failed attempt to stir up trouble in Iran. Skorzeny's operations came to Hitler's personal attention and in July 1943 Hitler assigned him to a scheme to liberate Mussolini along with a number of Luftwaffe officers. There is some controversy regarding his role in Mussolini's escape in September 1943, but he made the most of it and was decorated with the Knight's Cross. His next scheme was a plot to assassinate

Model is seen here consulting with Generalmajor Siegfried von Waldenburg, commander of the 116th Panzer Division in the Ardennes. (Military History Institute)

Stalin, Churchill, and Roosevelt at the Teheran conference in October 1943, which was uncovered by Soviet counterintelligence. A spring 1944 scheme to capture Yugoslav partisan leader Josip Tito using a Waffen-SS paratroop force was a bloody flop. Skorzeny had more success in October 1944 when Hitler sent him to Budapest to deal with the possible defection of Hungary from the Axis. Skorzeny abducted Admiral Miklos Horthy's son, forcing his abdication and replacement by Ferenc Szalasi who kept Hungary in the war on Germany's side. For the Ardennes offensive, Skorzeny came up with the idea of infiltrating a force in American uniforms using American vehicles as a means to seize key bridges ahead of the Panzer columns. Operation *Greif* also proved to be a flop, and was followed by an unsuccessful scheme to demolish the Rhine bridge at Remagen in March 1945 after it was captured by the US Army. Although tried after the war for war crimes connected with Operation *Greif*, Skorzeny was not convicted. He became involved in schemes to help SS men escape to South America, though it is often difficult to separate Skorzeny's schemes and self-promotion from his actual accomplishments.

AMERICAN COMMANDERS

The US field commanders in the Ardennes lacked the combat experience of their German counterparts. Even the most experienced commanders such as Patton had been in combat only a small fraction of the time of the average German commanders.

The senior American field commander was Lieutenant General Omar Bradley, who commanded the 12th Army Group. This consisted of Lieutenant General William H. Simpson's Ninth Army which abutted Montgomery's 21st Army Group on the Dutch frontier, Lieutenant General Courtney Hodges' First Army in the center from Aachen through the Ardennes, and Lieutenant General George Patton's Third Army in the Saar. Bradley had been one of Eisenhower's classmates in the West Point class of 1913, and both commanders were younger than the subordinate army commanders, Patton and Hodges. Bradley was typical of the meritocratic system of US army field commands in World War II, having grown up the son of a poor Missouri sodbuster and having been selected for the US Military Academy by intellectual promise and hard work. Like Eisenhower, Bradley was a quintessential staff officer rather than a field commander, more comfortable studying maps and planning the logistics of an operation than leading men in the field. Eisenhower tended towards accommodation with British demands in operational and strategic planning, and Bradley played an important role behind the scenes in reminding Eisenhower of US interests in these deliberations, especially in early 1945.

When Bradley was booted upstairs to command 12th Army Group in August, command of First Army fell to his aide, Lieutenant General Courtney Hodges. Hodges was in Patton's class at the US Military Academy at West Point but fell out for academic reasons. He enlisted in the army and earned his lieutenant's bar shortly after he would have graduated. Bradley had considerable confidence in Hodges, though other American commanders felt that he was not assertive enough and that he might be overly influenced by his dynamic chief of staff, Major General William Kean. His inactivity in the first days of the Ardennes fighting is something of a mystery – in the charitable view being attributed to the flu, and in the more skeptical view to nervous exhaustion. However, he had an able staff, and

Bradley played a central role in the first few days of fighting, keeping an eye on First Army HQ and involving himself in the details. Bradley continued to support Hodges even after his poor performance in the early days of the Ardennes offensive, but Bradley probably would have sacked any other commander. Hodges was neither as flamboyant or aggressive as his neighboring army commander, Patton, but one Patton was enough for Bradley. Hodges' lack of aggressive spirit was partly balanced by the presence of some of the US Army's best corps commanders in First Army.

Lieutenant General George S. Patton Jr. arrived on the scene when his Third Army was diverted from Operation *Tink* to relieve Bastogne instead. Patton is one of America's legendary commanders, if for no other reason than his colorful and heroic personality amongst a

Lieutenant General Courtney Hodges commanded the First US Army in the Ardennes. (NARA)

generation of faceless managerial commanders and organization men. General Patton was a study in contrast to the other two senior US commanders. Bradley and Eisenhower were from mid-western farm families with little military tradition. Patton was from a wealthy southern family; his grandfather and namesake had been a distinguished commander in the Confederate Army during the US Civil War. Graduating from West Point six years before Eisenhower or Bradley, Patton served under "Black Jack" Pershing in the Mexican punitive expedition in 1916 and commanded the infant US tank force in combat in France in 1918. He was a prominent cavalry officer during the inter-war years and his past tank and cavalry experience led to his command of the new 2nd Armored Division in 1940 at a time when mechanization of the army was a central concern. He attracted national attention for the exploits of his tank units in pre-war exercises, even gracing the cover of *Life* magazine. The army chief of staff George C. Marshall planned to retire many of the older commanders before their deployment to combat, but Patton's exceptional leadership in the wargames kept him in action. Patton was a natural choice to lead the I Armored Corps in North Africa in 1942, and when it became time to replace the II Corps commander after the Kasserine debacle, Patton was selected. Patton's inspirational leadership gave the troops confidence, and Eisenhower selected him to lead the US Seventh Army in the campaign on Sicily in July–August 1943. His extravagant behavior got him into serious trouble when, during two visits to field hospitals on Sicily, he slapped soldiers with battle fatigue. In an army of citizen-soldiers this would not do, and cast a shadow over Patton's future. Eisenhower still valued his aggressiveness and facility with mobile forces, but his impetuousness and impolitic style both on and off the battlefield limited his rise beyond army command. He was widely regarded as the US Army's most aggressive and skilled practitioner of mobile warfare, a reflection of his cavalry background.

The First Army's two corps facing the Ardennes were the V Corps to the north, and the VIII Corps to its south. Major General Leonard Gerow was a few years older than Bradley, and was in the Virginia Military Institute class of 1911. He served in the Mexican campaign in 1916, and was a signals officer in France in 1918 where he was involved in the early use of the radio

Major General Troy H. Middleton commanded the VIII Corps from Bastogne to the Schnee Eifel. (NARA)

by the US Army. He graduated first of his class from the Advanced Course at Ft. Benning's Infantry School; second was Bradley. He subsequently attended the US Army Command and General Staff School where Eisenhower was his study partner; Eisenhower graduated first, Gerow eleventh. He later commanded Eisenhower in 1941 while heading the war plans division of the general staff. Following the outbreak of the war, he commanded the newly formed 29th Division that would later serve under his corps command at Omaha Beach. The V Corps was the first large US Army formation created in Britain for the Allied invasion of France, and Eisenhower picked Gerow for its command in July 1943. As a result, he was deeply involved in planning for the D-Day invasion, and V Corps was assigned Omaha Beach. He was highly regarded by both Eisenhower and Bradley though not especially popular with his subordinate divisional commanders due to his propensity to micromanage operations. Gerow was a by-the-book commander lacking Eisenhower's political subtlety. He led V Corps during the D-Day landings on Omaha Beach and the liberation of Paris in August 1944.

Major General Troy Middleton of the VIII Corps had commanded the corps since Normandy. Middleton had entered the army as a private in 1909

Major General Troy H. Middleton (right), commander of the VIII Corps in the Bastogne sector, is seen here talking with General Dwight Eisenhower at St. Vith in the autumn of 1944. (NARA)

Major General Matthew Ridgway commanded the XVIII Airborne Corps, which was the only theater reserve in the ETO at the time of the Ardennes attack. His corps headquarters took over the St. Vith sector, but his two airborne divisions were scattered, with the 82nd Airborne Division going to the Malmédy sector and the 101st Airborne Division to Bastogne. (NARA)

and had risen through the ranks to become the army's youngest regimental commander in World War I. Although he had retired before the outbreak of World War II to become a college administrator, he returned to the Army and commanded the 45th Division in Italy with distinction. Though he was old for a corps commander, the army chief of staff remarked that he would "rather have a man with arthritis in the knee than one with arthritis in the head." When the issue of retirement was raised in 1944, Eisenhower quipped that he wanted him back in command even if he had "to be carried on a stretcher."

As reinforcements arrived following the German attack, a number of other corps commanders arrived on the scene. Major General Matthew Ridgway led the XVIII Airborne Corps and was the US Army's most experienced paratroop commander. He had commanded the 82nd Airborne Division since June 1942 when it had first converted from a regular infantry division into a paratroop division. Ridgway had led the unit during its first major combat jump over Sicily in 1943 as well as the D-Day landings in the Normandy operation and was assigned to lead the XVIII Airborne Corps in time for Operation *Market Garden* in September 1944. After the war, he would go on to a distinguished career as supreme NATO commander and army chief of staff.

The VII Corps was commanded by Major General J. Lawton Collins, better known by his nickname, "Lightning Joe." Collins graduated from West Point in April 1917, but did not arrive in Europe until after the Armistice. He received a divisional command in May 1942, taking over the 25th Division in the Pacific. Formed from cadres of the peacetime Hawaiian Division, this unit had a poor reputation. Collins whipped it into shape for its first assignment, relieving the 1st Marine Division on Guadalcanal in early 1943. The codename for the division headquarters on Guadalcanal

When command of the First US Army units northeast of Bastogne passed to Montgomery, he took control of the counterattack force of VII Corps commanded by Major General J. Lawton Collins to the left and XVIII Airborne Corps led by Major General Matthew Ridgway to the right, seen here at the VII Corps HQ on December 26. (NARA)

was Lightning, from which Collins picked up his nickname. He had been brought back from the Pacific theater to provide combat experience. Bradley described him as "independent, heady, capable, and full of vinegar," and he would prove to be one of the most aggressive and talented US field commanders in Europe. He led VII Corps in the D-Day landings on Utah Beach, and was responsible for the first US Army victory in Normandy when the port of Cherbourg was captured in June 1944. Collins proved to be an especially able practitioner of mobile warfare, and was instrumental in the Operation *Cobra* break out from Normandy in late July 1944. He later served as the army chief of staff during the Korean War.

When Patton's Third Army arrived on the scene around Christmas, it was spearheaded by Major General John Milliken's III Corps. Milliken was by far the least combat experienced of the major corps commanders of the Ardennes campaign. He commanded the 2nd Cavalry Division early in the war before assuming command of III Corps in October 1943. The III Corps was transferred to Patton's Third Army in October 1944 and its first major combat action was in the final phase of the fight for the Metz fortified zone, when it captured Fort Jeanne d'Arc on December 13, 1944. Patton

Eisenhower talks with Major General Norman Cota, hero of Omaha Beach, and later commander of the 28th "Keystone" Division during the fighting in the Hürtgen forest and the Ardennes. (NARA)

recommended him for the Oak Leaf Cluster to the Distinguished Service Medal for his leadership in the Ardennes fighting. Milliken's III Corps remained under Patton until late February 1945 when it was transferred to Hodges' First Army. Milliken did not get along well with Hodges and he was sacked after the capture of the Remagen bridge owing to his handling of the bridgehead build-up, a controversial decision at the time and since. Paradoxically, he was awarded the Silver Star for his leadership at the Remagen bridge. Milliken asked for a combat command, and served the remainder of the war as head of the 13th Armored Division under Patton's command.

Of the US Army tactical commanders in this sector of the Ardennes fighting, none made a stronger impression than Brigadier General Bruce C. Clarke. He began his career in the National Guard and received an appointment to the Military Academy at West Point. He spent most of the inter-war years as an engineer officer, and was transferred to the new armor branch at the beginning of the war. He commanded one of the early armored engineer battalions and was instrumental in the development of a treadway pontoon bridge that could be used easily by armored units. In 1943, he became chief of staff of the 4th Armored Division, a unit that would later become the spearhead of Patton's Third Army. By the time of the Normandy fighting in July 1944, he had been appointed to lead the division's Combat Command A (CCA). He became famous for his skilled leadership in Normandy and in the subsequent fighting in Lorraine where he often commanded the tank columns from the back seat of a Piper Cub observation aircraft. His unit was responsible for the defeat of the German Panzer counteroffensive around Arracourt. As an engineer rather than an infantryman, Clarke endured very slow career advancement. Patton jokingly told him that he was a "nobody" since the army chief of staff, George C. Marshall, had

The defense of the northern shoulder of the Bulge held in no small measure because of the skilled leadership of officers like Major General Walter Robertson (right), commander of the 2nd Infantry Division. Here he is seen talking with the 12th Army Group commander, General Omar Bradley (left), shortly before the Ardennes campaign. (NARA)

not recognized his name when he had pushed to get him a general's star. A similar situation befell another gifted engineer, Brigadier General William Hoge, who ended up commanding the CCB of 9th Armored Division alongside Clarke at St. Vith. Patton succeeded in advancing Clarke to brigadier general, but he was obliged to switch units since there were no slots in the 4th Armored Division. Bradley had been very unhappy with the performance of the 7th Armored Division, and to rejuvenate the unit he elevated Robert Hasbrouck to command, and shifted Clarke to lead its CCB. Hasbrouck and Clarke straightened out the problems in the division during November 1944 shortly before it was put to its greatest test at St. Vith. There were a number of other excellent commanders in this sector as well, such as Major General Walter Robertson of the 2nd Infantry Division.

OPPOSING ARMIES

WEHRMACHT

The Wehrmacht was an emaciated shadow of the force that had conquered most of Europe in 1939–41. The war on the eastern front had bled the army white, yet it remained a formidable fighting force and particularly tenacious in its defense of German soil. Its weaknesses became more evident in an offensive operation such as the Ardennes campaign where its lack of motorization, poor logistics, shortage of fuel, and lack of offensive air power severely hampered its striking power.

The attack force earmarked for the Ardennes offensive consisted of three field armies, the strongest of which, Dietrich's 6th Panzer Army, was on the right (northern) flank, Manteuffel's 5th Panzer Army in the center, and Brandenberger's 7th Army on the left (south).

The shock force of the 6th Panzer Army was the 1st SS-Panzer Corps, composed of the 1st SS-Panzer Division "Leibstandarte Adolf Hitler" and the 12th SS-Panzer Division "Hitlerjugend" (Hitler Youth). Dietrich's 6th Panzer Army had two more corps, the 2nd SS-Panzer Corps, and the 67th Army Corps. The 2nd SS-Panzer Corps, including the 2nd SS-Panzer Division "Das Reich" and the 9th SS-Panzer Division "Hohenstaufen," was in army reserve waiting until the 1st SS-Panzer Corps completed the breakthrough to the Meuse. It saw no fighting in the initial stage of the campaign. The 67th Army Corps was located on the northern flank and consisted of Volksgrenadier units intended to serve as a blocking force.

Manteuffel's 5th Panzer Army was not as lavishly equipped as the 6th Panzer Army and had the usual uneven mix of divisions. In general, the army

Opposite:
The Panzergrenadiers of the 1st SS-Panzer Division were still wearing their autumn-pattern camouflage jackets during the initial phase of the Ardennes attack. This NCO is armed with an StG44 assault rifle, an innovation in infantry small arms and forebear of modern assault rifles. This photo is from a well-known series staged along the Poteau–Recht road on December 17 after a column from the 14th Cavalry Group had been ambushed. (NARA)

(Heer) Panzer divisions had been kept in the line longer than the Waffen-SS Panzer divisions, and had less time to rejuvenate before the start of the Ardennes offensive. Lüttwitz's 47th Panzer Corps was the strongest element of Manteuffel's 5th Panzer Army while the neighboring 58th Panzer Corps had less strength. Of the three field armies taking part in the offensive, Brandenberger's 7th Army was the weakest and had little Panzer support.

Dietrich's 6th Panzer Army, although it would later be redesignated as the 6th SS-Panzer Army, was in fact an amalgam of units from three combat arms – the regular army, the Waffen-SS, and the Luftwaffe's ground combat formations. This conglomeration was the result of the factional in-fighting of Hitler's cronies as they sought greater personal power in the final years of the Third Reich.

The Waffen-SS had originally been organized as the praetorian guard of the Nazi Party and used primarily as a bodyguard force. At the beginning of the war in 1939, they were derided by the regular army (Heer) as "asphalt soldiers" good for little more than parade ground performances. As the war dragged on, the Waffen-SS increased substantially in size, eventually including a significant number of well-equipped Panzer and Panzergrenadier divisions. The SS-Reichsführer, Heinrich Himmler, saw to it that "his" divisions received the best equipment. In the early days, the Waffen-SS had the pick of the best troops, preferring German volunteers. By 1944, this personnel policy had collapsed and not only did the divisions increasingly rely on conscripts, but a number of divisions were composed of foreign troops or ethnic German *Volksdeutsche* from eastern Europe. The diminishing fighting power of these once formidable formations was evidence of the steady erosion of German military capabilities in 1944. Even though German industry was at its peak in the production of tanks and other weapons, the German armed forces were unable to transform this industrial windfall into increased combat power due to shortages of fuel and trained personnel.

The senior commanders in the regular army did not hold Waffen-SS combat leadership in high regard. The anti-Christian Nazi ideology promulgated within the Waffen-SS alienated many Protestant and Catholic officers who chose to remain in the regular army in spite of incentives to switch to the favored Waffen-SS. In addition, the Waffen-SS was imbued with the radical social views of the Nazi Party, which did not sit well with the conservative, aristocratic Prussian officer corps which formed a leading element within the regular army's leadership cadre. The Waffen-SS was regarded as the vanguard of the Nazi Party, favoring political loyalty over professional expertise. This was particularly the case in the wake of the July 1944 bomb plot against Hitler, which raised serious doubts about the loyalty of the regular army. After the bomb plot, the importance of the Waffen-SS increased, and it was Waffen-SS corps and divisions that were given the key roles in the Ardennes offensive.

The Waffen-SS divisions had won their reputation for stubborn defensive fighting in 1943–44 and had far less experience in offensive Panzer operations during the great

The shortage of manpower led the Waffen-SS to abandon their recruitment of volunteers and depend instead on draftees and transfers from the Luftwaffe and Kriegsmarine. Age restrictions were also loosened, as these two young soldiers from the 12th SS-Panzer Division suggest. They were captured during the fighting around Bütgenbach and a few prisoners were as young as ten. (NARA)

Blitzkrieg victories of 1939–41. Due to the decline in training, tactics were unsophisticated and tended towards the brute force approach. The chief of staff of the neighboring 5th Panzer Army complained that neighboring Waffen-SS Panzer divisions lacked road discipline, which was a major cause of the traffic jams that hindered the initial advance. Their reconnaissance skills were also judged to be poor, which was a significant issue in offensive Panzer operations. Instead of reserving the reconnaissance units for their main tasks, the Waffen-SS Panzer commanders often converted them into offensive battle groups which were used to carry out other combat assignments instead of their primary role of scouting for the division. Commanders of the Panzer spearheads such as Peiper were remarkably indifferent to the requirements for bridging and other engineering support during offensive operations, which would prove to be short-sighted when they encountered water obstacles and other terrain obstructions. Engineer troops are a critical lubricant in offensive operations to keep the mechanized formations moving in spite of terrain obstructions, but once again this was not an institutional memory within the Waffen-SS Panzer divisions due to their preponderant experience on the defensive. The regular army officers also complained that Waffen-SS units lacked discipline, based to some extent on the populist Nazi attitudes and greater fraternization between officers and enlisted men in the Waffen-SS compared to the more traditional relations in the army.

The other odd element of the Wehrmacht in the Ardennes was the presence of Luftwaffe ground units. This can partly be explained by the German decision to organize the paratroop (Fallschirmjäger) force under the Luftwaffe. Following the Pyrrhic victory of the German airborne force on Crete in 1941, the Fallschirmjäger divisions were usually used as elite light infantry. The US Army, after encountering them in Italy at Monte Cassino and in Normandy during the hedgerow fighting, regarded them as the best German infantry force. Besides the elite Fallschirmjäger divisions, the Luftwaffe also organized a growing number of field divisions which were normal infantry formations without the airborne training or specialized equipment. This was largely the doing of the Luftwaffe chief, Hermann Göring, and symptomatic of the "empire building" within the feudal Nazi political structure. Although the Fallschirmjäger divisions had been amongst the best German units in the summer of 1944, by December 1944 their quality had dropped precipitously. The most serious problem was the lack of experienced junior officers and NCOs due to the savage losses of the summer 1944 fighting. Ironically, manpower was not a major issue for the Luftwaffe divisions since there were large numbers of able young Luftwaffe ground crews who were idle due to the fuel shortage and the retirement of so many bomber and other Luftwaffe squadrons. Nevertheless, the sudden influx of these ground crew and Luftwaffe technical personnel had some odd consequences. These transfers included many junior officers and NCOs who were often assigned similar positions in the Fallschirmjäger units. The problem was that these men had no infantry experience at all. No matter how well motivated they may have been, they had suddenly been thrust into difficult combat leadership positions with no idea of their new trade. This problem will become more evident in the combat narrative which follows.

The Panzer Divisions

The success or failure of the Ardennes offensive depended very heavily on the spearhead Panzer divisions, so it is worth taking a detailed look at their preparation for the campaign.

The central task facing the Wehrmacht in the autumn of 1944 was rebuilding the divisions that had been destroyed in the summer 1944 fighting. The Wehrmacht had a fundamentally different replacement policy from the US Army in 1944. Divisions were kept in the line, receiving few replacements, with the combat elements shrinking into smaller and smaller *Kampfgruppen* (battle groups). At some convenient point, or when the division was decimated to the point of uselessness, the remaining "shadow division" would be pulled back for complete refitting. In the case of most of the Panzer divisions deployed in the Ardennes, they were scoured out by the Normandy campaign and pulled out of the line in September 1944 for refitting. It should be kept in mind that in a typical wartime Panzer division only about a third of the troops were engaged in direct combat including the Panzer crews, Panzergrenadiers, and some other units such as the reconnaissance battalion. So of the 14,700 men in a Type 44 Panzer division about 2,000 were in the Panzer regiment, of which about 750 were crewmen and another 5,400 were in the two Panzergrenadier regiments and reconnaissance battalion. Other elements such as the divisional engineers and artillery might be exposed to combat occasionally, but casualties tended to be heaviest in a narrow slice of the division. The administrative and support elements of the division often remained intact even in disasters such as the Falaise Gap encirclement, and so divisions were rebuilt around an experienced core. So when it is said that a division "suffered 50 percent casualties," these casualties were not evenly shared in the division and fell hardest on the combat elements. The Panzergrenadier regiments tended to suffer worst of all due to the usual hazards of infantry combat combined with the mobility of these units which led to their frequent commitment. Most of the Panzer regiments lost a third or more of their crewmen in Normandy and most if not all of their tanks.

The problem facing the Wehrmacht in the months before the Battle of the Bulge was that there were neither the time nor the resources to rebuild the divisions properly and many corners were cut. One of the 1st SS-Panzer Corps officers later wrote: "The level of training of the troop replacements was very poor. The Panzergrenadiers had been soldiers for only four to six weeks but instead of receiving basic training in this period, they had been employed cleaning away debris in towns damaged by air raids.

Replacements in the Panzer regiments had never ridden in a tank, let alone driven one, or fired from one, or sent messages from one by radio. Furthermore, the majority of the drivers have not had more than one or two hours' driving lessons before obtaining their driver's license. The casualties in officers had been exceptionally high during the hard battles of the summer, so that including the battalion and regimental commanders, it was mostly officers inexperienced in combat who had to lead these troops." The two Panzer divisions of 1st SS-Panzer Corps, the elite spearhead, were rated only as *Kampfwert III*, that is suitable for defensive operations, *Kampfwert I* indicating suitability for offensive operations.

In total, eight Panzer divisions were assigned to Operation *Wacht am Rhein*, each equipped with a single Panzer regiment and two Panzergrenadier regiments. This organization was somewhat different from the comparable US armored division, being lighter in tanks, but heavier in infantry. The Panzer division had a regiment with two tank battalions; the US armored division had three tank battalions. The Panzer division had two Panzergrenadier regiments each with three battalions for a total of six; the US armored division had only half as many infantry, three battalions. The German configuration was better suited to defensive operations than the American configuration which was usually found wanting in defensive fighting due to the shortage of infantry. Aside from the paper organization, there were some substantial differences between the divisions in terms of equipment. US armored divisions usually operated near full strength; German divisions even in the Ardennes often fought with significant shortfalls in equipment compared to the authorized equipment tables. By 1944, the Panzergrenadier regiments were often poorly mechanized due to a shortage of half-tracks and had to substitute commercial trucks with little cross-country capability.

In terms of tanks, the Panzer divisions had some advantages and disadvantages. Although the Panther was supposed to completely replace the PzKpfw IV by 1944, shortages of the Panther led to the continued use of the older PzKpfw IV, so each Panzer regiment nominally had a battalion each of Panther and PzKpfw IV. The PzKpfw IV had been the workhorse of the Wehrmacht since 1942 and was fairly comparable to the US Army's M4 Sherman medium tank in terms of firepower, armor, and mobility. The Sherman had some advantages in terms of mobility and reliability; the

PzKpfw IV had some modest advantages in terms of firepower. The Panther was a substantially better tank than the M4 Sherman in terms of armor and firepower, though this did not always directly translate into combat advantage on the battlefield. The Panther's main problem was a weak power-train that was particularly susceptible to breakdown in the hands of poorly trained drivers. A Panther on the prowl was a formidable opponent; a Panther broken down on the roadside with no spare parts was a logistics burden. Of 47 Panther tanks in the Ardennes inspected by Allied intelligence after the fighting, 20 (42 percent) had been abandoned or destroyed by their crew. Although detailed statistics are lacking, a number of German prisoners of war indicated that Panther tank losses had been higher due to mechanical breakdown than enemy action.

Although US troops tended to call any German armored vehicle a "Tiger" tank, in fact Tiger tanks were very uncommon. A handful of the original Tiger I tank saw service in the Ardennes, but the more common type seen in the Battle of the Bulge was the newer Kingtiger. It is best known for its use with Kampfgruppe Peiper. Although powerfully armed and thickly armored, it was not an especially useful vehicle in offensive operations due to its clumsy performance, high fuel consumption, and poor reliability. Peiper stuck his Kingtigers at the rear of his column in despair.

The most powerful tank to see combat in the Ardennes was the Kingtiger which served with s.SS.Pz.Abt. 501 attached to Kampfgruppe Peiper. This broke-down near Bourgomont during the Ardennes campaign and was later shipped to Aberdeen Proving Grounds where it is seen here, shortly after the war. (Military History Institute)

Aside from tanks, one of the most common German armored vehicles during the fighting on the northern shoulder was the Jagdpanzer IV/70 tank destroyer. This one from the 1st SS-Panzerjäger Battalion is seen in action with Kampfgruppe Hansen during the fighting with the 14th Cavalry Group along the Recht–Poteau road on December 18, 1944. (NARA)

Besides these tanks, the Wehrmacht was also beginning to employ the Panzer IV/70 in the tank role. This had originally been called the Jagdpanzer IV, and was a tank destroyer armed with the same powerful 75mm gun as the Panther, but mounted on a PzKpfw IV in a fixed casemate. Although very well armed and with excellent frontal armor, this vehicle was very clumsy in mobile operations as the long gun protruded very far forward and was prone to accident.

Aside from the tanks, the most important German medium Armored Fighting Vehicle (AFV) from a numerical standpoint was the StuG III. This was an assault gun consisting of the same 75mm gun used on the PzKfw IV, but mounted in a fixed casemate on the older PzKpfw III hull. It was primarily used in infantry divisions and separate battalions for infantry support and could also be employed for antitank fighting. The related StuH used a 105mm howitzer in place of the 75mm gun. A new, low-cost assault gun, the Jagdpanzer 38(t), was being introduced in the winter of 1944, though it was less common in the Ardennes than in Alsace. It consisted of the Czech PzKpfw 38(t) light tank chassis armed with a 75mm gun. Although cheaper to build than the StuG III, it was weakly armored and its cramped fighting compartment degraded its combat performance.

The Wehrmacht was very poorly provided with mechanized artillery in the Ardennes. The standard light self-propelled gun was the Wespe, consisting of a 105mm gun on an obsolete PzKpfw II chassis, while the medium Hummel mated a 150mm gun with a PzKpfw IV chassis.

The Wehrmacht used two different half-tracks. The SdKfz 250 was a light half-track used primarily for scouting and support roles. The more common SdKfz 251 was the standard medium half-track and was used primarily for transporting Panzergrenadiers. It also existed in a wide range of specialized sub-variants, including an assault gun version armed with a short 75mm howitzer.

Of the eight Panzer divisions eventually assigned to the Ardennes offensive, five were kept off line for three months to refit. Three army divisions, the Panzer Lehr, 9th, and 116th Panzer divisions, remained in combat until days before the offensive and hastily replenished. The table below summarizes the re-equipment of the critical Panther tank battalions prior to the Ardennes offensive. It is illustrative of how late the re-equipment took place, with the battalions at barely a third of strength in November 1944.

PANTHER TANK/PERSONNEL STATUS, AUTUMN 1944

Date (1944)	September 1–5		October 1		November 1		December 16		Ardennes losses*
	Panthers	Troops	Panthers	Troops	Panthers	Troops	Panthers	Troops	Panthers
3rd Panzer Regiment (2nd Panzer Division)	3	43%	0	68%	5	67%	64	96%	20
33rd Panzer Regiment (9th Panzer Division)	26	76%	53	85%	45	97%	60	100%	16
16th Panzer Regiment (116th Panzer Division)	1	68%	28	83%	44	92%	64	96%	30
130th Panzer Regiment (Panzer Lehr Division)	13	54%	0	85%	16	99%	29	95%	6
1st SS-Panzer Regiment (1st SS-Panzer Division)	4	74%	3	81%	25	95%	42	100%	30
2nd SS-Panzer Regiment (2nd SS-Panzer Division)	6	58%	1	79%	1	100%	58	100%	24
9th SS-Panzer Regiment (9th SS-Panzer Division)	5	35%	19	54%	2	100%	58	124%	30
12th SS-Panzer Regiment (12th SS-Panzer Division)	4	29%	3	75%	23	89%	41	100%	24
Total (average percent)	62	55%	107	75%	161	92%	416	101%	180

*Does not include broken-down tanks still in German hands

Aside from a shortage of equipment and training, the Panzer divisions were plagued by fuel shortages. At the outset of the campaign, the divisions carried enough fuel with them to travel 60 miles (100km) under normal conditions. But in the move from staging areas to the front in the days before the attack, the divisions found that the terrain and the drivers' inexperience led to such high consumption that only 30–40 miles (50–60km) could be covered with the remaining fuel. A resupply of another 60 miles-worth was brought up on the morning of December 16, 1944. Although a significant

WEHRMACHT AFV STRENGTH IN THE ARDENNES, DECEMBER 1944–JANUARY 1945

Armored fighting vehicle	December 16, 1944	December 26, 1944	January 6, 1945	January 16, 1945
Pzkfw IV	317	219	169	172
Panther	341	219	173	170
Tiger	14	14		
Kingtiger	52	39	13	35
Sub-total tanks	*724*	*491*	*355*	*377*
StG III	304	281	229	264
StuH (105mm)	42	42	26	37
Hetzer	99	110	73	68
Panzer IV/70	171	130	97	99
Jagdpanther	21	18	17	17
Sub-total assault gun/tank destroyer	*637*	*581*	*442*	*485*
105mm SP	20	18	14	12
150mm SP	24	30	27	20
Sturmtiger	8	8	8	8
Brummbar	21	18		
Heavy infantry gun SP	33	21	14	13
Sub-total SP Arty	*106*	*95*	*63*	*53*
Light armored car	176	170	137	131
Heavy armored car	41	27	15	13
Sub-total armored cars	217	197	152	144
Sdkfz 250	369	330	251	215
SdKfz 251/75mm	135	129	108	97
Sdkfz 251	1,239	1,092	895	852
Sub-total half-tracks	*1,743*	*1,551*	*1,254*	*1,164*
Sub-total heavy & medium AFVs	*1,467*	*1,167*	*860*	*915*
Sub-total light AFVs	*1,960*	*1,748*	*1,406*	*1,308*
Total AFVs	**3,427**	**2,915**	**2,266**	**2,223**

stockpile of fuel had been built up for the offensive, it was far behind the front lines and difficult to move forward. The fuel situation was exacerbated by the use of tanks such as the Panther and Kingtiger that consumed 75–100 gallons (350–500 liters) of fuel per 60 miles (100km) of road travel. By comparison, the PzKpfw IV consumed only 45 gallons (200–210 liters) of fuel – between 40 and 60 percent of a Panther's or Kingtiger's consumption.

The 1st SS-Panzer Division "Leibstandarte" provides a good example of the difficulties faced in re-equipping and training the Panzer regiments prior to the Ardennes offensive. The division had not been committed to Normandy until July and so suffered lower casualties than other Waffen-SS units such as 12th SS-Panzer Division which had been in action since D-Day. "Leibstandarte" was scoured of most of its heavy equipment during the fighting and its Panther battalion, the 1st Battalion of the 1st SS-Panzer Regiment, lost nearly all its tanks in Normandy and about a third of its men. Of the regiment's officers, its commander, Joachim Peiper, was in hospital from combat exhaustion, its two battalion commanders were in hospital and would not return to the regiment, four company commanders were wounded, and one company commander and at least four platoon commanders had been killed. The division was pulled off the line in early September with plans to make it operational by the end of October. The 1st SS-Panzer Regiment received its full complement of new recruits, but the standards of late 1944 were not comparable to previous years and the Waffen-SS received draftees as well as volunteers. The new recruits had undergone basic training but specialist training had been minimal and few of the trainees had ever been in a tank or fired a tank gun. Driver training was elementary with only two hours of actual armored vehicle driving to receive a license, usually on obsolete tanks. Under the new reduced tables of equipment, the 1st Battalion of the 1st SS-Panzer Regiment initially had two companies of Panther tanks (17 each) plus command tanks for a total of 38 Panthers while its counterpart second battalion had PzKpfw IV tanks; tank shortages meant that the four companies were merged into a mixed battalion instead of the usual pattern of one Panther and one PzKpfw IV battalion. Since the 1st SS-Panzer Division and its neighbor the 12th SS-Panzer Division were assigned the principal route of the attack, they were assigned a battalion of Tiger II heavy tanks instead of a standard full-strength Panzer regiment.

German Panzer regiments in the Ardennes were of mixed composition including the PzKpfw IV as seen here in the center, and the later Panther Ausf. G seen above and to the right. In the foreground is an SdKfz. 251/9 (7.5cm), an assault gun version of the standard German armored half-track used to provide fire support in Panzergrenadier units. (USAOM-APG)

The 1st Battalion did not receive its new Panthers until mid-October at Grafenwöhr, which permitted training to begin at Wietzendorf in the last week of October 1944. The training was compromised by an almost total lack of fuel and ammunition. Gunnery training consisted of dry runs, with occasional use of co-axial machine guns. The surviving veterans of the Normandy fighting attempted to impart as much practical knowledge as possible to the new recruits. Only one actual live firing exercise was conducted in early November. The regiment was transferred by train to its forward deployment area around Weilerwist on November 14–18, 1944. Training continued in this area but was again hampered by a lack of fuel, which prevented any exercises above platoon level. Live fire was out of the question, and strict radio silence limited training in this area as well. Since the cover story for the deployment was to defend the area against an expected Allied advance, the training focused on defensive tactics. The Panther companies were finally moved forward by road on the night of December 13–14, 1944, to an area in the Blankenheim forest a short distance from the front line.

The 1st SS-Panzer Division's partner in the Ardennes attack was the 12th SS-Panzer Division "Hitlerjugend" which escaped from Normandy with heavy losses including over 4,400 wounded and more than 4,000 killed or captured; it had lost nearly 75 percent of the troops in its two Panzergrenadier regiments. Its Panther regiment, the 1st Battalion of the 12th SS-Panzer Regiment, had lost over 40 percent of its men and was moved to lower Saxony in October 1944 to refit. Replacements came from SS replacement units as well as Luftwaffe and Kriegsmarine troops freed up by the fuel shortages. Like the 1st SS-Panzer Regiment, it received only enough replacement tanks in October–November 1944 to equip four tank companies instead of eight, and so had to amalgamate them into a hybrid Panther/PzKpfw IV battalion. The Panther companies faced the same difficulties: little fuel or ammunition for training, no batteries for training radiomen. However, the divisional commander felt that the 12th SS-Panzer Regiment was in adequate shape with "good and front-tested soldiers, NCOs, and officers." His main worry was the Panzergrenadier regiment and reconnaissance battalion, which were not ready for combat when the division was moved westward in mid-November 1944.

In comparison with the US armored divisions, Panzer divisions in late 1944 were significantly weaker than their American counterparts in terms of tanks and armored fighting vehicles. So for example, the 1st SS-Panzer Division had 34 PzKpfw IV, 37 Panther and 30 Kingtiger tanks for a total of 101 tanks, and the 12th SS-Panzer Division had 39 PzKpfw IV and 38 Panthers for a total of 77 tanks. A comparable American division at the time such as the 9th Armored Division had 186 M4 medium tanks, while the two US heavy armored divisions (2nd and 3rd Armored divisions) had about 230 medium tanks. The 12th SS-Panzer Division was so weak in tanks that a tank destroyer formation, 560th Heavy Panzerjäger Battalion, equipped with Jagdpanzer IV and Jagdpanther tank destroyers, was attached. The Panzergrenadier battalions were supposed to be equipped with SdKfz 251 half-tracks, but in fact only one in four battalions was so equipped.

The 2nd SS-Panzer Division "Das Reich" had escaped from Normandy with relatively modest combat casualties of 4,000 though it had suffered especially heavy casualties in its 2nd SS-Panzer Regiment of about 40 percent and most of its heavy equipment lost in the Roncey pocket. In contrast to the two previous SS-Panzer regiments, it received no Panther tanks until late November. However, it was eventually refitted with four companies of Panthers so that the 2nd SS-Panzer Regiment went into combat in the Ardennes at full strength; its second battalion was full strength but with two of its four companies substituting StG III assault guns for PzKpfw IV tanks. The belated arrival of its Panther tanks compromised the training of the new recruits, but the division was in significantly better shape than the two Waffen-SS Panzer divisions of the 1st SS-Panzer Corps. The officer casualties suffered in Normandy led to most command positions being filled by elevating combat leaders one step. The Panther battalion commander, Obersturmbannführer Rudolph Enseling, was elevated to command of the entire 2nd SS-Panzer Regiment due to the death of Christian Tyschen; he was replaced by 26-year-old Wilhelm Matzke. Panther company commanders were new as well: Obersturmführer Karl Muhlek with 1/2nd SS-Panzer Regiment and Alfred Hargesheimer with 2/2nd SS-Panzer Regiment.

The 2nd SS-Panzer Division's partner in the 2nd SS-Panzer Corps was the 9th SS-Panzer Division "Hohenstaufen" which had suffered heavier losses than any of the other Waffen-SS divisions amongst its Panzer troops in Normandy, extricating barely a third of its Panzer crew. It was sent to the quiet Arnhem region in the Netherlands to rest and refit, only to become enmeshed in the famous battle for the "Bridge too Far" in September 1944. It did not receive its replacement Panther tanks until late November 1944 and so had little time for proper training of its new tank crews, which constituted more than half of its men.

Manteuffel's 5th Panzer Army included four Panzer divisions in its two Panzer corps. Manteuffel considered all three of his Panzer divisions to be "very suitable for attack" in mid-December even if they were not fully up to strength in armored vehicles. At the time, an army Panzer division had an authorized strength of 32 PzKpfw IV, 60 PzKpfw V Panthers, and 51 StuG III assault guns, but few of the divisions taking part in the Ardennes offensive had a full complement of equipment. Both the 9th and 116th Panzer divisions remained in combat against the US Army in the fighting from September to early December 1944 along the Siegfried Line. They had generally been kept near full strength in November 1944 in anticipation of the Ardennes offensive, and given a short break in early December to refit and fill out their ranks. Although they were the most battle-hardened and experienced Panzer divisions serving in the Ardennes, there is a thin line between battle-hardened and battle-weary.

The 116th Panzer Division had been fighting on the western front since the summer and had been repeatedly burned out and rebuilt. After taking part in the initial defense of Aachen, the division was withdrawn in the early autumn and rebuilt. Although it was close to authorized strength in personnel at the start of the offensive, it was short of tanks with only 26 PzKpfw IV, 43 PzKpfw V Panthers, and 13 Jagdpanzer IV tank destroyers. The 2nd Panzer Division had been destroyed in the Falaise pocket, and was rebuilt in the Eifel region in the autumn of 1944. The division's 3rd Panzer Regiment lost more than half its troops in France and most of its tanks. It was moved to the Fallingbostel area for refitting and began receiving new Panzers at the end of October. It was only slightly better equipped than the 116th Panzer Division, with 26 PzKpfw IV, 49 PzKpfw V Panthers, and 45 StuG III assault guns. The Panzer Lehr Division was destroyed in Normandy during the US breakout near St Lô, rebuilt again, and sent into action against Patton's Third Army in the Saar. Panzer Lehr's 130th Panzer Regiment had been virtually destroyed by the Allied bombing attacks at the beginning of Operation *Cobra* on July 24, 1944, but had been partially rebuilt after Normandy and brought back to full strength in November 1944, with the

The workhorse of the German infantry divisions was the StuG III Ausf. G assault gun. These provided direct fire support for infantry units, but were usually in short supply. (Military History Institute)

usual problems of too little fuel and ammunition for proper training of new recruits. At the start of the offensive it was close to authorized strength in personnel, but the weakest of Manteuffel's three Panzer divisions in tanks with only 30 PzKpfw IV, 23 PzKpfw V Panthers, and 14 Jagdpanzer IV tank destroyers. The army reserve was the Führer Begleit Brigade, which was relatively well equipped with 23 PzKpfw IV tanks, 20 StG III assault guns, and a near full complement of troops.

German Infantry Divisions

If the situation in the elite formations was discouraging, it was even worse in the infantry divisions. The fighting power of German infantry divisions had become increasingly illusory as the war progressed due to Hitler's insistence on maintaining a large order of battle. The nominal strength of these units does not adequately explain their combat potential. The severe personnel shortage in the wake of the 1944 summer debacles forced the Wehrmacht to hastily recreate the infantry divisions without adequate training. Older men, under-age recruits, troops from other services such as the Luftwaffe and navy, and men who had previously been excluded due to medical problems were all put into infantry units, with little or no specialized infantry training. In addition, manpower resources from the fringes of Germany were inducted including ethnic German *Volksdeutsche* from eastern Europe; Poles and Czechs from provinces incorporated into the Reich; Alsatians; and some volunteer foreign troops. Heavy equipment such as artillery was often an agglomeration of captured foreign types mixed with standard German types. To make matters worse, some of the divisions allotted to the Ardennes offensive had been involved in the furious fighting in the autumn of 1944, and were withdrawn only days or weeks before the start of the offensive without adequate time for rebuilding.

Germany's precarious manpower situation in 1944 led to the creation of Volksgrenadier divisions as an alternative to conventional infantry divisions. The new organization was intended to offer maximum firepower with minimum personnel and equipment. They were intended primarily for defensive missions on elongated fronts, and were not optimized for offensive missions due to inadequate mobile resources. Curiously enough, their development was the responsibility of Colonel Claus von Stauffenberg, the officer who planted the bomb during the July 1944 plot against Hitler. To cut down on personnel, the infantry component took one of two forms, either a three-regiment configuration with a cut-down regimental strength of only two grenadier battalions each, or a two-regiment configuration with the normal three battalions. In either case, the new binary organization proved awkward in combat compared to the traditional triangular configuration in the regular infantry divisions. In the case of the common two-battalion regiment, it compelled the commander to keep both battalions in the line instead of the usual practice of leaving one battalion free as a reserve or for rest and re-equipping.

The Volksgrenadier units were supposed to be favored in the appointment of regimental and battalion commanders and assigned young, combat-proven officers with a minimum of the German Cross in Gold, and preferably holders of the Knight's Cross or Iron Cross. As in so many other respects of the plans for these units, this often proved impossible due to shortages. To make up for its weakened force structure, one or two platoons in each rifle company were supposed to be armed with the rapid-fire StG 43 assault rifle instead of the standard 98k rifle. To enhance antitank defense, the units were equipped with large numbers of Panzerfaust antitank rockets. Efforts were also made to equip each division with a company of 14 Jagdpanzer 38(t) Hetzer, which, contrary to their tank hunter designation, were actually intended to be used as dual-purpose assault guns in place of the more expensive StG III.

Aside from their organizational problems, the new Volksgrenadier divisions suffered from poor manpower resources. Those used in the Ardennes campaign had many older personnel of very mixed quality with an

A Volksgrenadier captured during the fighting around Bütgenbach in January 1945. Many of the Volksgrenadier units were provided with snow suits or other forms of winter camouflage prior to the Ardennes offensive. (NARA)

The Jagdpanzer 38(t), better known as the Hetzer, was widely deployed in the new Volksgrenadier divisions as a combination assault gun and tank destroyer. On paper, the divisions were each supposed to have a company of 14 of these, though this was not always the case. This example is preserved at the Bastogne memorial museum. (Author)

average age of 35 years. Of the three infantry divisions of 1st SS-Panzer Corps that were expected to make the initial breakthrough, the best was the 12th Volksgrenadier Division (VGD), which was personally selected by Hitler to lead the attack due to its excellent performance in the defense of Aachen. Having suffered heavy casualties in the autumn fighting, it had been withdrawn into Germany only on December 2 for hasty refitting prior to the offensive. The 277th Volksgrenadier Division had been gutted in the Normandy fighting and reconstituted in Hungary in September 1944 after absorbing the remains of the shattered 374th Volksgrenadier Division. It was fleshed out with young Austrian conscripts who lacked the usual German basic training, along with ethnic German *Volksdeutsche* from eastern Europe, and Alsatians. The latter two groups were characterized by the divisional commander as "an untrustworthy element." This division was rated as *Kampfwert III*, suitable for defense. Though still under strength, the division was deployed for static defense along the Westwall for most of the autumn and gradually brought up to strength with transfers from the navy and air force with no infantry training. The US Army had faced the 3rd Fallschirmjäger Division in the hedgerows of Normandy the previous summer and considered the paratroopers to be some of the toughest opponents they had ever fought. As in the case of the Waffen-SS Panzer divisions, this division had been decimated in the Normandy fighting and was a shadow of its former self. Replacement troops came mainly from Luftwaffe support units with no infantry training to say nothing of paratroop training. Casualties among the officers and troop leaders had been crippling, and some senior command positions had been filled by Luftwaffe staff officers with no infantry experience. It had been further weakened by almost continual combat through the late autumn, and arrived in the Ardennes with little opportunity to rebuild.

The infantry divisions in Manteuffel's 5th Panzer Army were the usual varied assortment. The 18th Volksgrenadier Division was created in September 1944 in Denmark using remnants of the 18th Luftwaffe Field Division, surplus navy personnel, and army troops from units shattered on the eastern front. It was committed to action near Trier in November, and against the US V Corps during the Roer fighting in early December. It was pulled out of the line shortly before the offensive and brought up to strength. The 62nd Volksgrenadier Division was reconstituted after the disastrous summer 1944 fighting in the east, using inexperienced recruits from the 583rd Volksgrenadier Division. It was nearly at authorized strength at the start of the offensive but Manteuffel did not consider it suitable for offensive operations. The 560th Volksgrenadier Division was a new division formed in August 1944 from Luftwaffe personnel in Norway and Denmark and initially deployed in southern Norway. It was near full strength at the start of the offensive, though completely inexperienced. The 26th Volksgrenadier Division was recreated in October 1944 after its namesake division was decimated by the Red Army along the Baranow front in Poland in September 1944. It was rebuilt with troops from the 582nd Volksgrenadier Division, fleshed out with surplus navy and Luftwaffe troops.

Brandenberger's 7th Army in Luxembourg was by far the weakest of the three attacking German armies. When planning the campaign, General

Brandenberger had asked for a Panzer or Panzergrenadier division to spearhead the thrust along 7th Army's right flank plus six infantry divisions. He instead received only four infantry divisions due to the relatively low priority given to this sector. The main effort on the right flank was assigned to the 5th Fallschirmjäger Division, which had been recently rebuilt using only partially trained, surplus Luftwaffe personnel. Brandenberger glumly noted that: "In training and in the quality of its officers, both junior and senior, the division displayed notable deficiencies." To make matters worse, many of the senior paratrooper officers were contemptuous and sometimes insubordinate to the new divisional commander. But it was the largest of the divisions in his army, and the best equipped in heavy weapons including an assault gun battalion, so it was given the main mission. The 352nd Volksgrenadier Division was a reconstituted replacement for the division that had fought the US Army so well at Omaha Beach and in Normandy. But it had been badly beaten up in the autumn fighting along the Siegfried Line. It was close to full strength at the start of the offensive, though lacking about a quarter of its authorized NCOs. The 212th Volksgrenadier Division was a reconstruction of a division shattered in Lithuania in the summer of 1944, and rebuilt in Bavaria before the Ardennes campaign. It was closer to authorized strength than the other Volksgrenadier divisions and Brandenberger felt it was his best division. The 276th Volksgrenadier Division was a recreation of a division destroyed in the Falaise pocket in August 1944.

Firepower Support

The quality of German artillery support for the Ardennes offensive was uneven. Although the amount of artillery was extensive, shortages of ammunition and mobility problems plagued the artillery during the campaign. In November 1944, the Wehrmacht had only half of the 105mm howitzer ammunition and a third of the 150mm stocks they possessed when attacking Poland in September 1939.

One innovation that debuted in the Ardennes was the *Koppelungsgerät*, an automated fire direction system that was introduced by General der Artillerie Karl Tholte and his Special Artillery Staff. This was akin to the US Army's fire direction centers employed at battalion level, but on a much

grander scale. An associated fire direction battery selected the targets, and then the data was passed to subordinated batteries by means of radio-teletype or field telephone. The intention was to use the system to direct the fire of the army and corps level batteries, enabling some 300 to 400 guns to be directed against a single target. This never fully materialized due to the dispersion of the artillery, indifferent communication nets, and the general shortage of ammunition.

The Wehrmacht massed a considerable amount of artillery for the Ardennes offensive including 12 artillery brigades with 960 guns, seven Volks artillery corps, and eight Volks Werfer brigades. As was the case with most resources, preference went to the 6th Panzer Army with the other two armies receiving smaller allotments of these heavy artillery assets. The field armies deployed their Volks artillery corps and Volks Werfer brigades generally on a scale of one artillery corps and one Werfer regiment per corps.

The workhorse of the German field artillery was the 105mm field howitzer like these, which were captured by the 35th Division near Lutrebois on January 17, 1945. This is the improved leFH 18/40 which used the lighter carriage of the PaK 40 antitank gun. (NARA)

Heavy firepower for German artillery was provided by the schwere Feldhaubitze 18 150mm howitzer. These served in a heavy artillery battalion in German infantry divisions. (Military History Institute)

While the idea of an artillery corps may create the impression of a massive amount of artillery, in fact, these formations were far grander in name than reality since they were in fact regimental in strength. Each consisted of five medium and heavy artillery batteries and a heavy antitank battery with 88mm guns. The Volks Werfer brigades had been created in November 1944 and usually consisted of two regiments with a total of eight batteries and 108 210mm multi-barrel Nebelwerfer rocket launchers.

Each of the three corps in the 6th Panzer Army had an additional heavy artillery battalion with guns of between 150mm and 210mm caliber. The 1st SS-Panzer Corps was the most heavily reinforced of the corps, assigned a full Volks Werfer brigade and two of the army's Volks artillery corps. For the Ardennes offensive, the artillery was supposed to be allotted a 14-day supply of ammunition but in fact received about ten days' supply. Resupply after the start of the offensive was very meager since the dumps were near Bonn and subject to Allied air interdiction. German artillery in the Ardennes was adequate in number, but with feeble motorization and sparse ammunition supplies. After the first few days of the offensive, about half of the towed artillery was left behind by the advancing corps due to lack of motorization and road congestion.

Hermann Göring's Luftwaffe had promised to provide air support for the Ardennes offensive, but failed to do so. This was in part due to the weather, but also due to the enormous shift in composition that had been forced on to the Luftwaffe by the fuel shortage. Nearly all of the Luftwaffe bomber force, and much of the ground-attack force, was grounded by the lack of fuel. Top priority went to "Defense of the Reich" fighter units, which were the only units given priority for fuel and training. By December 1944, the Luftwaffe simply didn't have a force well configured for close air support. Long-range bombardment was left to pin-prick attacks with unreliable and inaccurate V-1 and V-2 missiles. Battlefield interdiction of Allied supply lines and communication networks was impossible due both to the lack of operational medium bomber units and to Allied air superiority. The "Defense of the Reich" formations were concentrated in industrial regions of Germany, not near the front lines.

The distorted organizational structure of the Luftwaffe in late 1944 led to plans to concentrate the fighter force for a surprise attack on Allied airfields, codenamed Operation *Bodenplatte* (Base Plate). Hitler ordered a significant shift in Luftwaffe resources to support the Ardennes operation by transferring a large number of fighters from strategic air defense over the Reich to tactical fighter missions over the battlefield. As a result, Luftwaffe Command West's fighter component went from only 300 single-engine fighters in October 1944 to 1,770 at the time of the offensive. This did not provide much solace for the Wehrmacht, however, since there were only 155 ground-attack aircraft available. The majority of fighter pilots were poorly trained compared to their Allied adversaries, and what training they had received focused on ground-controlled intercepts of heavy bombers, not the rough-and-tumble of dogfights and ground strafing. In the event, the poor weather in the first week of the offensive severely limited Luftwaffe operations and forced the postponement of *Bodenplatte* until New Year's Day by which time it was irrelevant. The Ardennes offensive also saw the use of a number of German wonder weapons, including the bomber version of the Me-262 jet fighter, the first use of the Arado Ar-234 jet bomber. *Bodenplatte* was finally launched at 0930hrs on New Year's Day 1945. Although the attack did catch many Allied airbases by surprise, the attack was a disaster for the Luftwaffe with heavy losses amongst the inexperienced pilots.

Wehrmacht Order of Battle

The Wehrmacht order of battle as listed here covers the forces available and present at the start of the campaign.

6th Panzer Army	**Oberstgruppenführer Josef Dietrich**
388th Volks Artillery Corps	
402nd Volks Artillery Corps	
405th Volks Artillery Corps	
4th Volks Werfer Brigade	
9th Volks Werfer Brigade	
17th Volks Werfer Brigade	
1st SS-Panzer Corps	**Gruppenführer Hermann Preiss**
1st SS-Panzer Division	Oberführer Wilhelm Mohnke
12th SS-Panzer Division	Standartenführer Hugo Kraas
12th Volksgrenadier Division	Generalmajor Gerhard Engel
277th Volksgrenadier Division	Oberst Wilhelm Viebig
3rd Fallschirmjäger Division	Generalmajor Walther Wadehn
150th Panzer Brigade	Obersturmbannführer Otto Skorzeny
2nd SS-Panzer Corps	**Obergruppenführer Willi Bittrich**
2nd SS-Panzer Division	Brigadeführer Heinz Lammerding
9th SS-Panzer Division	Brigadeführer Sylwester Stadler
67th Army Corps	General der Infanterie Otto Hitzfeld
272nd Volksgrenadier Division	Oberst Georg Kosmalia
326th Volksgrenadier Division	Generalmajor Erwin Kaschner
3rd Panzergrenadier Division	Generalmajor Walter Denkert
5th Panzer Army	**General der Panzertruppen Hasso von Manteuffel**
66th Army Corps	General der Artillerie Walther Lucht
18th Volksgrenadier Division	Oberst Gunther Hoffmann-Schönborn
62nd Volksgrenadier Division	Oberst Friedrich Kittel
Führer Begleit Brigade	**Oberst Otto Remer**
766th Volks Artillery Corps	
401st Volks Artillery Corps	
7th Volks Werfer Brigade	
15th Volks Werfer Brigade	
16th Volks Werfer Brigade	
58th Panzer Corps	General der Panzertruppen Walter Krüger
560th Volksgrenadier Division	Oberst Rudolf Langhäuser
116th Panzer Division	Generalmajor Siegfried von Waldenburg
47th Panzer Corps	General der Panzertruppen Heinrich von Lüttwitz
2nd Panzer Division	Oberst Meinrad von Lauchert
Panzer Lehr Division	Generalleutnant Fritz Bayerlein
26th Volksgrenadier Division	Oberst Heinz Kokott

7th Army	General der Panzertruppen Erich Brandenberger
406th Volks Artillery Corps	
408th Volks Artillery Corps	
8th Volks Werfer Brigade	
18th Volks Werfer Brigade	
85th Army Corps	General der Infanterie Baptist Kneiss
5th Fallschirmjäger Division	Generalmajor Ludwig Heilmann
352nd Volksgrenadier Division	Oberst Erich Schmidt
80th Army Corps	General der Infanterie Franz Beyer
212th Volksgrenadier Division	Generalleutnant Franz Sensfuss
276th Volksgrenadier Division	Generalmajor Kurt Möhring

US ARMY

One young officer described the Ardennes sector as the US Army's "kindergarten and old-age home" – the sector where the newest and most battle-weary divisions were deployed. This choice was deliberate since Bradley felt that this sector was likely to remain quiet. Besides having inexperienced and worn-out divisions, the Ardennes deployment was thinly spread with four divisions covering about 40 miles (60km) of front line, far beyond what was considered prudent in US tactical doctrine.

US Infantry Divisions

In the northern sector opposite the 6th Panzer Army, the principal US units were two green infantry divisions, the 99th and 106th divisions. The 99th Division, nicknamed the "Battlin' Babes," was the southernmost unit of Gerow's V Corps, stretching along the Siegfried Line from Hofen to Lanzerath. It had arrived in Belgium in mid-November, replaced the 9th Division on the front line, and had become reasonably well acclimatized to the front. The division had been formed in 1942, but in March 1944, 3,000 riflemen were pulled from its ranks to make up for combat losses in Italy. Their places were filled by young men from the Army Specialized Training Program (ASTP).

The ASTP was an effort by the army chief of staff, General George C. Marshall, to divert the smartest young soldiers into advanced academic training. At a time when less than 5 percent of young men went to college, Marshall did not want to waste their talents and had them sent for further schooling rather than to the battlefield. ASTP came to abrupt end in 1944 when rising infantry casualties created an immediate need for troops, so 100,000 ASTP college students were transferred to active service. Some were sent as engineers to the secret atomic bomb program, others to technical branches of the army, but most ended up as riflemen.

Although the Ardennes was a quiet front compared to the Hürtgen forest, the division suffered moderate casualties during its first month at the front. The US Army had not paid enough attention to the need for winter clothing or boots, and what resources were available in Europe were scandalously mismanaged. Some of the division's rifle platoons had suffered 30 percent casualties in the latter half of November, more than half due to trench foot. On the positive side, the division's forward rifle companies had time to dig in, creating a network of foxholes and shelters with log roofs that would reduce artillery casualties in the ensuing battle. The division covered a 12-mile (19km) wide sector from the hilly Monschau forest, south to the more open country near Losheim.

The 106th Division had a less fortunate experience. The division was formed in early 1943 and by the spring of 1944 was ready to take the field. However, from April to August 1944, the division was gutted as more than 7,000 of its riflemen were shipped off to serve as replacements. They were replaced at the last minute by a mixture of ASTP students, gunners from antiaircraft and coastal artillery units, military policemen, and service personnel. This process had hardly ended when the division was shipped off to England in October 1944. Not only did the 106th Division have less unit cohesion than the 99th Division, but it arrived much later. It took over the northern sector of Middleton's VIII Corps from the 2nd Infantry Division on December 11, a few days before the German attack. To make matters worse, the division was thinly spread along a 15-mile (24km) front projecting into German lines on the Schnee Eifel plateau. The previous tenants of this position, the battle-hardened 2nd Infantry Division, had complained about its precarious location, but higher headquarters were reluctant to pull the units back as they sat within the German Westwall defensive belt.

The 99th and 106th divisions sat on the boundary between Gerow's V Corps to the north and Middleton's VIII Corps to the south. Between them was the 8-mile (13km) Losheim Gap. This area was covered by the 14th Cavalry Group with two armored cavalry reconnaissance squadrons. These

The 82nd Airborne Division was rushed to fill the gap created by the collapse of the 106th Division on the Schnee Eifel, and here a BAR squad automatic weapons team from Co. C, 325th Glider Infantry, is seen in action in Belgium on December 23, 1944. (NARA)

cavalry groups, as their name suggests, were intended for scouting and not positional defense. Although they had considerable firepower for such small units, this was mostly mounted on the squadrons' jeeps and light armored vehicles and was of little use when the unit was deployed in a dismounted defensive position. The squadrons' tactics were summarized as "sneak and peek," and they were spread much too thinly to create any sort of credible barrier. It was not unusual for a cavalry group to be placed along a corps boundary during offensive operations, since they could be used for mobile screening, but they were not well suited to this role when the mission became defensive. The first of its squadrons deployed on December 10 and the second did not follow until December 15. As a result, the corps boundary, which happened to be situated on a traditional invasion route, was weakly protected by a unit very ill-suited to a defensive role. It was no coincidence that the German plan aimed its heaviest strike force through this area.

In view of the composition of the attacking German forces, it is worth mentioning the antitank capabilities of the US Army. The organic antitank defense of the infantry divisions was a license copy of the British 6-pdr, the 57mm antitank gun. There were 57 in each division, with 18 in each regiment. By 1944 this gun was obsolete, and the official history of the campaign pungently describes them as "tank fodder." A more useful weapon was the 2.36in antitank rocket launcher, more popularly called the bazooka. There were 557 in each division, and they were generally allotted on a scale of one per rifle squad. Their warhead was not as effective as comparable German weapons such as the Panzerfaust or Panzerschreck, but in the hands of a brave soldier, they could disable German tanks by a well-placed side or rear hit. Most infantry divisions had an attached tank destroyer battalion equipped with 36 3in antitank guns. Unfortunately, in the spring of 1943, the organization of these units was changed, and a portion of the force was converted from self-propelled M10 3in gun motor carriages to towed 3in guns based on a mistaken assessment of the Tunisian campaign. These towed battalions proved to be poorly suited to conditions in the European theater, and the two battalions attached to the infantry in the St. Vith sector were this configuration, as was the battalion attached to the unfortunate 14th Cavalry Group.

There were a few bright spots in the American dispositions in the northern sector. The battle-hardened 2nd Infantry Division had been pulled off the Schnee Eifel in early December with the arrival of the 106th Division, and had been shifted northward to take part in the V Corps offensive against the Roer

US Army antitank defense was poorly served by the cumbersome 3in antitank gun which had indifferent performance against contemporary German tanks and was too heavy to be easily maneuvered by its crew. This gun belonged to the 801st Tank Destroyer Battalion, attached to the 14th Cavalry Group, and was knocked out in Honsfeld during an encounter with the spearhead of Kampfgruppe Peiper on the morning of December 17. (NARA)

dams in mid-December. Some elements of the division were still intermixed with the 99th Division or stationed on the nearby Elsenborn Ridge. The proximity and combat readiness of this unit would play a crucial role in the US Army's subsequent ability to hold the northern shoulder of the Bulge.

In the center, the VIII Corps had three infantry divisions and two of the three combat commands of the 9th Armored Division. Its northernmost unit, the 106th Division, was covered above. The 28th Division was deployed along an extended front that largely coincided with the attack sector of the 5th Panzer Army from near the junction of the Belgian–Luxembourg–German borders, south along the Luxembourg frontier. The division was based around a Pennsylvania National Guard division, and was commanded by the hero of Omaha Beach, General Norman Cota. The division had been shattered by the fighting in the Hürtgen forest in early November and had suffered 6,184 casualties in two weeks of fighting, one of the most ferocious bloodlettings suffered by any US Army division in World War II. The division had been sent for rebuilding to the Ardennes front and by mid-December was back near authorized strength. All three infantry regiments were in the line with the 112th Infantry in the north, the 110th in the center, and the 109th in the southern sector. The front was grossly overextended: for example, the 110th held 10 miles (16km) of front with only two battalions, with the third in divisional reserve. Under such circumstances, the best the units could do was to create a thin defensive screen. So, typically, the infantry battalions strung out their companies in a few villages a mile or so behind the front on Skyline Drive, the road that ran along the ridge line that paralleled the frontier. Each company had a few outposts closer to the front that were manned only during daylight hours. With so few forces to cover such a broad front, the regiment was concentrated to bar access to the best routes westward. The heavily forested and hilly front line was in reality a no man's land, and both sides sent out small patrols at night to take prisoners and harass their opponents. Combat Command A of the 9th Armored Division held the area south of the 28th Division. The 9th Armored Division was divided into its three combat commands, with CCA fighting in the south between the 28th and 4th Infantry divisions, the CCB fighting in the defense of St. Vith, and the CCR positioned in reserve. The CCA, 9th Armored Division, had a relatively narrow sector about 2 miles (3.2km) wide along the Our River. Due to its defensive mission, the 60th Armored Infantry Battalion held the front line with the 19th Tank Battalion and 89th Reconnaissance Squadron behind it. The division arrived in Europe in September 1944, but was not committed to action as a whole until the Ardennes fighting.

The 12th Infantry Regiment of the 4th Infantry Division held the southernmost area of the German attack zone. The regiment was spread along a sector about 9 miles (14.5km) wide, with the neighboring sector to the south being held by the division's 8th Infantry Regiment. The 4th Infantry Division had landed at Utah Beach on D-Day, and had fought in the brutal hedgerow battles in Normandy through the summer, suffering 100 percent casualties in its infantry companies. The division had recuperated in the early autumn, only to be subjected to the horrific fighting in the Hürtgen forest in November 1944. In two weeks of fighting in late November, the division suffered 6,000 casualties, leaving it a hollow shell. It was deployed on the "ghost front" to recuperate and rebuild. Many of its rifle companies were at half strength, and the attached 70th Tank Battalion had only 11 of its allotted 54 M4 medium tanks. The 12th Infantry, which would bear the brunt of the fighting, had been rated as "a badly decimated and weary regiment" in the days before the German offensive.

Even if the US forces stationed in the Ardennes were not especially impressive, the US Army had ample resources in the European Theater of Operations, and the mobility to quickly move them when necessary. The most critical phase of the Ardennes campaign was the first week, and it would be a race to see whether the Wehrmacht could penetrate the American defense and reach Liège before the US Army could mobilize its considerable resources and bring them to bear against the German attack force.

Supreme Headquarters Allied Expeditionary Force (SHAEF) had very modest theater reserves due to the extended front from the North Sea to the Mediterranean. Two divisions were held in strategic reserve, the 82nd and 101st Airborne divisions, which had been beaten up in prolonged defensive operations in the Netherlands in the wake of the failed *Market Garden* operation. They were rebuilding when the Ardennes campaign started. Nevertheless, they were both excellent units with high morale, and could be moved quickly by truck.

The Armored Divisions

The rest of the US Army was heavily motorized, and the most mobile of all were the armored divisions. The First Army had very modest tank resources in the Ardennes at the time of the German attack. The usual pattern was to attach a single tank battalion and a single tank destroyer battalion to each infantry division. This was considerably more lavish than German infantry divisions, which by the end of 1944 were lucky to have a company of StuG III or Jagdpanzer 38(t) assault guns. Indeed, the combined strength of tanks and tank destroyers in most US infantry divisions rivaled the Panzer strength in many of the badly depleted German Panzer and Panzergrenadier divisions.

There were several US armored divisions on either side of the Ardennes in mid-December 1944, and they had the mobility to intervene quickly. US tactical doctrine employed the armored division in a combined-arms fashion and the division regularly fought in triangular fashion, organized into combat commands (CCA, CCB, and CCR/reserve). The idea was that two combat commands would be in action with the third (CCR) kept in reserve or for rebuilding and maintenance. Each combat command typically was built around a tank battalion, armored infantry battalion, and armored field artillery battalion, with additional engineer, signals, and other units added as necessary. These combat commands were relatively self-contained fighting forces and, as will become evident in the campaign narrative below, the First Army would regularly break off a combat command from a division and send it off on its own assignment.

The US Army armored divisions were primarily intended as offensive formations. Under ideal scenarios, the infantry divisions conducted the breakthrough and then the armored divisions were injected to conduct the breakout and the exploitation phases. US doctrine was adamantly opposed to the use of armored divisions in conducting the initial breakthrough, as it was felt that by this stage of the war infantry seldom suffered the sort of "tank panic" that facilitated Blitzkrieg operations in 1939–41. By 1944, well-emplaced infantry formations bolstered with embedded antitank guns and antitank rocket launchers were a formidable defensive barrier against tank attack. US armor divisions were regularly used in defensive operations, but were not optimally configured for such tasks. Their main problem was that they were too light in infantry for defensive purposes with only three battalions of armored infantry. They had less than a third the riflemen of an infantry division since the armored infantry battalions had fewer rifleman than "leg" infantry battalions. This was apparent in some of the skirmishes described in the campaign narrative here, and helps to explain the predicament of the 7th Armored Division in trying to hold St. Vith early in the campaign.

The two exceptions to the general rules were the 2nd and 3rd Armored divisions which played a central role in the defeat of the German offensive around Christmas. All the other armored divisions were organized under the "light" 1943 tables of organization and equipment and so had three each of tank, armored infantry, and armored field artillery battalions. The 2nd and 3rd Armored divisions were already in Britain when this organization change took place in the autumn of 1943, and the theater commander at that time, General Jacob Devers, got into a spat with the promulgator of the new organization, Lieutenant General Lesley McNair of the Army Ground Forces, and refused to convert the two divisions from the "heavy" 1942 tables. As a result, these two divisions were still in the heavy configuration in December 1944, meaning that they had six tank battalions instead of three. While this added a considerable amount of mechanized power to the divisions, their use in combat in the spring and autumn of 1944 showed that the 1942 organization was indeed flawed, with far too little infantry for most operations. As a result, the US Army tended to employ these divisions as mini-corps, teaming them up with an infantry division with individual infantry regiments assigned to the combat commands. These formations were amongst the most powerful tools in the hands of skilled corps commanders, and the US Army was fortunate to have "Lightning Joe" Collins of VII Corps to handle these two divisions during the critical phase of the Ardennes battle. The table below summarizes the tank strength in the First Army through the autumn. This does not include the tank forces of Simpson's Ninth Army to the north or Patton's Third Army to the south, which were of comparable size and strength. This is of some consequence as both neighboring armies served as reserves of armored force during the battle. For example, the 2nd and 3rd Armored divisions came into the Ardennes from the Ninth Army, while the 10th Armored Division came from the Third Army.

The US Army enjoyed quantitative advantages over the Wehrmacht in tanks, but qualitative inferiority. The US Army in 1943 had failed to

US FIRST ARMY SHERMAN TANK STRENGTH/LOSSES, AUTUMN 1944

	September		October		November		December	
	Operational*	Losses	Operational	Losses	Operational	Losses	Operational	Losses
2nd AD	221	7	197	17	n/a		187	26
3rd AD	193	74	193	12	196	51	176	44
5th AD	137	20	143	10	142	3	131	48
7th AD	n/a		117	37	n/a		102	72
9th AD	n/a		167	0	167	0	158	45
10th AD	n/a		n/a		n/a		156	7
70th TB	48	3	52	0	41	23	31	9
707th TB	54	0	52	0	43	26	40	26
709th TB	n/a		38	0	36	5	33	12
740th TB	n/a		n/a		9	0	17	5
741st TB	40	5	41	0	49	0	47	18
743rd TB	43	1	34	22	n/a		40	9
745th TB	44	7	35	17	31	5	27	5
746th TB	42	17	34	16	33	4	37	8
747th TB	40	5	45	1	47	16		
750th TB	n/a		n/a		n/a		47	7
771st TB	n/a		n/a		n/a		42	9
774th TB	n/a		53	0	52	0	49	17
Total	862	139	1,201	132	846	133	1,320	367

AD = Armored Division *TB = Tank Battalion*
* Average daily operational strength *n/a: Not assigned to First Army this month*

US TANK STRENGTH IN THE ARDENNES, DECEMBER 1944–JANUARY 1945*

Type	December 16, 1944	December 26, 1944	January 6, 1945	January 16, 1945
M4 (75mm) medium tank	490	649	1,190	1,205
M4 (76mm) medium tank	297	237	558	511
M4 (105mm) assault gun	104	128	249	247
M5A1 light tank	501	617	1,016	945
M8 75mm HMC	60	94	137	131
Total	1,452	1,725	3,150	3,039

*Data for January 6 and 16, 1945 includes Third Army minus its XX Corps units

appreciate the dynamics of German tank development, and so had dragged its feet in the deployment of more powerful tank guns or better tank armor. Although the Panther tank had been first deployed in the summer of 1943, the

US Army had seriously misunderstood its role, expecting it to be used like the Tiger heavy tank in relatively modest numbers in special corps-level regiments or brigades. In actuality, the Wehrmacht planned to use the Panther as its principal tank, and it was only its industrial problems which prevented the Wehrmacht from doing so by 1944. As a result, the bulk of the US tank battalions were still equipped with versions of the M4 Sherman tank armed with the 75mm gun, and essentially similar in performance to the Sherman tanks which first entered service in North Africa in 1942. An improved version with a 76mm gun had entered combat in the summer of 1944, but the gun development had been half-hearted due to the intelligence failure, and its performance was markedly inferior to the 75mm gun on the German Panther or the 17-pdr (76mm) gun on the modified British Sherman Firefly tank. The accompanying charts give some idea of the relative scale of issue of the newer 76mm Shermans. To make matters worse, the Sherman had not seen any significant increase in armor protection, so it was vulnerable to virtually all

The workhorse of the US field artillery was the M2A1 105mm howitzer, seen here in action with the 915th Field Artillery Battalion, 90th Division, after the Battle of the Bulge. (NARA)

German antitank weapons, from the lowly Panzerfaust antitank rocket to the powerful 88mm gun. On the positive side, the Sherman was available in large numbers and by 1944 it was a durable and reliable design. Tank-vs-tank fighting was not as common as is popularly assumed, and the Sherman was an adequate weapon in the majority of its encounters with German forces.

SHERMAN TANK STRENGTH, US 12TH ARMY GROUP 75MM VS 76MM MEDIUM TANKS, 1944–45

	November	December	January	February
75mm tanks	1521	1377	1695	1749
76mm (armored division)	406	418	350	542
76mm (tank battalion)	166	177	259	216
Sub-total 76mm	572	595	609	758
Total M4	2,093	1,972	2,304	2,507
% 76mm tanks	27.3	30.1	26.4	30.2

ARMORED DIVISIONS IN THE ARDENNES, NOVEMBER 1944–FEBRUARY 1945: SHERMAN TANK STRENGTH (75MM GUN / 76MM GUN)

Division	November	December	January	February
2	128/60	125/60	117/21	143/66
3	138/60	165/48	138/40	155/44
4	132/18	128/17	68/16	112/42
6	157/2	122/11	139/11	66/44
7	78/32	77/49	61/36	94/41
9	167/0	0/168	13/95	51/116
10	114/51	116/49	85/34	84/49
11			98/44	81/58
Avg. % 76mm	18.6	33.1	27.3	34.5

Besides the basic gun tanks, the Sherman was also built with a turreted 105mm howitzer, called an assault gun, that was used in tank battalions to provide additional indirect fire support. This assault gun should not be confused with the M7 105mm howitzer motor carriage (HMC) which was a field artillery weapon consisting of a 105mm howitzer in an open-topped carriage mounted on the M4 Sherman chassis. The M7 105mm HMC was the standard weapon of the armored field artillery battalions, with three battalions of these in each armored division. Each US tank battalion had three companies of M4 medium tanks, plus a single company of M5A1 light tanks. The M5A1 light tank was the final version of the M3 Stuart light tanks which traced their ancestry back to pre-war light tanks. These small, poorly armed vehicles were not at all popular as their 37mm guns were not adequate against German armored vehicles and not particularly effective against non-armored targets such as buildings either. Most tank battalions used their light tank company for scouting or flank security due to their limitations in close combat. As in the case of the Sherman, there was an assault gun version, the M8 75mm HMC, which mounted a short 75mm howitzer in an open turret on an M5A1 chassis. These were most widely used in mechanized cavalry units. The M5A1 was scheduled to be replaced by the new M24 Chaffee light tank in 1945. At the time of the Ardennes offensive, there were a small number of M24 light tanks being transported to the Ninth Army north of the Ardennes. At least one of these was stolen by the 740th Tank Battalion which had been given a blank check to equip itself after arriving in Belgium without any tanks. As a result, the M24 saw a premature combat debut in the fighting around La Gleize and Malmédy with this unit.

The US Army also deployed a significant number of tank destroyer battalions in the Ardennes. Generally, each infantry division had a single tank destroyer battalion attached. The subject is too complicated to describe in detail here, but there had been a debate in the US Army in 1943 over whether towed or mechanized tank destroyers were preferable, and the head of US Army Ground Forces, Lieutenant General Lesley McNair, foisted the towed guns on the army. This was a deeply unpopular decision and the combat use of towed and mechanized tank destroyers in Normandy in 1944 made it clear that the towed 3in antitank gun was ineffective. Although the 12th Army Group intended to replace all the towed 3in guns in the tank destroyer battalions, some battalions still had these weapons. There were three different mechanized tank destroyers in service in 1944. The original M10 3in gun motor carriage (GMC) consisted of a 3in antitank gun in an open-top turret on a Sherman hull. It offered firepower comparable to the 76mm version of the Sherman tank, but had inferior armor protection. An improved version, the M36 90mm GMC, began to arrive in the ETO in the autumn of 1944 and by the time of the Ardennes offensive was the only US Army armored fighting vehicle with a good probability of defeating the

heavier German tanks such as the Panther in a frontal engagement. The third type, the M18 76mm GMC, was an entirely new design based on a very light and fast chassis. It offered no advantages over the M10 3in GMC in terms of firepower or armor, and so the 12th Army Group proved reluctant to accept it, wanting more of the M36 90mm GMC instead. A few tank destroyer battalions in the Ardennes used the M18 76mm GMC.

Field artillery was the one ground combat arm where the US Army had unquestioned tactical and technological superiority over the Wehrmacht in 1944. The US field artillery was fully motorized and partly mechanized while the German artillery was still relying on horse transport for some of its field artillery until the end of the war. Each US infantry division was supported by three motorized 105mm howitzer battalions and a 155mm howitzer battalion. At corps level, there were additional howitzer battalions but there were also 155mm gun battalions which offered longer range.

A major advantage enjoyed by US forces in the Ardennes campaign was superior artillery. This is a 155mm howitzer of the 254th Field Artillery Battalion providing support to the 82nd Airborne Division near Werbomont on January 2, 1945. (NARA)

The US Army's development of innovative field artillery tactics such as the use of fire direction centers networked by radio enhanced its lethality. The US Army typically deployed a forward observer at company level to help direct fire, and the availability of modern FM radios added substantial tactical flexibility to this system. The quality of its field artillery was further extended by its sheer quantity: more field artillery battalions, more ammunition, better ammunition. Quantity has a very special quality in field artillery. Some idea of how much artillery was available can be seen from the fighting in the Bastogne sector around Christmas. Patton's two corps brought with them 35 artillery battalions which fired 94,230 rounds in five days; the First Army had about a hundred artillery battalions during the Ardennes fighting.

The demoralizing effect of American artillery was encapsulated in a German letter home: "You have no idea what is going on here. Simply by using his artillery, the Americans are finishing us off here. Such massed artillery fire I have not even seen in Russia. Day after day, the earth is flying

Long-range firepower for the US Army was provided by the 155mm gun, which was assigned to separate battalions at corps or army level. This is a 155mm gun of the 981st Field Artillery Battalion in action near Heppenbach in the Schnee Eifel towards the end of the Ardennes campaign in late January 1945. (NARA)

around our ears. Slowly, one loses nervous energy. I am amazed that I am still alive and in possession of my limbs."

One of the technical innovations used in the Ardennes was the VT (variable time) fuze, the cover name for a revolutionary proximity fuze. This fuze was developed originally for antiaircraft use, and its use was forbidden in the ETO for fear that a fuze might fall intact into German hands. If reverse manufactured, such a fuze would have been deadly against Allied strategic bombers and turned the tide of the air war. However, the exclusion rule was dropped during the Ardennes fighting, partly due to the desperate circumstances, and partly due to the recognition that it was unlikely that the Germans could manufacture such a device at this late stage of the war. Artillery projectiles are substantially more lethal against infantry if detonated overhead, since in this event even a deep trench offers little or no protection. The VT fuze could be set to air-burst at a pre-determined height over the ground, substantially increasing its effect compared to a ground-detonated projectile.

US Army Order of Battle, mid-December 1944

The US Army order of battle as listed here covers the forces available and present at the start of the campaign.

First US Army	Lieutenant General Courtney H. Hodges
V Corps	Major General Leroy T. Gerow
2nd Infantry Division	Major General Walter M. Robertson
99th Infantry Division	Major General Walter E. Lauer
VIII Corps	Major General Troy Middleton
106th Infantry Division	Major General Alan Jones
28th Infantry Division	Major General Norman Cota
4th Infantry Division	Major General Raymond Barton
9th Armored Division (minus CCB)	Major General John Leonard
XVIII Airborne Corps (December 20)	Major General Matthew B. Ridgway
82nd Airborne Division	Major General James M. Gavin
7th Armored Division	Major General Robert W. Hasbrouck
30th Infantry Division	Major General Leland S. Hobbs

The Aerial Dimension

By 1944, the United States Army was a much more modern force than the Wehrmacht, which had become impoverished and outdated by its gross overextension. The US Army included three branches, the Army Ground

Forces (AGF), the Army Air Force (AAF), and the Army Service Force (ASF). These other two forces help to explain some of the American advantages in the Ardennes. The Army Service Force was responsible for the production and supply of war materiel and there was no directly comparable organization in the Wehrmacht. The ASF was the outcome of the logistics experiences of the American Expeditionary Force in France in 1918 which suffered from severe shortages of equipment due to poor industrial mobilization. As a result of this experience, the US Army shifted substantial resources to industrial preparation. American numerical superiority in equipment, ammunition, and supplies was not a casual accident but a deliberate shift in policy after World War I that placed more emphasis on the logistical side of modern war than did the German Army.

The other branch, the Army Air Force, provided the US Army with one of its most powerful battlefield edges. The US Army devoted a disproportionate share of its resources to air power not only in terms of industrial production, but also in terms of manpower resources, training costs, and operating funds. Neither the German nor Soviet armies could compete with the US Army in this regard due to the sheer expense; only the British armed forces made a comparable effort. In 1941–45, the US Army spent almost six times as much on aircraft as tanks, $36 billion versus $6 billion.

The Wehrmacht, meaning the Heer (army) and Luftwaffe (air force), did attempt to create a modern three-dimensional art of war, and also devoted a disproportionate level of resources to air power. However, this attempt was largely overwhelmed by the Allied strategic bombing campaigns, which forced the Wehrmacht to strip much of its tactical air power from the Russian front in 1943–44 and concentrate its attention on strategic air defense of the Reich. The US Army Air Force doctrine was focused on destroying enemy air power as a prerequisite to further operations. This led to Operation *Pointblank* in the autumn–winter of 1943–44 aimed at destroying the Luftwaffe in the air and crippling its related aviation plants. By the spring of 1944, prior to D-Day, this mission had been largely accomplished. The lack of Luftwaffe air power over the battlefields in France was due not to Wehrmacht negligence, but to its defeat in repelling Operation *Pointblank* in 1943–44.

The US art of war that had emerged by 1944 was three-dimensional, consisting of traditional two-dimensional ground warfare supplemented by the third dimension of air power. The industrial focus of the US art of war led to a dominant mission of strangling the enemy's economy by means of heavy "strategic" bombers which struck into the depths of the German Reich. In the operational depths, the mission was primarily focused on strangling the Wehrmacht by interdicting its supply of men and materiel from Germany to the battle area through the use of medium bombers. At the tactical level, air power had the mission of tactical interdiction to deprive the Wehrmacht of its mobility, as well as tactical air support, to provide firepower beyond the range of traditional artillery.

The US Army Air Force in Europe was organized to carry out strategic bombing of German industry with dedicated forces, the Eighth Air Force based in Britain and the Fifteenth Air Force based in Italy. It had a separate force to attack the Wehrmacht at operational depths, the Ninth Air Force based in Europe. Each US Army's army group was assigned its own air force, which in the case of Bradley's 12th Army Group was Major General John

Supplementing the 105mm howitzer in the divisional artillery was the 155mm howitzer. These are from Battery C, 108th Field Artillery Battalion, 28th Division, on January 11 near Arsdorf. (NARA)

Cannon's Twelfth Air Force. In turn, each field army had its own tactical air command (TAC), which in the case of the First Army was Major General Elwood "Pete" Quesada's XI Tactical Air Command. These tactical air commands typically deployed four or more fighter groups, each with 36 P-47 fighter-bombers and a similar number of medium bomber groups, generally equipped with the B-26 Marauder.

American air power was so potent that the German Ardennes plans were heavily distorted to avoid its wrath. The Ardennes was chosen in no small measure since the forested terrain offered the German forces better ability to hide from the prying eye of Allied reconnaissance aircraft. Mid-December was chosen as the launch date due to the likelihood of overcast weather. In this respect, the German planning largely succeeded since US reconnaissance did not uncover the full extent of German deployment prior to the attack. As expected, the early winter weather prevented much Allied air support in the opening week of the campaign. However, with the arrival of the Russian high front on December 22 came crystal clear skies, and the air over the Ardennes was quickly swarming with P-47 fighter-bombers while the railroad yards in neighboring Germany were hammered by B-26 bombers. The effectiveness of Allied fighter-bombers against Panzers is largely a myth, but fighter-bomber attacks had a profoundly demoralizing effect on German army units, hampered tactical movement in daytime, and frequently led to the loss of vital transport which in turn starved the infantry and Panzers of food, fuel, and ammunition. The German Ardennes offensive depended on a rapid victory since once the attack started the Allied medium and heavy bombers would inevitably begin a campaign to isolate the battlefield by smashing the railway network supporting it. Bomber strikes against bridges and rail-yards paralyzed traffic in the rear areas and deprived German units of fuel and ammunition reserves that had been built up in anticipation of the offensive.

TACTICAL DILEMMAS IN THE WINTER OF 1944–45

The changing tactical environment in late 1944 posed distinct tactical dilemmas for both armies that are worth exploring to help clarify the conduct of the Ardennes campaign. These revolve around the proper use of armor and infantry to secure a breakthrough.

One of the most critical tactical decisions in 1944 involved the use of armored divisions in offensive operations. Should they be used to conduct the initial breakthrough? Both the German and American answer to this question was decidedly no. The British experience around Caen in Normandy in the summer of 1944 provides the reason why. With the proliferation of antitank weapons, an attempt by a tank heavy force to secure a breakthrough of enemy infantry positions was apt to be extremely costly and unsuccessful. Ideally, the infantry would be used to secure the breakthrough, and then the tank force injected to exploit it. While the doctrinal preference was quite clear in both the German and the American case, by December 1944 the Wehrmacht was faced with the problem of poor-quality infantry that had a hard time securing the breakthrough. This will become more evident in the combat narrative which follows. Under these circumstances, there is always the temptation to prematurely commit the armor force before the breakthrough has been secured, with the tanks

The M1 155mm gun was one of the most effective pieces of US field artillery, and was usually deployed in corps-level battalions. This battery is seen in action east of Bastogne on January 17 while supporting Patton's drive to link up with the First Army near Houfallize. (NARA)

becoming caught up in a costly infantry defense. This outcome will be seen in the conduct of the breakthrough in the northern sector near Elsenborn ridge by the 1st SS-Panzer Corps.

The difficulty of the German infantry in securing breakthroughs of American infantry defenses in December 1944 raises the issue of tank support to assist in the breakthrough. In contrast to the use of armored divisions, this involves the use of small tank formations to support the infantry. In the German case, armored support of the infantry was not a doctrinal question but a supply question. Ideally, the Wehrmacht would have liked to provide more armored support to the infantry, but the equipment was simply not available. Each German infantry division was supposed to have a company of assault guns, and at corps level there were supposed to be additional assault gun battalions that could be attached to the lead attack force. In practise, the shortage of assault guns meant that this type of support was difficult or impossible to provide. The Wehrmacht devoted about the same fraction of its armored fighting vehicles (AFVs) to the infantry support role as the US Army, about a third of the total strength of medium and heavy armored fighting vehicles. However, the available number of AFVs was simply so much smaller that German infantry divisions could seldom provide more than a company of assault guns per division or roughly a platoon per regiment. In contrast, US infantry divisions received a tank battalion and a tank destroyer battalion for support, or roughly two companies per regiment, a six-fold difference.

To further amplify the American advantage, the US Army was working out the critical technical problem facing tank-infantry support: the difficulty the infantry faced communicating with supporting tanks. Through a combination of tank telephones and additional radios, this vexing tactical problem was finally being solved, which substantially enhanced the effectiveness of AFVs supporting infantry. In contrast, the Wehrmacht had not yet addressed this problem in any comprehensive fashion, and lacked both tank telephones and sufficient tactical radios to permit small unit communication with supporting AFVs.

These communication problems became especially acute when armor attempted to support infantry in built-up areas, these days called MOUT (mechanized operations in urban terrain). Close cooperation between infantry and their supporting AFVs was especially necessary in built-up areas since the infantry could warn or protect the supporting AFVs from enemy antitank threats such as bazookas and Panzerfausts. In return, the supporting AFVs could provide the firepower necessary to overcome the enemy use of cellars and stone buildings as improvised field fortifications. These tactics required timely communication between the infantry and supporting AFVs, and the only practical means of such communication was by radio or field telephone. This tactical problem was not particularly decisive in the Ardennes as there were few cases where it occurred. But when it did occur, such as at Krinkelt-Rocherath, it could decisively influence the outcome of the skirmish.

DECISION IN THE NORTHERN SECTOR

The center of gravity for the Ardennes offensive was the northern sector, the attack corridor of the 6th Panzer Army. The success or failure of the Ardennes offensive depended on the results in this sector, since it contained the best and fastest route to Antwerp via Liège and was conducted by the best-equipped German Panzer divisions.

There were two principal thrusts in the northern sector, the 12th SS-Panzer Division towards Elsenborn Ridge on the right flank, and the 1st SS-Panzer Division assault towards the Losheim Gap and Malmédy on the left flank. The failure of the Panzer spearheads in this sector doomed the Ardennes offensive. However, the early disappointments in this sector did not bring the Battle of the Bulge to a close. Successes in the neighboring 5th Panzer Division sector, while not offering the potential tactical opportunities of the northern sector, helped prolong the campaign into January.

The artillery of 1st SS-Panzer Corps opened fire in the pre-dawn hours of Saturday, December 16, 1944, at around 0530hrs. The initial barrage fell on the forward lines of American trenches. The projectiles as often as not exploded in the trees overhead: a deadly pattern for exposed troops but not for the US infantry who were in log-covered trenches. Five minutes after the barrage began, the forward edge of the battlefield was illuminated by German searchlight units, which trained their lights upward against the low cloud cover, creating an eerie artificial dawn. After 15 minutes of firing, the artillery redirected their fire against secondary defensive lines and key crossroads. The fire strikes on crossroads had more effect since they often succeeded in tearing up field telephone networks. There were two more

Opposite:
An SdKfz 234/1 eight-wheel reconnaissance armored car of Kampfgruppe Knittel is seen moving forward with SS troops on its rear deck during the fighting on December 18. (NARA)

barrages, each directed further into the US defenses, finally concluding around 0700hrs. The promised Luftwaffe support failed to materialize due to the low cloud cover. The 6th Panzer Army plan assigned five advance routes for the Panzer spearheads, labeled Rollbahn A through E.

OPENING ROLLBAHN A AND B: BATTLE FOR THE TWIN VILLAGES

The northernmost element of the German attack was an attempt by the 67th Corps in the Monschau forest to push through the left wing of the 99th Division's defenses from Hofen to Wahlerscheid. This attack was carried out by the 326th Volksgrenadier Division through forested, hilly terrain not unlike the neighboring Hürtgen forest. Without any significant Panzer support, the attack was stopped cold by the 395th Infantry of the 99th Division. The positions of the forward rifle platoons had been registered by the US regimental artillery, and in the cases where the German infantry reached the forward trench lines they were pummeled mercilessly while the US infantry remained within the cover of their foxholes. This was the one sector of the front where the German offensive made no significant inroads. An attack the following day met the same results, and the division was withdrawn to its start line where it remained for the remainder of the campaign.

An aerial view of Krinkelt (to the left) and Rocherath (to the right). This view looks westward. (Military History Institute)

The most significant objective in the northern sector of the 1st SS-Panzer Corps zone was the small village of Krinkelt, which blended into the neighboring village of Rocherath. As a result, fighting for Krinkelt-Rocherath is frequently called the battle for the Twin Villages. Krinkelt sat near the junction of two roads which led towards the old Belgian army camp at Elsenborn and the ridge line in front of the Hohes Venn moor.

The initial assault was conducted by the 277th Volksgrenadier Division through a wooded area covered by the 393rd Infantry of the 99th Division. The US regiment had only two battalions, its 2nd Battalion having been assigned to the aborted Roer dam attacks a few days before. These were initially deployed in a trench line on the eastern edge of woods along the International Highway. Their defensive focus was two forest trails, the Schwarzenbruch and Weissenstein trails that led to the open farm country in front of the villages. Two of the 277th Volksgrenadier Division regiments took part in the first day's attack, the 989th Grenadier Regiment from Hollerath along the Schwarzenbruch trail, and the 990th Grenadier Regiment from Neuhof towards the Weissenstein trail. A plan for the third

Riflemen of the 393rd Infantry, 99th Division during the fighting around Rocherath. This regiment was deployed in the woods east of the Twin Villages, and after suffering heavy casualties retreated into the towns. (NARA)

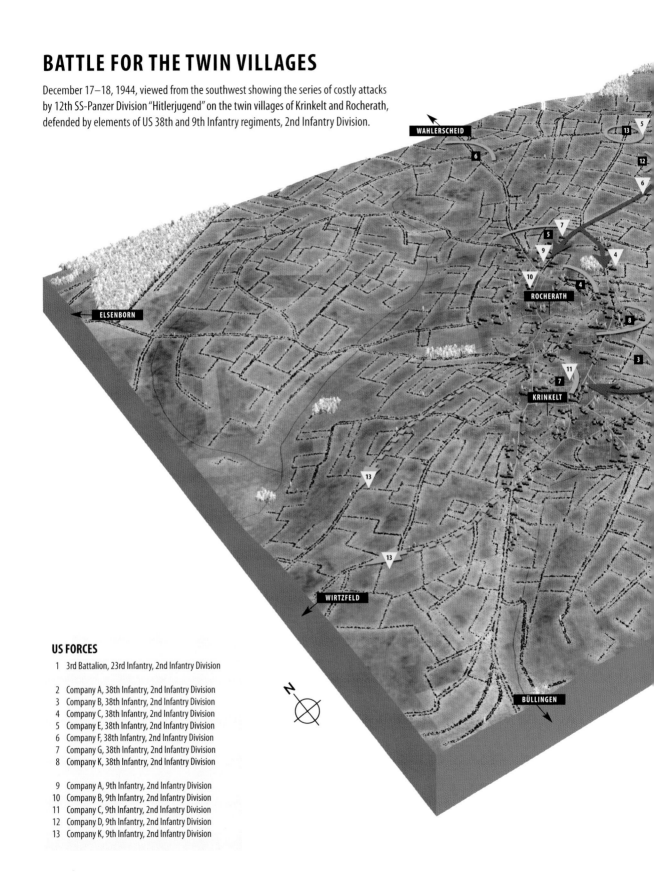

BATTLE FOR THE TWIN VILLAGES

December 17–18, 1944, viewed from the southwest showing the series of costly attacks by 12th SS-Panzer Division "Hitlerjugend" on the twin villages of Krinkelt and Rocherath, defended by elements of US 38th and 9th Infantry regiments, 2nd Infantry Division.

WAHLERSCHEID

ELSENBORN

ROCHERATH

KRINKELT

WIRTZFELD

BÜLLINGEN

US FORCES

1 3rd Battalion, 23rd Infantry, 2nd Infantry Division

2 Company A, 38th Infantry, 2nd Infantry Division
3 Company B, 38th Infantry, 2nd Infantry Division
4 Company C, 38th Infantry, 2nd Infantry Division
5 Company E, 38th Infantry, 2nd Infantry Division
6 Company F, 38th Infantry, 2nd Infantry Division
7 Company G, 38th Infantry, 2nd Infantry Division
8 Company K, 38th Infantry, 2nd Infantry Division

9 Company A, 9th Infantry, 2nd Infantry Division
10 Company B, 9th Infantry, 2nd Infantry Division
11 Company C, 9th Infantry, 2nd Infantry Division
12 Company D, 9th Infantry, 2nd Infantry Division
13 Company K, 9th Infantry, 2nd Infantry Division

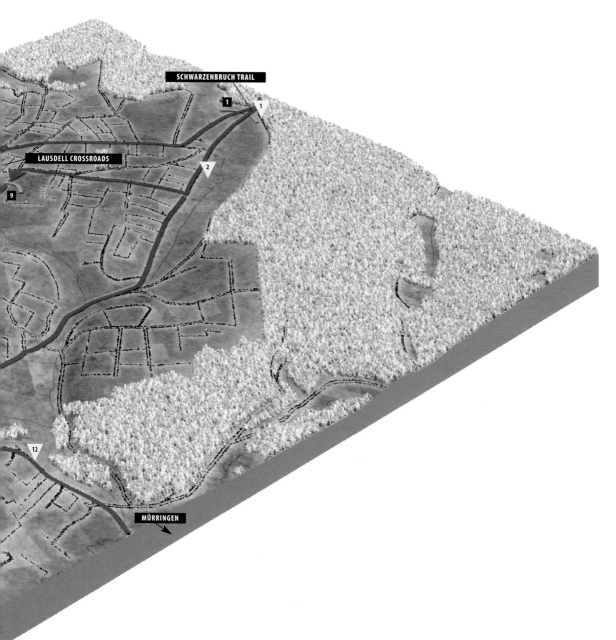

SCHWARZENBRUCH TRAIL

LAUSDELL CROSSROADS

MÜRRINGEN

EVENTS

1. 1230hrs, December 17: Kampfgruppe Müller, 12th SS-Panzer Division "Hitlerjugend" emerges from woods along Schwarzenbruch trail having pushed back the 3rd Battalion, US 393rd Infantry, 99th Division.

2. December 17: The forest opening at Roppenvenn "Sherman Crossroads" is defended by 3rd Battalion, US 23rd Infantry Division and two M4 tanks of 741st Tank Battalion. These US positions are overcome by dusk.

3. 2030hrs, December 17: Kampfgruppe Müller attacks 1st Battalion, US 9th Infantry, 2nd Infantry Division who have established a blocking position on Lausdell crossroads. This begins 17 hours of intense fighting.

4. December 17: Four Jagdpanzer IVs and a platoon of Panzergrenadiers under Helmut Zeiner elude Lausdell crossroad defenses and get into Rocherath after dark.

5. 0830hrs December 18: Company K, 9th Infantry finally overwhelmed by tank attack; only around one officer and ten soldiers withdraw.

6. 1300hrs, December 18: 1st Battalion, 9th Infantry finally withdraws with cover of four tanks from 741st Tank Battalion.

7. 1840hrs, December 17: German armor avoids Laudell crossroads and begins assault on Company A, 38th Infantry positions.

8. Morning, December 18: Commander of "Hitlerjugend," Hugo Kraas, decides to commit his tank regiment to the battle, along with additional grenadiers.

9. Morning, December 18: German tanks begin to penetrate into Rocherath in strength; many supporting Panzergrenadiers are killed by US fire. The Germans lose numerous tanks to bazooka fire.

10. December 18: Struggle most intense inside Rocherath as Panzers supported by Panzergrenadiers attempt to clear US infantry in house-to-house fighting.

11. December 18: About five Panther tanks penetrate into the center of the village, shell the US command post, but lose four tanks in the process. One escapes to the southeast and is knocked out by M10 tank destroyer.

12. Afternoon, December 18: German infantry from 12th Volksgrenadier Division join the fray.

13. After dusk, December 18: Major General Walter Robertson, commander of 2nd Infantry Division, orders withdrawal to Wirtzfeld.
December 19: Hermann Preiss, commander of 1st SS-Panzer Corps orders "Hitlerjugend" to pull back and leave the clean up to 3rd Panzergrenadier Division.

regiment to create a route to Rollbahn B through a southern trail towards Mürringen was abandoned due to the late arrival of the regiment, and instead both routes were redirected through the villages. The "Hitlerjugend" commander, Standartenführer Hugo Kraas, was concerned that the attack groups were not strong enough, and assembled a small battlegroup consisting of a battalion from the 25th SS-Panzergrenadier Regiment supported by Jagdpanzer IV tank destroyers to stiffen the attack if necessary.

During the first day's fighting, the 989th Grenadiers managed to overrun a company of the 3/393rd Infantry in the first rush, and infiltrated through the woods between the two battalions, reaching the Jansbach stream about half way through the woods. Although the German attack had been halted well short of its objective, casualties in the 3/393rd Infantry amounted to nearly half its troops.

Further south, the attack of the 990th Grenadier Regiment began half an hour after the artillery barrage had lifted and the US infantry was well prepared. As the German infantry moved through the fog in the fields approaching the woods, they were hit by concentrated small arms and artillery fire. The divisional commander attempted to restart the attack by reinforcing it with some Jagdpanzer 38(t) but this attack also failed. In frustration, the divisional commander ordered the reserve regiment, the 991st Grenadiers, into action in the hope of outflanking the American positions. This attack was also stopped without any significant gains, but the 1/393rd Infantry suffered about 30 percent casualties in the process. German casualties had been heavy, especially among the officers. Due to the poor training and poor quality of the new troops, the senior officers were forced to lead from the front and in three days of fighting the 277th Volksgrenadier Division lost all its battalion commanders and 80 percent of its company commanders, along with the majority of its NCOs, rendering the division unsuitable for any further offensive combat.

Frustrated by the delays, the corps commander, Gruppenführer Preiss, ordered "Hitlerjugend" to commit its task force to assist in clearing the route the next day. On the US side, the 2nd Infantry Division was ordered to continue its attacks towards the Roer dams on the first day of the German offensive, with First Army commander Hodges believing the attack was only a spoiling action. But by afternoon the divisional commander, Major

General Walter Robertson, realized that a major attack was underway and that it was imperative that the flank be secured. He began to redeploy units to reinforce Elsenborn Ridge. The 3/23rd Infantry was alerted to move to Krinkelt on December 16 and arrived in the late afternoon, deploying at the edge of woods where the two main trails emerged.

In the early morning hours of December 17, the commander of the 3/393rd Infantry ordered a counterattack down the Schwarzenbruch trail. In the meantime, the Panzer reinforcements had reached 989th Grenadier Regiment. The two attacks were launched in the early morning and careened into one another. Even though a pair of German tank destroyers were damaged by bazooka fire, the weaker American attack was halted. Under pressure, the US battalion withdrew to the western forest edge towards a roadblock covered by a newly arrived company from the 3/23rd Infantry and a pair of M4 tanks. The neighboring 1/393rd Infantry was ordered to withdraw at 1100hrs to prevent it from being cut off by Volksgrenadiers who continued to move forward through the gap between the two battalions in the woods. The continuing attack by the battalion from the 25th SS-Panzergrenadier Regiment along the Schwarzenbruch trail suffered heavy

Trucks of the 372nd Field Artillery Battalion, 99th Infantry Division withdraw through crossroads at Wirtzfeld on December 17 as the "Hitlerjugend" attacks neighboring Rocherath. The junction is covered by an M10 from the 644th Tank Destroyer Battalion. The M10s from this unit repulsed a probe by Kampfgruppe Peiper that day along a neighboring road. (NARA)

INITIAL ATTACKS BY 6TH PANZER ARMY

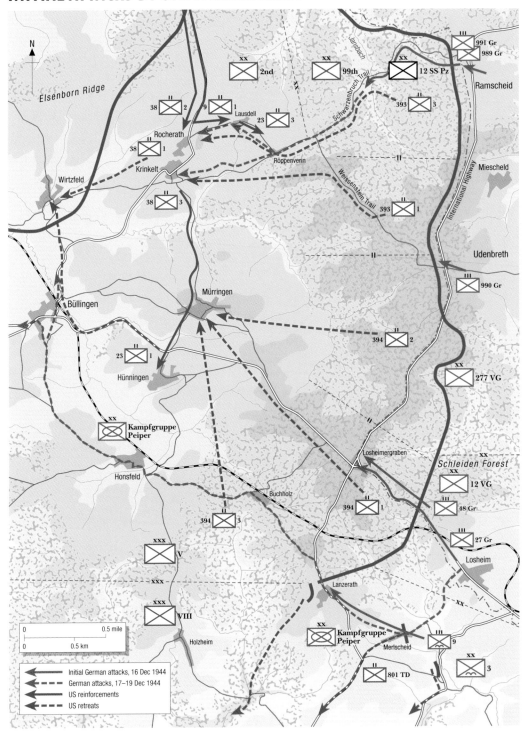

casualties on encountering the fresh 3/23rd Infantry, but the arrival of the tank destroyers settled the matter and overwhelmed the American positions. On reaching the edge of the woods, the Panzers came under fire from two M4 tanks of the 741st Tank Battalion, but both US tanks were quickly knocked

Panzer Graveyard: 2nd Infantry Division vs 12th SS-Panzer Division in Krinkelt, December 18, 1944

In his impatience to get his division back on schedule, the commander of the 12th SS-Panzer Division "Hitlerjugend," General Kraas, decided to commit his Panzer regiment to help rout out the American infantry in the streets of Krinkelt. The town was enshrouded in fog and icy rain, and the green GIs of the recently arrived 99th "Battlin' Babes" Division were intermixed with the hardened veterans of the 2nd Infantry Division. The Twin Villages of Krinkelt and Rocherath were typical of farm communities in this rural region, with sturdy buildings made of stone. They proved to be ideal defensive positions for the US infantry. Most of the German Panzergrenadiers who were supposed to accompany the tanks into the town were stripped away from the Panzers by small arms fire before they reached the village. The Panther tanks blundered down the narrow streets, nearly blind, and with no infantry support. Although it was probably the best tank of World War II, the Panther tank was not suited for urban warfare. Its sides and rear could be penetrated by the unreliable bazooka rocket launchers used by the US infantry, and the Panzers were mercilessly hunted by US antitank teams all day long. The bazooka gunner seen here would operate as part of a team with the other infantrymen providing cover against the small number of German infantry who made it through the gauntlet of fire at the edge of town. (Artwork by Howard Gerrard) out. By the end of the day, the Panzergrenadier battalion had lost so many officers in the intense fighting that "companies were being commanded by sergeants." Shortly before noon, Kraas, the 12th SS-Panzer Division commander, decided to commit a battalion of Panther tanks, the remainder of the Panzergrenadier regiment and an assault gun battalion to reinforce the attack, hoping to reinvigorate the stalled and badly delayed advance.

By dusk on December 17, the 989th Grenadier Regiment of 277th Volksgrenadier Division had finally pushed out of the woods and the stalled 990th Grenadier Regiment was ordered to withdraw from its fruitless attack and fall in behind it. Frustrated by the poor performance of the infantry in breaking through the woods, Kraas ordered his SS-Panzergrenadiers to continue the attack through the night.

As the remnants of the 3/23rd Infantry and 3/393rd Infantry were pulling back from the forest line, about 600 men of Lieutenant Colonel William McKinley's 1/9th Infantry, 2nd Infantry Division had been moved behind them and set up defensive positions near the Lausdell crossroads on the outskirts of Rocherath. The crossroads covered the trails leading into the northern end of Rocherath from the woods. The battalion had suffered

Kraas' decision to commit his Panzer regiment to the fight led to heavy tank casualties in the streets of Krinkelt. The nearest of these two Panther Ausf. G, probably that of SS-Hauptsturmführer Kurt Brodel, has been burned out and had its barrel ripped off. They were knocked out in the fighting opposite the village church. (NARA)

nearly 50 percent casualties in several days of fighting at Wahlerscheid in the Roer dams operation, and even after Co. K, 3/9th Infantry was added, the battalion was still under strength. McKinley, the grandson and namesake of the former US president, organized bazooka teams and had his troops lay antitank mines along the road.

The first German probe by four Jagdpanzer IV tank destroyers and infantry exited the woods after dark in the midst of a snow squall, and they evaded the Lausdell roadblock, reaching the town square in Krinkelt. A confused fight began with a handful of M4 medium tanks and M10 tank destroyers, and house-to-house fighting erupted between the GIs and Panzergrenadiers.

Subsequent German columns were brought under fire by American artillery, directed by McKinley's units at the crossroads. But in the dark and fog, some German units continued to infiltrate past the defenses into the villages. Confused fighting engulfed Lausdell but the US infantry disabled a number of German armored vehicles with bazookas and chains of mines pulled in front of advancing German columns. The German commander reinforced his spearhead and launched a concerted attack against the

This was one of five Panthers of the first company of the 12th SS-Panzer Regiment which fought their way into Krinkelt around 0730hrs on December 18. Four were knocked out by bazooka teams and antitank guns and this vehicle escaped down the Büllingen road where it was knocked out by an M10 3in GMC of the 644th Tank Destroyer Battalion at around 1100hrs. It had 11 bazooka hits, several 57mm hits, and three 3in impacts in the rear. (NARA)

crossroads at 2230hrs. The Lausdell position was so vital to the American defense that all the available artillery, numbering some seven battalions with 112 howitzers, was directed to break up the attack even though radio communication with McKinley's battalion had been lost. After a pulverizing artillery concentration fell on all the roads leading into Lausdell, the German attacks finally bogged down around 2315hrs. McKinley's defense of the Lausdell crossroads on December 17 allowed the 2nd Infantry Division to move its 38th Infantry Regiment into Krinkelt-Rocherath to defend the approaches to the Elsenborn Ridge. It was reinforced by companies from the 741st Tank Battalion and the 644th Tank Destroyer Battalion.

To finally overcome the American roadblock, Kraas committed the remainder of his Panzer regiment to the fray in the early morning of December 18 along with another Panzergrenadier battalion. Colonel McKinley had been ordered to withdraw back to the villages before dawn, but the Germans struck first. In the early morning drizzle and fog, Panther tanks overran the forward defenses, firing point-blank into the trenches with their guns. One infantry company called in artillery fire on its own positions, which stopped the German attack but only a dozen GIs survived the barrage. McKinley's decimated battalion held its ground, and most of the German forces bypassed the crossroads to the south and charged directly into

Another view of the Panzer graveyard inside the Twin Villages, in this case another of "Hitlerjugend's" destroyed Panther Ausf. G tanks. (Military History Institute)

Rocherath. McKinley's force was finally extracted at 1115hrs when an artillery barrage was ordered to shield it from any further attacks from the woods while a local counterattack by four M4 tanks cleared a path into Rocherath past the Panzers. Of the original 600 men, only 217 returned to US lines. Charles B. McDonald, present at the battle as a young company commander with the 23rd Infantry and later a senior US Army historian, wrote: "for all the defenses of many other American units during the German counteroffensive, probably none exceeded and few equaled McKinley's battalion in valor and sacrifice."

Besides the attack against the Lausdell crossroads, additional assaults backed by Panzers broke into the villages from north and south. During the course of the day, the assaults were reinforced by units of the 12th Volksgrenadier Division, which had come up from the south via Mürringen. Much of the German infantry was stripped away by artillery and small arms fire. With little infantry support, the Panther tanks became involved in

Although not of the best quality, this photo shows a dramatic moment during the Battle of the Bulge as this M7 105mm HMC has been positioned along a road junction leading to the Elsenborn Ridge on December 20, 1944 with the assignment of stopping any approaching German units after Krinkelt-Rocherath has been abandoned. (NARA)

Artillery played a vital role in the defense of Krinkelt-Rocherath, and as the battle reached its peak, eight US artillery battalions took part, firing nearly 30,000 rounds during the fighting. This is the 38th Field Artillery Battalion, 2nd Infantry Division, on the Elsenborn Ridge on December 20. (NARA)

deadly cat-and-mouse games with US bazooka teams scurrying through the stone buildings in the villages. A German tank commander later described the town as a "Panzer graveyard." House-to-house fighting continued inside the villages for most of the day, but at nightfall, Krinkelt and Rocherath were still in American hands, with pockets of German infantry and Panzers at the edge of the villages.

By the evening of December 18, both sides were reassessing their options. Sepp Dietrich, realizing that he was badly behind schedule, suggested to Preiss that he disengage from Krinkelt-Rocherath and move "Hitlerjugend" via the southern routes. Preiss was unwilling to do so, as Rollbahn C and D already went through Büllingen to the south. This would lead to all four columns being funneled through a very narrow corridor and his northern column needed to get on to the Elsenborn Ridge. As a compromise, Preiss agreed to pull out "Hitlerjugend" and to substitute the 3rd Panzergrenadier Division to continue the attack on to the Elsenborn Ridge once Krinkelt and Rocherath were finally cleared. At roughly the same time, Major General Robertson had concluded that the defense of Krinkelt-Rocherath had become untenable and it was time to withdraw to the Elsenborn Ridge.

The German infantry, with tank support, resumed their attacks in the villages the following morning but were greeted with heavy fire from eight field artillery battalions. Around 1345hrs, Robertson radioed his commanders in the Twin Villages and told them that the withdrawal would begin after nightfall at 1730hrs with the units from the northern edge of Rocherath pulling out first, followed by a gradual withdrawal of the units from the center and the southern edge of Krinkelt. The withdrawal would be to the next largest town to the west, Wirtzfeld. The rearguard consisted of a small number of M4 tanks and M10 tank destroyers and was successfully executed in the dark.

The fighting for Krinkelt-Rocherath had effectively blocked the 12th SS-Panzer Division "Hitlerjugend" for three entire days. Although the German plans had expected "Hitlerjugend" to reach the Meuse on the second day, they had barely reached a depth of 6 miles (10km). The defense of the Twin Villages enabled the V Corps to build up an impregnable defense along the Elsenborn Ridge, thereby denying the Germans the shortest route to the Meuse. A later US study concluded that "Hitlerjugend" lost 111 tanks, assault guns, and other armored vehicles in the fighting, which is an exaggeration. German records are far from complete and it would appear that about 60 AFVs were knocked out, of which 31 tanks and assault guns and 14 light armored vehicles were total losses. But time was far more precious than hardware, and the loss was unredeemable.

While other elements of the 2nd Division were engaged in the savage fighting in Krinkelt-Rocherath, the 2nd Battalion, 9th Infantry was shifted from the "Heartbreak Crossroads" near Wahlerscheid to cover the gap west of Krinkelt near Wirtzfeld. Here, the unit is seen on December 20 while in transit on the Elsenborn Ridge. (NARA)

OPENING ROLLBAHN C AND D: LOSHEIMERGRABEN AND BUCHHOLZ STATION

Of all the road networks in the 6th Panzer Army sector, none were more important than those leading west out of Losheim. Originally, the plan had called for a regiment of the 277th Volksgrenadier Division to open a route from Udenbreth to Mürringen for "Hitlerjugend" but its late arrival made this impossible. Instead, Losheim became the start point of both Rollbahns C and D, and so, in theory, the start points of the heavy battle groups of both the 1st SS-Panzer and 12th SS-Panzer divisions. In the event, "Hitlerjugend" became bogged down in fighting at Krinkelt-Rocherath, and later at Dom Bütgenbach, and so its planned Panzer drive along Rollbahn C never materialized.

The German assault to capture this road-net was led by the 12th Volksgrenadier Division from Losheim along the International Highway where it met Losheimergraben and the route to Büllingen. The division attacked with two regiments, 27th Grenadier Regiment up the International Highway, and 48th Grenadier Regiment through the Schleiden forest. US forces in this region consisted of the 394th Infantry Regiment, 99th Division, with its three battalions stretched out in a line on the eastern side of the

The 99th Division's rifle squads built log-reinforced shelters along the front line during November 1944, usually consisting of a two-man fighting trench, and a large but shallower bunker for sleeping like this one near Losheimergraben. These substantially reduced casualties from the initial artillery barrage of December 16. (Military History Institute)

International Highway from Weissenstein to the Buchholz railroad line, a distance of about 3 miles (5km).

The attack by the 48th Grenadier Regiment went badly when one of its battalions stumbled into the opening barrages, suffering 60 percent casualties. As a result attacks were weakest in the northern sector against 2/394th Infantry. The attack along the key route out of Losheim progressed more smoothly and by afternoon had overrun one company of the 1/394th Infantry and inflicted heavy casualties on the others. The intensity of these attacks decreased when trouble to the south forced the 27th Grenadier Regiment commander to redirect a battalion in this direction.

Buchholz rail station, the southernmost position of the 99th Division, was held by the 3/394th Infantry. This company was not deployed in a trench line like its two northern neighbors, but left in an assembly area around the station to serve as a mobile reserve for the division. Shortly after the initial barrage, a battalion of the 27th Grenadier Regiment attempted to use the cover of the early morning ground fog to rush the station. They were caught in the open and withdrew with serious casualties. Around 1100hrs reinforcements arrived but failed to overcome the US positions. The US battalion commander realized the precariousness of his position, and with

The task of clearing the way into the Losheim Gap for the 1st SS-Panzer Corps was assigned to the 12th Volksgrenadier Division, commanded by Generalmajor Gerhard Engel, seen here conversing with the head of Army Group B, Walter Model. (Military History Institute)

regimental consent, withdrew his unit back towards a more defensible position near Losheimergraben after dusk, leaving two platoons behind at Buchholz station as a security force. By evening, the 27th Grenadier Regiment had patrols on the fringes of the American positions in front of Losheimergraben.

After dark, the 12th Volksgrenadier Division officers were visited by the irate 1st SS-Panzer Corps commander who insisted that they take Losheimergraben in a dawn attack. Preceded by artillery strikes, their attacks were renewed before dawn. Intense fighting enveloped the town and surrounding woods, and though the 1/394th Infantry positions held, the battalion suffered serious casualties. By late morning, the US regimental commander decided to withdraw from the woods and set up new defensive positions on the hills east of Mürringen. The German attack failed in part because the promised support from the division's StuG III assault guns did not materialize when they got stuck in the massive traffic jam behind the lines. When the attacks on the town resumed with armored support at 1300hrs there was hardly any resistance except for a small rearguard. A battalion of the 48th Grenadier Regiment began racing up the highway towards Mürringen but ran into elements of the 2/394th Infantry that had not yet received instructions

Among the most famous of the photos taken by an anonymous German military cameraman is this shot of a Waffen-SS Schwimmwagen pulled up to the road signs at the Kaiserbaracke crossroads leading towards Poteau on December 18, 1944. Often misidentified as Joachim Peiper, it is in fact a team from Fast Gruppe Knittel with SS-Unterscharführer Ochsner to the left and SS-Oberscharführer Persin behind the driver. This photo was one of those from four rolls of film later captured by the US 3rd Armored Division. (NARA)

to withdraw. The last American rearguard in the customs houses in Losheimergraben did not surrender until 1500hrs.

While the fight was going on in Losheimergraben, reinforcements in the form of the 1/23rd Infantry from the 2nd Infantry Division moved into the town of Hünningen before dawn on December 17. They covered the afternoon withdrawal and prevented the 12th Volksgrenadier Division from emerging from the woods. A hasty defense was set up in the neighboring village of Mürringen by the remnants of the 394th Infantry, but a night attack supported by ten StuG III assault guns captured the town around midnight. One of the routes was finally open, two days late.

OPENING ROLLBAHN E – KREWINKEL AND LANZERATH

The 3rd Fallschirmjäger Division was assigned the task of opening the southernmost corridor for the 1st SS-Panzer Corps. This should have been the easiest of the breakthroughs due to the extreme imbalance between German and US forces. The objective was the corps boundary, which was screened by nothing more than the 14th Cavalry Group. Normally, a gap this size would be assigned to an entire infantry division, not to a unit with a deployable strength roughly that of a single infantry battalion. Furthermore, the cavalry commander, Colonel Mark Devine, decided to keep one of his two squadrons in reserve almost 20 miles (32km) behind the front. A defensive plan had been developed for the Losheim Gap when the 2nd Infantry Division had been responsible for the sector earlier in the month, which consisted of a withdrawal of the forward outposts to the Manderfeld Ridge, pre-registered artillery strikes forward of these defenses, and a counterattack from the Schnee Eifel. When the 106th Division took over this sector on December 11,

A Kubelwagen utility vehicle of the 1st SS-Panzer Division passes a disabled US 3in antitank gun of the 820th Tank Destroyer Battalion, knocked out in the fighting for the Losheim Gap, in the hamlet of Merlscheid on December 18, 1944, with the village church in the background. (NARA)

this plan went into limbo in spite of the efforts of the cavalry. In contrast to the conditions in the V Corps sector to the north, with forests along the frontier, this sector consisted of open farmland.

Generalmajor Wadehn's badly depleted 3rd Fallschirmjäger Division was deployed with both available regiments up front. The 9th Fallschirmjäger Regiment was assigned to seize the small village of Lanzerath, while the 5th Fallschirmjäger Regiment was assigned the capture of Krewinkel, the nominal start point of Rollbahn E.

Defense of Lanzerath was nominally in the hands of a towed 3in antitank gun platoon attached to the 14th Cavalry Group. However, once the initial barrage lifted, the platoon evacuated the village when it saw the German paratroopers marching down the road towards the town. The only other US force in the area was an understrength intelligence and reconnaissance (I&R) platoon of the 1/394th Infantry under the command of Lieutenant Lyle Bouck, which served as a screening force for the southern boundary of the 99th Division. After a brief scouting foray into the village, Bouck deployed his force, now down to a squad in size, in a trench line on the edge of the woods outside Lanzerath. To the surprise of the GIs, a paratrooper battalion emerged from the village in marching order. About a hundred paratroopers deployed in a skirmish line 110 yards (100m) in front of their line and charged across an open field. A slaughter ensued. Through the course of the day, the Germans launched two more frontal charges with equally ghastly results. Although Bouck's men held their position, most were wounded, little ammunition remained, and their machine guns had been put out of action. In the late afternoon, the German tactics changed when a veteran NCO, infuriated by the casualties, pointedly told the commander, an inexperienced rear echelon Luftwaffe staff officer, that they should outflank the American position and not continue to attack it frontally. This time the American position was quickly overwhelmed and the survivors, including Bouck, captured. Bouck's platoon was later awarded the Presidential Unit Citation and he and his men were decorated with four Distinguished Service Crosses and five Silver Stars making it the most decorated unit of the war. An under-strength platoon had held off a regiment for an entire day, in turn blocking the advance of 1st SS-Panzer Division.

The defense of Krewinkel was more short-lived. The village was held by a platoon from C Troop, 18th Cavalry Squadron, in a series of foxholes. As at Lanzerath, the 5th Fallschirmjäger Regiment attacked frontally, resulting in heavy casualties. However, the American positions were so thin that German units simply continued their march westward past the defenses. The 14th Cavalry Group commander, Colonel Mark Devine, asked the 106th Division to send reinforcements as per the earlier defensive plan, but the 106th Division, largely unaware of the plan, refused. In the late morning Devine ordered his men to withdraw to Manderfeld. The cavalry began withdrawing from Krewinkel at 1100hrs, as did neighboring garrisons in Abst and Weckerath. The garrison at Roth was overrun and the troops in Kobsheid had to wait until dark to withdraw. Reinforcements from the 32nd Cavalry Squadron arrived near Manderfeld in the late afternoon, but by this stage, German troops were already pouring past. The surviving elements from the 18th Cavalry abandoned Manderfeld around 1600hrs, heading for the squadron headquarters at Holzheim. For all intents and purposes, Rollbahn E and the Losheim Gap were wide open with no appreciable American defenses remaining.

A Kingtiger drives past US prisoners, mostly from the 99th Division, captured during the fighting on December 17. The village of Merlscheid lies in the background and the Kingtiger is on its way towards Lanzerath, the start point for Kampgruppe Peiper. (NARA)

COMMAND PERSPECTIVES

From the perspective of Generalfeldmarschall Model of Army Group B, the breakthrough in the northern sector had finally been accomplished by December 19, but two days behind schedule. The configuration of the breakthrough had not conformed to the plan. The anticipated breakthrough along the northern routes on the Elsenborn Ridge had been stopped cold by the prolonged fighting in Krinkelt-Rocherath, stalling the assault by "Hitlerjugend's" powerful battlegroup. The penetrations of the Losheim Gap around Büllingen were very narrow, resulting in considerable traffic congestion along these routes, which was delaying the exploitation of the breakthrough by the heavy Panzer formations. The quickest and most devastating breakthrough had not occurred in the 6th Panzer Army sector as expected, but in the 5th Panzer Army sector due to Manteuffel's more prudent tactics, as will be detailed in the next chapter. While this attack appeared to be progressing well, there was the worrisome matter of St. Vith. This town sat astride the main road network leading westward, and its capture would be essential to fully exploit the breakthrough in this sector.

A column of US prisoners from the 99th Division trudge towards the rear between Lanzerath and Merlscheid following the fighting on December 17. This photo was one of the series taken by a German combat cameraman accompanying Fast Gruppe Knittel along Rollbahn D. (NARA)

The commander of Fast Group Knittel was Sturmbannführer Gustav Knittel, commander of the 1st SS-Panzer Reconnaissance Battalion. He is seen here consulting a map along with the chief of his headquarters company, Heinrich Goltz, to his left while near La Vaux-Richard on December 18, 1944, on the approaches to La Gleize. (NARA)

Therefore, by the third day of the offensive, the German objectives were threefold: to try to push on to the Elsenborn Ridge from points further west such as Bütgenbach; to try to exploit the breakthrough in the southern portion of the 6th Panzer Army sector by the spearhead of the 1st SS-Panzer Division, Kampfgruppe Peiper; and to develop the breakthrough in the 5th Panzer Army sector by securing the St. Vith crossroads.

Hodges' First US Army headquarters, located at Spa in the Ardennes, began receiving reports of the German attacks on the morning of December 16. Middleton's VIII Corps headquarters at Bastogne had a difficult time providing a clear picture of the unfolding events due to poor communications with its forward units. As mentioned earlier, Middleton requested that the CCB of the 9th Armored Division, located near Faymonville to support the Roer dams operation, be returned to support VIII Corps, a request that was granted. However, Hodges refused to call off the Roer dams offensive at 1100hrs, arguing that the activity in the Ardennes was only a spoiling attack. By early afternoon, the First Army headquarters received a copy of Rundstedt's order of the day which began "Your great hour has arrived... We gamble everything!" This changed the view of

German intentions, but even late in the day, many in the headquarters still felt it was nothing but a diversion to discourage the two US offensives in the works – the Roer dams operation in the north, and Patton's planned attack in the Saar to the south. Nevertheless, a regiment of the 1st Infantry Division was transferred to Gerow's V Corps, which would prove instrumental two days later in the defense of Dom Bütgenbach.

The reaction in the 12th Army Group headquarters, located in Luxembourg City, was more vigorous. Bradley was in Paris that day conferring with Eisenhower, and first word of the offensive arrived in the afternoon. Bradley knew that the 12th Army Group had minimal reserves, so he immediately telephoned Patton and told him to transfer the 10th Armored Division from his planned Saar offensive to Luxembourg. He then phoned the 12th Army Group headquarters and instructed them to transfer the 7th Armored Division from Ninth Army to the Ardennes. The only other reserves were the two airborne divisions of Major General Matthew Ridgway's XVIII Airborne Corps, the 82nd and 101st Airborne divisions. These were refitting around Reims after prolonged deployment, and though not ready, were ordered to move by truck to the Ardennes immediately. Bradley's prompt actions would have vital consequences over the next few days.

The debate over German intentions at the First Army headquarters ended on December 17 when the first reports emerged of German Panzers racing through the Losheim Gap. It was finally recognized that this was no spoiling attack. The Roer dams attack was called off, and Gerow was given a free hand to organize a defense of the Elsenborn Ridge. By 0930hrs, the first reports began to arrive that two regiments of the 106th Division had been surrounded. The rest of the day was spent attempting to secure additional reinforcements. Within First Army, the remainder of 1st Infantry Division and a regiment of the 9th Infantry Division were transferred to Gerow's embattled V Corps. General William Simpson of the Ninth Army telephoned and offered the 30th Infantry Division and the 2nd Armored Division. The 30th Infantry Division was the first of the two units to begin moving. By midnight December 17/18, 80,000 troops and 10,000 vehicles were on their way to the Ardennes, a much prompter response than the Germans had anticipated. The CCB/9th Armored Division and 7th Armored Division were committed to Middleton's VIII Corps, originally with plans to help rescue the two trapped regiments of the 106th Division. The 1st Infantry Division was used to buttress the defenses on the Elsenborn Ridge. The 30th Infantry Division was dispatched to the Malmédy area and the 82nd Airborne Division to Werbomont to seal off the Losheim Gap.

When a copy of the German operational plan was captured late on December 16, First Army headquarters learned that the German offensive would eventually depend on captured fuel. As a result, on December 17 an effort began to remove the several large fuel dumps in the Ardennes especially the truck-head at Bütgenbach and the network of dumps south of Malmédy. Most of these were withdrawn except for 124,000 gallons (564,000 liters) near Stavelot which were burned to prevent them from falling into German hands.

A bazooka team from Co. C, 325th Glider Infantry, 82nd Airborne Division, guards a road near Werbomont on December 20, after a probe from Kampfgruppe Peiper reached as far as Habiemont, 2½miles (4km) to the east. This was the furthest west reached by Peiper, and his forces pulled back to Stoumont later in the day due to increasing US attacks. (NARA)

On the afternoon of December 18 word arrived that a spearhead from Kampfgruppe Peiper had reached to within 6 miles (10km) of the First Army headquarters in Spa, a rumor that proved untrue. Nonetheless, the proximity of the German forces down the road in La Gleize convinced them to evacuate the headquarters at 2200hrs to Chaudfontaine in the suburbs of Liège. The haste with which this was done left a bad impression, especially among subordinate commands who found themselves temporarily cut off from instructions or support. Even though the move helped improve the headquarters security from immediate German attack, it posed another threat as the new site was in the flight path of V-1 buzz bombs being launched at Liège and Antwerp. The G-4 traffic headquarters was hit en route by a V-1.

During the fighting in Stavelot, this Kingtiger of the 501st Heavy SS-Panzer Battalion stalled while climbing the hill on Rue Haut-Rivage, and then rolled back down the hill into this house where it became stuck. A couple of GIs from the 30th Division look it over after the town was retaken. (NARA)

One of the most effective efforts by the headquarters was the unconventional activity of the section chiefs. Colonel William Carter, the engineer chief, mobilized his units to prepare roadblocks, lay minefields, demolish bridges, and construct barrier zones in the northern sector of the front. These were mostly rear area service units, normally assigned to construction and road building, but trained for secondary combat roles. The Germans would soon curse the "damned engineers" for harassing the Panzer spearheads and blowing key bridges. The 49th Antiaircraft Brigade responsible for defense against V-1 flying bombs moved a number of its units of 90mm antiaircraft guns to defend the approaches to key locations including Huy, Liège, and Spa. Even the armor section got in on the act, taking the crews of the newly arrived 740th Tank Battalion and outfitting them with a motley selection of British Shermans, tank destroyers, DD tanks, and whatever else was available, and dispatching them to the front. This unit would later serve as the cork in the bottle when Kampfgruppe Peiper was trapped at La Gleize.

On December 19, Eisenhower met with the senior commanders including Patton, Bradley, and Devers at Verdun to discuss ways to deal with the German attack. The two basic options were to establish a secure defensive line to make a stand, or to begin counterattacking as soon as forces were available. Eisenhower made it clear he desired the second option, and wanted the initial attack to come from the south. Eisenhower was surprised by Patton's eagerness to shift a corps of three divisions in only three days, but this was possible due to the preparation of these units for the abortive Saar offensive. In addition Patton had shown foresight in planning for such an eventuality some days previously based on the assessments of his G-2 of the likelihood of a German attack in the Ardennes.

On the evening of December 19 Bradley received a telephone call from Eisenhower's chief of staff, Lieutenant General Walter Bedell Smith, suggesting that Eisenhower wanted to turn over control of the US First and Ninth armies on the northern shoulder of the Bulge to Montgomery since this would avoid problems if communications were cut by the German advance. The main repeater station at Jemelle was located in the path of Manteuffel's advancing Panzers between Bastogne and Dinant. Bradley was concerned that the switch would discredit the American command at a very

KAMPFGRUPPE PEIPER

December 18–23, 1944, viewed from the southwest, showing the increasingly desperate attempts by the battlegroup to open a viable route west towards the Meuse as the cordon of US units tightens around it.

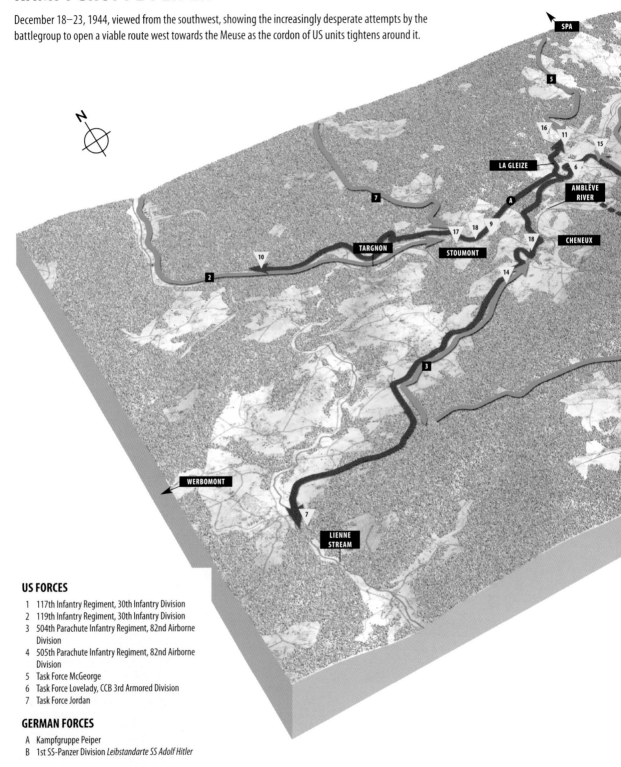

SPA

LA GLEIZE

AMBLÉVE RIVER

CHENEUX

STOUMONT

TARGNON

WERBOMONT

LIENNE STREAM

US FORCES

1 117th Infantry Regiment, 30th Infantry Division
2 119th Infantry Regiment, 30th Infantry Division
3 504th Parachute Infantry Regiment, 82nd Airborne Division
4 505th Parachute Infantry Regiment, 82nd Airborne Division
5 Task Force McGeorge
6 Task Force Lovelady, CCB 3rd Armored Division
7 Task Force Jordan

GERMAN FORCES

A Kampfgruppe Peiper
B 1st SS-Panzer Division *Leibstandarte SS Adolf Hitler*

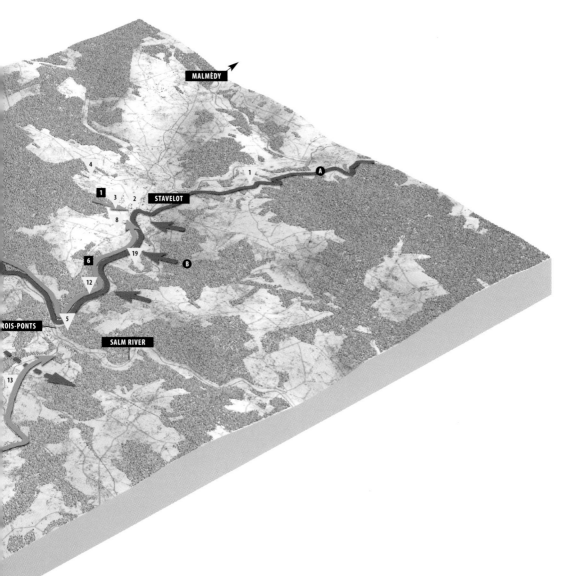

EVENTS

1. 1930hrs, December 17: Peiper decides to halt for the night after encountering a roadblock from 291st Engineer Battalion.

2. Night, December 17: The 526th Armored Infantry Battalion arrives in Stavelot and begins to set up defenses.

3. 0800hrs, December 18: Kampfgruppe Peiper attacks Stavelot, capturing town by 1000hrs. Columns begin to move on Trois Ponts.

4. December 17: US troops burn fuel dump to prevent its capture by Peiper.

5. 1145hrs, December 18: Kampfgruppe's lead tank is knocked out by a 57mm antitank gun. Amblève and Salm river bridges are blown by US engineers, forcing Kampfgruppe Peiper towards La Gleize instead of the direct route west to Werbomont.

6. 1300hrs, December 18: Kampfgruppe Peiper reaches La Gleize.

7. Probe from Kampfgruppe Peiper finds a bridge over the Lienne stream, but it is blown up by a patrol from US 30th Infantry Division.

8. Evening, December 18: US 30th Infantry Division retakes Stavelot, cutting off Kampfgruppe Peiper and part of Kampfgruppe Knittel in La Gleize.

9. 0900hrs, December 19: Kampfgruppe Peiper attacks 3/119th Infantry, 30th Infantry Division at Stoumont and captures the town.

10. Kampfgruppe Peiper is finally halted near Stoumont railway station on the outskirts of Targnon by 119th Infantry reinforced by the 740th Tank Battalion and 90mm antiaircraft guns. A company of Panzergrenadiers holds Targnon until nightfall and then withdraws to Stoumont.

11. Not realizing First US Army HQ is at Spa, Peiper sends a weak probe up the road, but it withdraws after encountering a roadblock.

12. Early evening December 19: Kampfgruppe Knittel returns from La Gleize and attempts to clear the road back to Stavelot.

13. December 20: 505th Parachute Infantry, 82nd Airborne moves on Trois Ponts.

14. December 20: 504th Parachute Infantry, 82nd Airborne moves on Cheneux, capturing a toehold in the town that afternoon.

15. Afternoon, December 20: Task Force Lovelady, CCB 3rd Armored Division moves down the Francorchamps road and seizes road behind La Gleize.

16. Afternoon, December 20: Task Force McGeorge is stopped by a roadblock near Borgoumont.

17. Afternoon, December 20: Task Force Jordan is stopped by Panzers in outskirts of Stoumont.

18. December 21: Peiper withdraws forward positions in Cheneux to La Gleize in afternoon, and from Stoumont after dark.

19. December 22: The remainder of 1st SS-Panzer Division near Wanne attempts to break through to La Gleize, but is frustrated by an encounter with Task Force Lovelady.

20. 0200hrs, December 24: Peiper begins evacuating La Gleize, moving south through the woods.

German Panzergrenadiers of 1st SS-Panzer Division move through Honsfeld on December 17 after the town was captured by Kampfgruppe Peiper. To the right is an SdKfz 251 Ausf. D, the standard German infantry half-track, while to the left is a captured example of its American counterpart, the M3 half-track. The vehicle in the background is a Mobelwagen 37mm antiaircraft vehicle, one of two of 10th Company, 1st SS-Panzer Regiment knocked out during the fighting by a US antitank gun. (NARA)

sensitive moment, and reluctantly agreed in the hopes that the British would commit their reserves to the campaign. He also received assurances that the reorganization would only be temporary. Bradley was deeply suspicious of this change as a result of Montgomery's interminable campaign to be appointed the main Allied ground commander.

The handover took place on December 20 and Montgomery strode into Hodges' HQ at Chaudfontaine later in the day like "Christ come to cleanse the temple." Though Montgomery's theatrics and arrogance infuriated the American officers, his energy and tactical skills helped to stabilize the command situation on the northern shoulder, which he took command of on the 22nd. He began to move the reserve XXX Corps to the Meuse to make certain that no German units would penetrate into central Belgium, and he dispatched liaison officers from the Phantom service to coordinate the

This PzKpfw IV Ausf J from the spearhead of Kampfgruppe Peiper was knocked out by US M10 tank destroyers on the road from Büllingen to Wirtzfeld on December 17. (NARA)

defensive actions along the front. American tactical commanders such as Hasbrouck and Clarke of the 7th Armored Division were later effusive in their praise of his role in restoring control.

EXPLOITING THE BREAKTHROUGH: KAMPFGRUPPE PEIPER

The first attempt to exploit the breakthrough in the northern sector was made by the 1st SS-Panzer Division. The delays in opening up the main approach avenue through Losheimergraben on December 16 prompted Hermann Preiss, the 1st SS-Panzer Corps commander, to re-arrange the route allotments and direct Joachim Peiper to move his Kampfgruppe through Lanzerath to the rail station at Buchholz, leaving the direct road to Losheimergraben open for the stalled "Hitlerjugend."

The spearhead of Peiper's formation began moving towards Buchholz at 0330hrs on December 17, and quickly overran the two hapless platoons from 3/394th Infantry who had been left behind when the rest of the battalion had pulled back. As the column cleared the woods approaching Honsfeld, the only opposition was the scattered elements of the 14th

Cavalry Group and its attached 801st Tank Destroyer Battalion. The town itself had been used as a rear area rest camp for the 99th Division and stragglers had drifted in the previous day. There were also a dozen towed 3in antitank guns, some still limbered for travel. Kampfgruppe Peiper's column moved past a pair of 3in antitank guns in the dark that were then overrun

Attack in the Ardennes: Kampfgruppe Peiper, December 17, 1944

Probably the most vivid image to have emerged from the Battle of the Bulge was the sight of the massive Kingtiger tanks advancing through the snowy pine forests of the Belgian border, immortalized by a series of photographs taken by a German combat cameraman on the morning of December 17 near the German–Belgian border. In many accounts of the battle, these images have symbolized the armored spearhead of Kampfgruppe Peiper as it steamrolled through American defenses at the start of the Ardennes offensive. In reality, the image highlights the underlying problems of the German offensive. The Kingtigers of the 501st Heavy SS-Panzer Battalion were not in the vanguard of the German attack, but brought up the rear of

Kampfgruppe Peiper due to the difficulties of moving such awkward and accident-prone tanks on the narrow country roads of Belgium. Peiper's spearheads were the old, reliable, and more fleet-footed PzKpfw IV medium tanks. The troops on the Kingtiger wear the distinctive camouflage smocks of the elite Fallschirmjäger paratroopers, long respected by the US Army as the best of the German light infantry. However by December 1944 they were a pale reflection of their former glory. Decimated in the summer 1944 fighting, the divisions were reconstructed using surplus Luftwaffe ground personnel and other recruits who would have been rejected in years past by such an elite formation. But the division's real problem was its leadership, with many of its units led by inexperienced Luftwaffe staff officers, not combat-hardened veterans. (Artwork by Howard Gerrard) by infantry, and encountered small arms fire on reaching the town. Resistance quickly evaporated, and about 250 GIs were captured. While being marched back to Lanzerath a number of American prisoners of war and Belgian civilians were randomly killed, the beginning of the 1st SS-Panzer Division's loathsome record of atrocities during the campaign.

Peiper pushed his column forward to Büllingen, where there was little organized defense of the town except for the 254th Engineer Battalion, which hastily deployed a company along each of the main roads leading into town. Peiper's column reached the town before dawn and there was sporadic fighting between the engineers and the lead Panzers. Bazooka teams and 3in antitank guns knocked out a few German tanks. Peiper's column also overran two airfields used by divisional spotting aircraft, but those from the 2nd Infantry Division mostly managed to escape.

The engineers withdrew to a manor farm along the Bütgenbach road dubbed "Dom Bütgenbach" that would later figure in the fighting, but which for now was ignored by the German advance. There are two roads out of Büllingen, one towards Elsenborn Ridge via Bütgenbach (currently called N632), and the other, N692, to the southwest. Peiper moved to the southwest, as the other route to the northwest was allotted to the neighboring "Hitlerjugend" which was still entangled in the Krinkelt-Rocherath fighting.

The spearhead of Peiper's columns moved through open farm country from Moderscheid to Thirimont. To save time, some tanks and half-tracks tried to go across the farm fields, only to find the ground so muddy that they stalled. The columns, which stretched all the way back to the German border, were subjected to at least three strafing attacks by US P-47 fighters during the morning, but with little damage.

During this advance, Peiper captured some US military police and was told there was a major American headquarters in the village of Ligneuville. Peiper decided to investigate, and ordered a company to take a short-cut along minor farm roads but it became trapped in the mud. As a result, Peiper ordered his armored spearhead under Werner Sternebeck to go the long way around via Waimes, and the Baugnez crossroads. While approaching the crossroads, it ran into a column of trucks from B/285th Field Artillery Observation Battalion, one of the elements of the 7th Armored Division moving to St. Vith. As the columns met around 1300hrs, the lead German PzKpfw IV tanks fired on the trucks, bringing them to a halt. Sternebeck's men quickly captured the lightly armed Americans and about 90 men were herded together in a field near the crossroads, joined later by additional prisoners when more American trucks stumbled into the ambush. After most

Peiper was infuriated by the failure of the 3rd Fallschirmjäger Division to seize Honsfeld on December 17, 1944, and appropriated a battalion of paratroopers for his column. Some of these troops ended up riding on the engine deck of a Kingtiger tank commanded by Oberscharführer Sowa of the 501st Heavy SS-Panzer Battalion near Ligneuville on December 18, 1944, as seen here. (NARA)

of Peiper's column had passed the crossroads, a massacre took place of the prisoners, the details of which remain controversial to this day. It would appear that the massacre started around 1500hrs when a tank crew assigned to guard the prisoners began taking random pot shots at the prisoners, a vile amusement repeated from earlier in the day at Honsfeld. This was followed by machine gun fire from the two tanks. For a while, troops from passing vehicles continued to fire randomly at the wounded and the dead, and finally troops from the SS-Pioneer Company were sent into the field to finish off any survivors. In total, some 113 bodies were found in the field in January when the US Army recaptured the crossroads. The incident has become infamous as the Malmédy massacre and a post-war trial was conducted of Peiper and many of his surviving officers and men.

In fact there was no major US headquarters in Ligneuville and at the time the village had been abandoned by the service elements of CCB/9th Armored Division, which had set off earlier in the day towards St. Vith. The lead Panther of the column was knocked out by an M4 dozer tank under repair,

During the fighting in Büllingen on December 17, the spearhead of Kampfgruppe Peiper, a company of PzKpfw IV tanks led by SS-Obersturmführer Werner Sternebeck, became disoriented and headed out of town north instead of west towards Wirtzfeld. About a mile (1.6km) out of town the two lead Panzers were knocked out by some M10 3in GMCs of the 644th Tank Destroyer Battalion. (NARA)

but the town was taken with little fighting. Through dusk Peiper's columns snaked their way through the foothills of the Amblève valley without encountering any opposition. On the approaches to the town of Stavelot around 1800hrs, they encountered a small engineer roadblock and came under small arms fire. Surprisingly, Peiper decided against a night attack into the town. The exhaustion of his troops after two days with little sleep was probably a more important factor than the feeble resistance encountered. At the time, the town was held only by a single engineer company. Peiper's delay in attacking Stavelot gave the US defenders time to prepare. A small task force from the 526th Armored Infantry Battalion arrived after dark, but with so little knowledge of the layout of the town, the defense was poorly prepared and the key Amblève bridge weakly defended and not prepared for demolition.

Kampfgruppe Peiper resumed their attack at 0400hrs on December 18 deploying Panzergrenadiers in the southern fringes of the town opposite the bridge. As the newly arrived GIs attempted to set up roadblocks with antitank guns at 0600hrs, they were brought under fire. A Panzergrenadier

The focus of much of the fighting in Stavelot was over the Amblève stone bridge seen here to the right, the only one still intact. To the left of the picture under a heavy coat of snow can be seen Kingtiger number 222 of the 501st Heavy SS-Panzer Battalion, which was knocked out while supporting Kampfgruppe Sandig's attack on December 19. This photo was taken on January 10, 1945, after heavy snow had set in; during most of the Stavelot fighting the area was relatively free of snow. (NARA)

platoon made its way over the bridge but was quickly forced back to the southern side. In the meantime, German engineers determined that the bridge was not prepared for demolition. After receiving reinforcements, another attack was made at dawn but control of the north side was in question until the first Panther tanks arrived. The first Panzer was hit by a 57mm antitank gun positioned up the street, which failed to penetrate, and the tank drove over the gun. The German troops advanced rapidly through the town, losing one Panzer to a 3in antitank gun, but by 1000hrs the town was in their hands. The remnants of the US task force retreated north to a large fuel dump on a side road outside the town. To prevent the Germans from capturing it, 124,000 gallons (563,715 liters) of gasoline were poured into a gully and ignited. Peiper, in a rush to seize the critical bridges at Trois Ponts, had not realized it was there.

The three bridges in Trois Ponts for which the town received its name had all been prepared for demolition by US engineers. A lone 57mm antitank gun guarded the road from Stavelot and managed to knock out the lead German tank when it approached around 1145hrs. Although the gun was

Although desperate for fuel, Kampfgruppe Peiper was unaware of the US fuel dump on the Francorchamps road above Stavelot. Fearing it might fall into German hands, US troops set all 124,000 gallons (564 liters) on fire. It was the only major fuel dump not evacuated by the US Army. (NARA)

quickly destroyed and the small roadblock overwhelmed, the delay gave the engineers time to blow up both the Amblève bridge and one of the two bridges over the Salm River. Prevented from using the main route to Werbomont and having left his tactical bridging behind, Peiper redirected his columns along the more circuitous route up the Amblève valley through La Gleize. A small bridge on a poor secondary road was found near Cheneux, but in the late afternoon the weather cleared and the column was hit by US fighter-bombers. Two tanks and several half-tracks were damaged, blocking the road. As importantly, US observation aircraft slipped through the cloud cover and were able to pass back detailed information on the size and direction of Peiper's force for most of the rest of the afternoon.

By the time that the damaged vehicles at Cheneux were moved aside it was dusk. A bridge was found over the Lienne stream, but it was blown by US engineers as the German spearhead approached. After dark a small group of half-tracks and tank destroyers attempted to use small side roads to reach the road junction at Werbomont, but were ambushed by an advance patrol from the US 30th Infantry Division. As Peiper had been moving through the Amblève valley, newly arrived American reinforcements had begun to block the main exits towards Liège. Instead of facing small rearguards made up of

Kampfgruppe Peiper left Stavelot on its way northwest, and was followed later on December 18 by Kampfgruppe Knittel which fought a losing battle against the 30th Infantry Division for the town later in the day. This SdKfz 251/9 75mm assault gun half-track was knocked out by a rifle grenade in the fighting. (NARA)

engineers and scratch defense forces, Peiper would now begin to face more substantial opposition.

A new threat began to emerge behind him. He had expected that the bulk of the 3rd Fallschirmjäger Division would close up behind his columns and occupy Stavelot. But a battalion from the US 30th Division joined the remnants of the task force that had fought for Stavelot earlier in the day and launched an attack on the town in the late afternoon. A Panzer column returning from Trois Ponts through Stavelot became mixed up in the battle, as did a few Kingtiger heavy tanks. The fighting continued through the night and the next day Stavelot was back in US hands. The US control was still patchy so that some German forces were still able to infiltrate past to reinforce Peiper. Nevertheless, the recapture of Stavelot cut Peiper off from the rest of his division.

With his rear now under attack, Peiper frantically tried to find other routes to the west. Since the road out of La Gleize to the southwest was blocked, Peiper decided to try the better road towards Stoumont, even though there were already reports it was held in force by US troops. In fact, the lead elements of the 119th Infantry, 30th Division arrived in Stoumont after dark, shortly after the spearhead of Kampfgruppe Peiper had bivouacked outside the town.

The columns following behind Kampfgruppe Peiper's spearhead were held up by the demolished rail bridge on the Malmédy–Stadkyll rail-line. It was finally breached by a J-Gerät bridge which enabled trucks and other wheeled vehicles to follow. (NARA)

By the morning of December 19, Peiper's force in La Gleize had dwindled to a paltry 19 Panthers, six PzKpfw IVs and six Kingtigers, the remaining 86 Panzers having broken down, been knocked out, bogged down, or become lost during the previous days' odyssey. With thick fog covering the area, Peiper decided to strike Stoumont before the Americans could prepare their defenses. The US forces in Stoumont consisted of the 3/119th Infantry supported by eight towed 3in antitank guns and a 90mm antiaircraft gun. The attack began at 0800hrs with the Panzers going straight down the road, and the Panzergrenadiers advancing through the fog on foot. The 3in antitank guns were quickly overrun and in the ensuing two-hour battle one US infantry company was surrounded and forced to surrender, and the other two pushed out of town. The US regimental commander dispatched a

As can be seen in this aerial view of La Gleize, the town was heavily shelled. This view looks towards the northwest with the road to the left upper corner heading towards Stoumont and the road to the right center heading to Trois Ponts. (Military History Institute)

reserve infantry company to the scene, and, in conjunction with ten M4 tanks of the 743rd Tank Battalion, executed a fighting retreat along the road past Targnon with Panzers on their heels.

While attempting to exploit their success the Panzer spearhead ran into a 90mm antiaircraft gun situated on a bend to the west of the town, and was temporarily halted. A few Panzers reached the village of Targnon where a bridge led to the southwest and the Werbomont road junction. Peiper was hesitant to push his force in this direction, as by late afternoon, his armored vehicles were running very low on fuel. To reinforce the Targnon roadblock, the First Army cobbled together some tank support. The 740th Tank Battalion had recently arrived in Belgium without tanks and some of its officers were dispatched to a depot and told to requisition whatever tanks were available. This totaled 14 British M4 tanks, five M4A1 duplex-drive amphibious tanks, and an M36 90mm tank destroyer. A platoon from this unit arrived to the west of Stoumont at 1530hrs and was thrown into the fray to support an infantry attack on the Stoumont railroad station west of Targnon. Three Panthers were knocked out in the ensuing encounter and Peiper pulled his forces back into Stoumont. Whether he realized it at the time or not, this was his battlegroup's high-water mark.

The German offensive was going badly awry. By late on December 19, additional forces were closing in on Peiper from the north and west. The 82nd Airborne Division had already arrived at Werbomont and was moving towards the Amblève valley from the west. A combat command of the 3rd Armored Division was dispatched down the road from Liège and its three task forces approached La Gleize down three separate roads to prevent Peiper from moving towards the First Army headquarters in Spa. By the end of December 19 Kampfgruppe Peiper was low on fuel and trapped in the Amblève valley around La Gleize, 28 miles (45km) from Liège, and 40 miles (65km) from its initial objective on the Meuse River at Huy that Peiper had hoped to reach on the first day of the offensive.

The southern arm of 1st SS-Panzer Division had advanced with far less opposition. Kampfgruppe Hansen had cleared the border area near Krewinkel, and after a short delay in minefields along the front line, it began a rapid advance with the Jagdpanzer IV tank destroyers in the lead. Its route was through the Losheim Gap, weakly defended by retreating elements of

This aerial view of Stoumont is centered on the Sanatorium where much of the heaviest fighting took place. This view looks towards the east; the road to La Gleize is to the right and to Targnon to the lower left. (Military History Institute)

the hapless 14th Cavalry Group. By late on December 17 Hansen's battlegroup was only a short distance behind Peiper's and had encountered no serious opposition. The following day a small task force of the 18th Cavalry Squadron and some towed 3in antitank guns were ambushed by a group of Hansen's Panzergrenadiers bivouacked in a woods astride the road from Poteau to Recht. The column was quickly overcome. While this small encounter hardly figures in the larger picture of combat actions in the sector, the aftermath of the skirmish was caught by a German photographer whose film was later captured by the US 3rd Armored Division. These four rolls of film constitute most of the surviving images of the German Ardennes offensive, and are among the most famous of the battle. Kampfgruppe Hansen advanced no further as at 1400hrs he was ordered to withdraw his force to Recht with an aim to keep open this route for the planned advance of the 9th SS-Panzer Division, the lead element of the 2nd SS-Panzer Corps. Hansen was furious at the order, as the route to the Salm River crossing at Viesalm was weakly protected and his troops could have arrived there later in the day. Instead, the lead elements of the US 7th Armored Division arrived in Poteau late in the day – the opening phase of the battle for St. Vith. Hansen's troops remained idle through December 19, awaiting the 9th SS-Panzer Division.

On December 20, US forces were again pressuring Kampfgruppe Peiper's defenses. The main US concern was the threat posed to Spa, but Peiper was oblivious to the US headquarters there. Task Force McGeorge was sent down the road from Spa but was stopped before reaching La Gleize. Two companies of the 504th Parachute Infantry Regiment, 82nd Airborne Division attempted to secure Cheneux, but two attacks during the afternoon and evening left them with barely a toehold in the town.

Of more immediate consequence to Peiper, US actions at Stavelot were ending any hope of reinforcement. Task Force Lovelady from the CCB/3rd Armored Division seized control of the road from La Gleize to Stavelot on December 20 and engaged Kampfgruppe Knittel near Trois Ponts which controlled the only remaining access to La Gleize from the German side. Knittel made another attempt to wrest control of Stavelot from the 117th Infantry, but by the end of the day, the Americans were in firm control of the west bank of the Amblève. The following day, the 1st SS-Panzer Division's commander, Wilhelm Mohnke, ordered Kampfgruppe Hansen to reinforce Knittel for another try against Stavelot. The 1st SS-Panzergrenadier Regiment crossed the Amblève east of Trois Ponts but a Jagdpanzer IV following the grenadiers collapsed the bridge and left them isolated on the

During the fighting on December 18, in the Losheim Gap, Kampfgruppe Hansen overwhelmed a column from the 14th Cavalry Group that was moving on the road between Recht and Poteau. This shows two of the M8 armored cars that were abandoned, both from C Troop, 18th Cavalry Squadron. (NARA)

western bank without support. Attempts to bridge the Amblève were a failure. Task Force Lovelady linked up with the Stavelot defenders and was reinforced by two more companies from the 30th Division. After another hard day of fighting, the third German attempt to regain Stavelot was foiled.

Peiper's defenses were driven in by attacks on December 21. After failing to clear out the paratroopers in the outskirts of Cheneux in the morning, another battalion from the 82nd Airborne Division outflanked the town that afternoon, forcing Peiper to withdraw his infantry back to La Gleize. American attacks against the more heavily defended positions in Stoumont were frustrated by the heavy fog and Panther tanks. The road behind Stoumont was temporarily captured by US infantry, but a quick counterattack restored the situation in the afternoon. Although Kampfgruppe Peiper had managed to hold the village for another day, Peiper had too little infantry to defend the town and withdrew his forces back to La Gleize after dark.

The renewed attempts to relieve Peiper from the Stavelot area on December 22 were again frustrated by Task Force Lovelady. A counterattack near Biester in the late afternoon almost cut the task force in two, but instead resulted in heavy casualties for Kampfgruppe Hansen.

A column of M36 90mm tank destroyers moves forward in support of the 82nd Airborne Division's attempt to halt the advance of Kampfgruppe Peiper near Werbomont, Belgium on December 20, 1944. These were the only US Army vehicles capable of handling the Panther or Tiger tank in a frontal engagement. (NARA)

Riflemen of the 117th Infantry, 30th Division prepare to break down a door during street fighting in Stavelot on December 21, 1944. The two riflemen nearest the door have rifle-grenades fixed on their M1 Garand rifles, while the soldier to the left is armed with an M1 carbine. (NARA)

After consolidating in La Gleize, Kampfgruppe Peiper had been reduced to less than a third of its starting strength – some 1,500 troops – and a fifth of its original Panzers: 13 Panther tanks, six PzKpfw IVs, and six Kingtigers as well as an assortment of other vehicles. Fuel and ammunition were low. The day's fighting proved frustrating for both sides as they ineffectively probed each other's defenses. Late on December 22 Mohnke contacted Peiper and let him know that the attempt to reach him earlier in the day had failed again. Peiper consulted with his senior officers and asked Mohnke's permission to attempt a breakout. This was refused but the corps commander, Hermann Preiss, asked Dietrich for permission to divert the 9th SS-Panzer Division from its advance to clear out Stavelot and open up an escape route. Dietrich refused, and an attempt to airlift supplies to La Gleize that night proved ineffective as only about a tenth of the materiel parachuted from three Ju-52 aircraft landed within the German perimeter.

US forces began a major effort to clear the remaining German forces from the western side of the Amblève on December 23 but didn't manage to do so until the following day. Kampfgruppe Knittel withdrew its last forces before dawn on Christmas Day and by Christmas the Stavelot area was in US hands. This ended any plans to rescue Kampfgruppe Peiper.

Peiper was surrounded by about three battalions of infantry and four tank companies with US units probing eastward from Stoumont, and westward from the other side of La Gleize. These attacks were frustrated by Panzer fire from La Gleize, but Peiper's troops were on the receiving end of a punishing artillery bombardment. One of the most effective weapons was a single M12 155mm self-propelled gun that fired almost 200 rounds into the town from the outskirts at practically point-blank range. Although Dietrich had refused permission for Peiper to break out the day before, the grim situation around Stavelot led him to pass the buck down the chain of command to the divisional commander, Wilhelm Mohnke. Peiper was given permission to break out at 1400hrs on December 23 and began planning to escape that night. About 800 men were deemed fit enough for the attempt, and all the wounded were left behind. The walking wounded were given the task of setting fire to or disabling the surviving equipment after the evacuation had taken place. The retreat out of La Gleize began around 0200hrs on December 24 through the woods to the immediate south of the town. About 770 survivors reached German lines 12 miles (20km) away about 36 hours later, having had only brief encounters with paratroopers from the 82nd Airborne Division. US troops occupied La Gleize in the early morning hours of December 24 after brushing past some rearguards and were surprised to find the town abandoned except for the German wounded and 107 captured GIs.

The 1st SS-Panzer Division had failed in its mission and had suffered heavy casualties. Personnel casualties through Christmas were about 2,000 men of which more than 300 were prisoners. Equipment losses through Christmas were far heavier and included 11 Kingtigers, 27 Panthers, 20 PzKpfw IVs, and 12 Jagdpanzer IVs or about 65 percent of the division's initial tank and tank destroyer strength with a significant fraction of the remainder broken down or trapped in the mud.

SPECIAL OPS: OPERATIONS *GREIF* AND *STÖSSER*

The German special operations associated with the Ardennes offensive proved complete non-events, yet had consequences far beyond their meager accomplishments. Skorzeny's formation, 150th Panzer Brigade, had been formed in November 1944 in an attempt to recruit soldiers with a knowledge of English who could pass as American troops. Fewer than a dozen with colloquial American English were found, along with another 400 who spoke the language with less proficiency. As a result the size of the unit was scaled back to two battalions and the best speakers were segregated into a commando unit – the Steinhau team. Attempts to collect captured American equipment were not particularly successful as few German front-

Skorzeny's 150th Panzer Brigade was committed to the attack on Malmédy on December 21. The Panther tanks were disguised as American M10 tank destroyers, and this one was knocked out with a bazooka by Private F. Currey of the 120th Infantry who was later decorated with the Medal of Honor for his actions that day. (Military History Institute)

line units wanted to part with their much-prized jeeps, and the tanks and armored cars that were rounded up were in poor mechanical condition. Five Panther tanks were modified to look like M10 tank destroyers, and five StG III assault guns were modified to hide their identity. The brigade was assigned two separate missions. The Steinhau team totaling 44 soldiers was broken up into six groups, usually consisting of a few men in a jeep, with four groups to infiltrate behind US lines for reconnaissance and two groups to conduct diversionary tasks such as destroying bridges, misdirecting traffic, and cutting communications. The main body of 150th Panzer Brigade was positioned to the rear of 1st SS-Panzer Corps, and once the Hohes Venn was reached beyond the Elsenborn Ridge, the unit would be injected in front of the advancing German force, pretending to be fleeing US troops, and race to capture at least two bridges over the Meuse at Amay, Huy, or Andenne.

The Steinhau teams departed during the first two days of the offensive. At least eight commandos were captured, although American records suggest that a total of 18 were caught. The actual effect of the teams is difficult to calculate since they have become shrouded in myth and legend. While no major reconnaissance discovery or major demolition operation was carried out by the Steinhau teams, the capture of several of the groups caused chaos in American rear areas. The 106th Division captured a document outlining

Besides the five Panther tanks converted to resemble M10 tank destroyers, 150th Panzer Brigade also had five StuG III assault guns, painted in American markings, with an ineffective disguise. This one from Kampfgruppe Y was abandoned between Baugnez and Geromont. (NARA)

the general scheme of Operation *Greif* the first morning of the fighting, and several of the captured German commandos revealed their mission. One spread the rumor, entirely false, that a team was on its way to assassinate General Eisenhower, which led to his virtual imprisonment at his headquarters for a few days. A young American counterintelligence officer, Earl Browning, came up with the idea of asking suspicious characters trivia questions about sports or Hollywood that would only be known by someone living in the United States. The security precautions caused far more trouble than the Steinhau teams themselves.

After the 1st SS-Panzer Corps failed to make a significant dent in American defenses in the Elsenborn region, Skorzeny realized that there was little chance that his unit would actually be used as intended. On the evening of December 17, he was given permission for it to serve with the 1st SS-Panzer Division in an attempt to capture the key crossroads town of Malmédy, which had been bypassed by Kampfgruppe Peiper earlier in the day.

A trio of GIs of the 120th Infantry, 30th Division, in Malmédy on December 29, 1944. The town was originally held by a scratch force of engineers and the 99th Infantry Battalion until the arrival of the 120th Infantry prior to Skorzeny's attack. (NARA)

Von der Heydte's paratroopers were dropped into the Hohes Venn by Ju-52 transports like this one. This particular example, from Transport-Squadron 3, was abandoned near Asselborn in northern Luxembourg near a German field hospital. (NARA)

Malmédy was initially held by the 291st Engineer Battalion. Curiously enough it was then reinforced by a US unit specifically assigned to deal with rear area threats. In November 1944 the First Army had formed a Security Command around the 23rd Tank Destroyer Group to counter German guerrilla groups and saboteurs. Two of its units, the 99th (Norwegian) Infantry Battalion and "T Force" consisting of an armored infantry battalion with a supporting tank destroyer company, were dispatched to the Malmédy-Stavelot depot area to guard the junction until the 30th Division arrived. The 120th Infantry, 30th Division arrived in Malmédy before Peiper's attack began on December 21.

Peiper's force attacked before dawn along the two main roads into the town. In the early morning darkness, the columns were stopped by concentrated rifle and bazooka fire, reinforced with artillery. As dawn broke and the fog lifted, American artillery spotters were able to work over the German forces stalled near one of the bridges leading into town. By the afternoon both German battlegroups were forced to withdraw having lost many of their strange Panzers. Another attack was launched before dawn on December 22 but was quickly beaten back. Rather than risk any further German advances, the US engineers blew several of the key bridges later in the afternoon. One of the most tragic episodes of the Malmédy fighting occurred the next day when US bombers, mistakenly informed that Malmédy was in German hands, bombed the town, killing over 200 civilians as well as some US troops. The 150th Panzer Brigade remained in the lines until late December and was later returned to Germany and disbanded.

The German paratroop mission, Operation *Stösser*, was an even clumsier mess than Operation *Greif*. After having been delayed a day due to a lack of trucks to transport Colonel von der Heydte's paratroopers to the airbases, it finally set off at 0300hrs on December 17. One rifle company was dumped 30 miles (50km) behind German lines near Bonn and the signal platoon ended up immediately in front of German lines along the stalemated Monschau front in the north. The drop was hindered by severe crosswinds as well as poor navigation, and only about 60 paratroopers landed with von der Heydte himself in the Hohe Venn moors. This was too small a group to carry out the planned capture of Meuse bridges since such a small force could certainly not hold on to any bridge. Over the next few days, the paratroopers performed reconnaissance, conducted nuisance raids, and gathered another 300 paratroopers scattered over the Belgian countryside. With 1st SS-Panzer Corps nowhere near the Meuse River and not even on Elsenborn Ridge, the mission of the paratroopers was pointless. Late on December 21 they were ordered to cross back to German lines near Monschau.

Many of von der Heydte's units were dropped in the wrong location along with this airborne ammunition container which fell into American hands near Kornelimunster north of the Monschau forest. (NARA)

"HITLERJUGEND" HALTED

On the evening of December 18, after its costly attack on Krinkelt–Rocherath, the 12th SS-Panzer Division "Hitlerjugend" was ordered by the corps commander, Hermann Preiss, to shift the main direction of its attack towards Bütgenbach. Movement was slow due to the traffic jams in the Eifel and the wretched state of the roads through Losheimergraben after the past days' heavy traffic. The forest roads were not designed for this level of use, and in some areas, the constant travel of heavy tracked vehicles had worn down the road into muddy trenches with the road banks level with the Panzers' engine decks.

The 26th Infantry of "Big Red One" – the 1st Infantry Division – held the Bütgenbach approaches. The regiment was in rough shape after having fought along the fringes of the Hürtgen forest earlier in the month. It was deployed east of Bütgenbach, with its lead battalion, the 2/26th Infantry, on a hill overlooking the manor farm of Domane Bütgenbach, better known to the Americans as Dom Bütgenbach. The first element of "Hitlerjugend" to arrive in the area around noon of December 18 was Kampfgruppe Bremer, based around a reconnaissance battalion. A patrol consisting of an SdKfz 234 armored car and a Kubelwagen moved up the road towards Dom Bütgenbach and both vehicles were destroyed by a 57mm antitank gun hidden in the fog. The two trucks that followed disgorged their infantry into the woods to the south of the farm and they were decimated by an artillery barrage.

The main elements of "Hitlerjugend" reached Büllingen on the night of December 18/19 in three battlegroups. The first attack was launched around 0230hrs by Kampfgruppe Kühlmann consisting of 12 Jagdpanzer IV tank destroyers from the 560th Heavy Panzerjäger Battalion and two companies of Panzergrenadiers of the 26th SS-Panzergrenadier Regiment. With the armor in the vanguard and the grenadiers behind, the attack formed up 700 yards (640m) in front of the American positions, cloaked in the dark and thick fog. The 26th Infantry began firing illumination rounds from their mortars and then called in artillery. The potent combination of artillery and small arms fire stopped the Panzergrenadiers, and several of the tank destroyers became bogged in the muddy ground in front of the American positions. Three tank destroyers broke through into the manor itself, but they turned back when confronted with a 155mm artillery barrage. Two of the three were knocked out while trying to escape. The attack petered out after an hour leaving about a hundred dead, and three burning Jagdpanzers.

An infantry column from the 26th Infantry, 1st Infantry Division, is seen here moving down the Büllingen road on December 17, 1944, on its way to the Dom Bütgenbach manor farm. This regiment's defense of the road junction finally halted the attacks of the "Hitlerjugend". (NARA)

The American positions were pounded by German artillery until around 1015hrs. An attack from the south along the Morschheck road was spearheaded by an SdKfz 234 armored car and a tank destroyer. Both were knocked out at close range by a 57mm antitank gun and the Panzergrenadier company was almost wiped out in the ensuing artillery and mortar barrage. A second attack was launched shortly after from Büllingen but after two Jagdpanzers were knocked out the attack faltered. By this stage, the forward elements of "Hitlerjugend" were suffering from ammunition shortages, and further attacks were postponed until more supplies could be brought forward along the congested roads. "Hitlerjugend's" commander, Hugo Kraas, reinforced Kampfgruppe Kühlmann with the remainder of his available tanks and Jagdpanzers. The reinforced German battlegroup set off around midnight and was immediately subjected to US artillery fire even while forming up. The main thrust came from Büllingen with a supporting thrust from Morschheck. Once again spearheaded by tank destroyers from the 560th Heavy Panzerjäger Battalion, the attack again encountered very stiff resistance and heavy artillery fire. At least five Jagdpanzers broke through the infantry trench line and advanced into the manor farm itself.

Without infantry support, two were destroyed by bazooka teams and two more withdrew. Several of the German tank destroyers became stuck in the mud and the fighting finally ended around 0530hrs as both sides licked their wounds. The American infantry had held, but there were serious shortages in bazooka rockets and antitank mines. Casualties on both sides had been high, and about 12 Jagdpanzers had been knocked out or bogged down in the fourth attack on Dom Bütgenbach.

Rather than give the Americans time to recover and reorganize their defense, Kraas sent other elements from Kampfgruppe Kühlmann to attack the manor around 0600hrs. This included eight surviving Jagdpanzers from Morschheck, and about ten PzKpfw IVs and Panthers from Büllingen. The Jagdpanzers crunched into the American trench line, running over at least one 57mm antitank gun. As in the previous attacks, American artillery and small arms fire kept the Panzergrenadiers away from the American trench line, and when the German Panzers reached the forward defenses, they were hunted down in the fog by bazooka teams. The attack finally collapsed around dawn. It was the last major attack on December 20, though smaller infantry attacks continued through the day to little effect. The 560th Heavy Panzerjäger Battalion, which had been the backbone of the attacks on the manor, was reduced in strength to three Jagdpanthers and ten Jagdpanzer IVs, from an initial strength of 12 Jagdpanthers and 25 Jagdpanzer IVs.

In desperation Kraas decided to make one last assault with all his Panzergrenadier battalions and surviving armor. All four artillery battalions supported the attack with their remaining ammunition. The heavy artillery barrage hit the American positions around 0300hrs on December 21, causing severe casualties. The Americans responded by calling in their own artillery on suspected assembly points. The attack was postponed when a Panzergrenadier battalion became lost in the dark. It was finally located and the attack began around 0625hrs, three hours behind schedule. The attack began badly when the lead Panther tank and a Jagdpanther following it were destroyed by 57mm antitank gunfire. Nevertheless, the Panzers managed to knock out every surviving 57mm antitank gun defending the southern positions facing the Morschheck road. The attack continued until dawn, with eight PzKpfw IV tanks fighting their way into the manor itself. Two M4 tanks and two PzKpfw IV tanks were destroyed in a point-blank duel.

The farmyard of Dom Bütgenbach was littered with knocked-out equipment including this PzKpfw IV, one of the handful to reach the manor itself during the final skirmishes. In the foreground is an M36 90mm gun motor carriage of 613th Tank Destroyer Battalion. (NARA)

The remaining six began moving through the farm buildings, followed by a half-dozen Panzergrenadiers, the only German infantry to make it into the manor. They were quickly killed by headquarters staff from the regimental command post, and the PzKpfw IV tanks used the cover of the stone farm buildings to try to avoid being hit by tank fire from a pair of M4 tanks on a neighboring hill.

The pre-dawn attack had ripped open a gap in the American defenses along the southern side, but continual artillery fire prevented the German infantry from exploiting it. A renewed Panzer attack at around 1000hrs from the south side was stopped cold when an M10 tank destroyer knocked out several tanks in quick succession. The fighting continued intermittently through the late morning, with reinforcements finally arriving in the early afternoon on the American side in the form of four M36 90mm tank destroyers of the 613th Tank Destroyer Battalion. These were assigned to hunt down the surviving PzKpfw IV tanks lurking in the farm itself. They began firing their guns through the wooden walls of the barn, convincing the Panzer crews to retreat. Two of the three tanks were hit while withdrawing and only one escaped.

The road leading from Dom Bütgenbach towards Büllingen was strewn with destroyed and abandoned equipment including this Jagdpanther tank destroyer from the 560th Heavy Panzerjäger Battalion and an overturned PzKpfw IV from the 12th SS-Panzer Regiment. (Military History Institute)

This last attack convinced Kraas that it would be impossible to open Rollbahn C towards Liège. The "Hitlerjugend" Division was subsequently pulled out of this sector and sent into the southern sector, later becoming involved in an equally futile attack against Bastogne. Casualties in the attack on the Dom Bütgenbach manor were over 1,200 of which there were 782 dead. During the five days of fighting at Krinkelt-Rocherath and Dom Bütgenbach, "Hitlerjugend" lost 32 of its 41 Panthers, 12 of its 33 PzKpfw IV tanks, three of its 14 Jagdpanthers, and 18 of its 26 Jagdpanzer IV tank destroyers – almost 60 percent of its initial armored strength.

The losses in the 26th Infantry had been heavy as well, including 500 killed, wounded, or captured out of an initial strength of about 2,500 men. Equipment losses were heavy including five 57mm antitank guns, three M4 tanks, and three M10 3in tank destroyers. But the 26th Infantry had held the Bütgenbach manor and prevented a German breakthrough along the northern route. Divisional artillery, and supporting artillery from neighboring units on the Elsenborn Ridge, had been essential in the defense, and during the fighting about 10,000 artillery rounds were fired in support of the 26rd Infantry.

THE LOST GAMBLE

The failure of the 1st SS-Panzer Corps along the northern shoulder of the Ardennes salient doomed Hitler's plans. The reasons for their failures are many, ignoring for the moment the basic strategic problems with the plan. Dietrich had no "finger-feel" for the battlefield, underestimating the problems posed by the US infantry defenses in the wooded area along the forward edge of battle. The preliminary artillery barrage was a mistake since it caused few US casualties yet ensured that US defenses were alerted when the first wave of German infantry advanced into the forest. The lead infantry units were not given sufficient armored support to overcome the American defenses, as a result of which they faltered in the face of well-entrenched troops. The attacks were channeled down the handful of roads suitable for vehicle traffic instead of making use of the many smaller forest trails which would have allowed the use of more infantry units to infiltrate past the sparsely scattered US defenses and enveloped them from the rear. Once out of the woods, the 12th SS-Panzer Division became entangled in the defenses at Krinkelt-Rocherath. Skeptical of the fighting quality of the Volksgrenadier divisions after their failures in the forest fighting, "Hitlerjugend" failed to use them in overcoming the American defenses in the Twin Villages or later at Dom Bütgenbach. The use of isolated tanks in the built-up towns without sufficient infantry support led to a "Panzer graveyard."

Peiper was much more successful in sticking to the mission plan since he faced such paltry opposition in the opening days of the attack. Yet the delays of the first few days, first at Lanzerath, and then on the outskirts of Stavelot, proved fatal. The configuration of his force was ill suited to a contested advance, being encumbered by fuel-guzzling tanks, especially the Kingtigers, and bereft of bridging equipment or adequate infantry and artillery support. Although fuel shortages would help trap his group in La Gleize, German tactical intelligence was so poor that Peiper had no information on the location of significant US fuel dumps that were within his grasp.

THE BREAKTHROUGH IN THE CENTER

Of the three German armies that staged the Ardennes operation, the only one to gain a significant breakthrough was Manteuffel's 5th Panzer Army in the center. With the disintegration of the 106th Division on the Schnee Eifel, a substantial rupture was created in the American line. This rupture assisted the southern elements of the 6th Panzer Army, notably Kampfgruppe Peiper, and led to rapid advances by units of the 5th Panzer Army, especially the drive of the 116th Panzer Division on Houfallize. However, the full exploitation of this sector was hampered by an extended salient around the key road junction of St. Vith that acted as "a thumb down the German throat."

THE SCHNEE EIFEL AND THE 106TH DIVISION

The inexperienced 106th Division held a front line about 15 miles (24km) wide with the 14th Cavalry Group acting as a screening force to its north. Two of its regiments, the 422nd and 423rd Infantry, were positioned in a vulnerable salient on the Schnee Eifel, a wooded ridge line protruding off the Eifel plateau. The previous tenants, the 2nd Infantry Division, felt the position was poorly situated for defense and in the event of an attack planned to withdraw off the Schnee Eifel to a more defensible line along the Auw–Bleialf Ridge, freeing up a regiment to deal with the weak cavalry defense of the Losheim Gap. Although these plans were outlined to the 106th Division commander, Major General Alan Jones, his staff had been in position for too short a period of time to appreciate their predicament. The area forward of the two regiments was very suitable for defense since it consisted of rugged

Opposite:
In his frustration with their poor performance at the outset of the offensive, Peiper commandeered a battalion of paratroopers from the 3rd Fallschirmjager Division and ordered them to mount up on Kingtiger tanks of his Kampfgruppe to support his assault on December 17, 1944. (Corbis)

forest with no significant roads. But it was flanked on either side by two good roads, from Roth to Auw, and from Sellerich to Bleialf.

Recognizing the weakness of his infantry divisions, Manteuffel realized that 5th Panzer Army needed sound tactics to break through. Before the offensive, German patrols discovered that the inexperienced 106th Division had arrived on December 10. Contrary to Hitler's orders, Manteuffel permitted patrols that discovered a 1¼-mile (2km) gap to the north between the weak 14th Cavalry positions in Roth and Weckerath. He decided that the American positions on the Schnee Eifel were so precarious that a single division could bypass them, with the main thrust directed through the Losheim Gap to the north. The task was assigned to the 18th Volksgrenadier Division, which had been created from the remains of the 18th Luftwaffe Field Division destroyed in the Mons pocket in Belgium in September. While neither particularly experienced nor well trained, it had suffered few losses during its occupation duty at the front in the autumn. Its northern thrust through Roth would include two of its infantry regiments, the divisional artillery, and a supporting assault gun brigade, while its southern battlegroup had only a single infantry regiment supported by a self-propelled artillery battalion. The positions directly in front of the Schnee Eifel were held only by a replacement battalion since Manteuffel expected that an American counterattack eastward was unlikely. The US 106th Division's third regiment, the 424th Infantry, south of the Schnee Eifel, was the target of the 62nd Volksgrenadier Division.

As mentioned earlier, the tactics in the 5th Panzer Army sector for the initial assault differed significantly from those in the neighboring 6th Panzer Army sector and were based on infiltration prior to the main artillery barrage. As a result, the German infantry began moving in the dark at 0400hrs to infiltrate past the scattered defenses in the Losheim Gap. The morning was overcast with ground fog and rain that further aided this plan. Manteuffel firmly instructed his infantry officers that their men were to cut all communication wire that they found to isolate the forward US positions.

The main assault force in the northern sector made it past the cavalry outposts in Roth and Weckerath without being detected, reaching the outskirts of Auw before dawn. German artillery did not begin its fire missions until 0830hrs against the towns held by the American cavalry, and by this time, German troops had already begun their assaults. The 14th Cavalry garrisons at Roth and Kobscheid surrendered in the late afternoon. The remnants of the 14th Cavalry further to the north were given permission by the 106th Division to withdraw to a ridge line from Andler to Holzheim in the late afternoon. The remaining resistance in this sector came from the 592nd Field Artillery Battalion, which was subjected to a direct attack by StuG III assault guns. The attack was stopped by point-blank howitzer fire, but by nightfall the artillery were in a precarious position.

On the right flank, the first 106th Division unit to come under heavy attack was the isolated 424th Infantry. Its foxholes on the high ground near Heckhuscheid were attacked by the 62nd Volksgrenadier Division and Panzergrenadiers of the 116th Panzer Division. The first attack made little progress, but another attack up the Habscheid road began to isolate the 424th Infantry from the other two regiments on the Schnee Eifel.

One of the only organized groups to escape the encirclement of the 106th Division on the Schnee Eifel was the intelligence and reconnaissance platoon of Lieutenant Ivan Long (center) from the 423rd Infantry. About 70 men from the regiment refused to surrender and reached St. Vith on the night of December 20, as seen here. (NARA)

Casualties in the 424th Infantry were modest, but casualties in the inexperienced 62nd Volksgrenadier Division had been heavy, especially amongst the officers. The neighboring regiment of the 18th Volksgrenadier Division had similar experiences, fighting its way into Bleialf by late in the day, but at significant cost.

Manteuffel's infiltration tactics had been moderately successful. By nightfall the attack had made progress even if not as fast as hoped. The northern assault groups of the 18th Volksgrenadier Division held positions near Auw behind the northern flank of the 106th Division as well as the Roth-Kobscheid area. On the southern side of the Schnee Eifel, the penetration was not as deep, but significant inroads had been made along the Bleialf road. Manteuffel prodded the commanders to complete their missions even if it took all night.

Since the 106th Division had exhausted its reserves due to its overly extended front, the VIII Corps commander, Major General Middleton, allotted Combat Command B (CCB) of the 9th Armored Division near Faymonville to the division that evening. Recognizing the gravity of the situation, Bradley in turn committed the 7th Armored Division to Middleton's beleaguered corps.

That evening, Middleton telephoned Jones and the ensuing conversation was one of the most controversial of the campaign. Middleton promised to send the CCB of the 7th Armored Division to St. Vith but Jones misunderstood that it would arrive by dawn on December 18. Since it was facing a road march from the Netherlands along roads clogged with retreating troops and civilians, this was impossible. While Middleton and Jones were discussing future plans for the two regiments exposed on the Schnee Eifel, a switchboard operator accidentally disconnected the line and reconnected it moments later with unfortunate consequences. Middleton thought Jones understood that he wanted him to withdraw his two regiments off the Schnee Eifel, while Jones thought that his plans to leave the two regiments in place had been approved. As a result of all this confusion, Jones and his staff decided to deploy the CCB/9th Armored Division to the southern flank to reinforce the isolated 424th Infantry, and to use CCB/7th Armored Division to counterattack against the German penetration in the Losheim Gap, thereby defending the two regiments on the Schnee Eifel.

Although two of the 106th Division's regiments were surrounded on the Schnee Eifel, a third, the 424th Infantry, was further south and later served in the defense of St. Vith. Here, two soldiers of Co. C, 3/424th Infantry roll up their sleeping bags on December 28, 1944, near Manhay, where the unit withdrew alongside CCB/7th Armored Division after the defense of St. Vith. The Golden Lion divisional patch can be seen on the soldier on the right. (NARA)

The CCB/9th Armored Division moved through St. Vith around dawn with the intention of deploying near Winterspelt to block the German inroads between the 424th Infantry and the Schnee Eifel. Winterspelt was already in German hands, and first contact was made on the western bank of the Our River near Elcherath when the 14th Tank Battalion collided with the 62nd Volksgrenadier Division. During the subsequent fighting on December 17, the 424th Infantry became separated from the 28th Division to its south, and the intervention of CCB/9th Armored Division was not enough to bridge the gap to the Schnee Eifel. By early evening, Jones gave the 424th Infantry permission to withdraw west and set up defensive positions along the Our River with the CCB/9th Armored Division covering the area towards St. Vith.

The situation on the Schnee Eifel had become dangerous during the night of December 16/17 as the two battle groups of the 18th Volksgrenadier Division continued their push around the flanks of the two American regiments. On the southern flank, the town of Bleialf was hit hard at 0530hrs and was overrun shortly after dawn. This regiment, the 293rd, continued to move rapidly to the northwest against little opposition, aiming for the town of Schönberg. The US defense was further weakened by the lack of communications between Jones in St. Vith and his two regimental commanders, due in no small measure to the success of the German infantry in ripping up communication wires, as well as the failure of this inexperienced unit to establish a robust radio net prior to the attack. On the northern flank, the 14th Cavalry Group's defensive efforts had evaporated by the morning of December 18, and it began a series of uncoordinated withdrawals towards Andler and Schönberg. The northern remnants of the 14th Cavalry Group bumped into advancing columns from the 1st SS-Panzer Division. By noon, surviving elements of the 32nd Cavalry Squadron were at Wallerode on the approaches to St. Vith, and the 18th Cavalry Squadron were at Born, further to the northwest.

The first inkling that the two wings of the 18th Volksgrenadier Division were about to link up behind the Schnee Eifel came in the early morning when US artillery battalions attempting to retreat near Schönberg began to run into advancing German columns. By 0900hrs the German encirclement of the two regiments of the 106th Division on the Schnee Eifel was complete, though it was by no means secure. The leading German battalions were instructed to continue to move west, and there were no efforts to establish a firm cordon around the trapped American units. The two trapped regiments set up perimeter defense and attempted to contact divisional headquarters in St. Vith for further instruction. They were informed that reinforcements would attempt a breakthrough from the west on December 18 and that further supplies of ammunition would be dropped by air. Major General Jones at first believed that the imminent arrival of CCB/7th Armored Division would permit a relief of the units, and that prompt air supply would take care of their shortage of ammunition and food. As the day wore on, this seemed more and more unlikely. The call for air supply became caught up in red tape and no action was ever taken. The CCB/7th Armored Division became so entangled in traffic on its approach to St. Vith that there was never any chance of it intervening on the Schnee Eifel. By the time it arrived, the fate of St. Vith itself was in doubt. An order at 1445hrs to withdraw both regiments westward towards the Our River was so delayed by radio problems that it did not arrive until midnight by which time it was too late.

Further instructions arrived at 0730hrs on December 18 indicating that the units should break out towards St. Vith, bypassing the heaviest German concentrations around Schönberg. The regiments destroyed non-essential equipment such as field kitchens, left the wounded with medics in regimental collection stations, and started off to the west, both regiments abreast in a column of battalions. The first contact with German forces began around 1130hrs when 2/423rd Infantry encountered German infantry on the main Bleialf–Schönberg road. Requesting help, two more battalions moved forward but were not able to push through. Shortly after the attacks began the divisional headquarters ordered the attack redirected towards Schönberg. During the course of the day, contact was lost between the two regiments. That night, the 423rd Infantry formed a defensive position to the southeast of Schönberg. By this time, the unit was out of mortar ammunition, and had little rifle ammunition. The 422nd Infantry did not make contact with the German forces during the day, and when they bivouacked that evening, they mistakenly believed they were on the outskirts of their objective of Schönberg.

The German response to the American breakout attempts was made more difficult by the enormous traffic jam around Schönberg as units flowed west. As a result, the 56th Corps commander decided to counter the Americans with heavy artillery concentrations. As the 423rd Infantry formed for its attack shortly after dawn on December 19, it was hit hard by the German artillery, followed by an infantry assault. Two rifle companies reached the outskirts of Schönberg but were pushed back by German antiaircraft guns. By mid-afternoon, the attacks had collapsed, and the US infantrymen were down to fewer than a dozen rounds per rifle. With tactical control gone, the regimental commander gave the order to surrender around 1630hrs.

The 422nd Regiment moved out on the morning of December 19 across the Bleialf–Auw road near Oberlascheid but was brought under heavy small arms fire from German infantry in the woods west of the road. The 422nd had little success in advancing any further, and around 1400hrs the tanks of the Führer Begleit Brigade suddenly moved down the road on their way towards St. Vith. This trapped a portion of the regiment between the tanks on the road and the German infantry in the woods. Some of the regiment surrendered at 1430hrs, and most of the rest around 1600hrs. A number of groups tried to escape but most were eventually captured over the next few days. The surrender of the two regiments of the 106th Division, over 7,000 men, was the US Army's single greatest setback of the campaign in Europe.

A FINGER DOWN THE GERMAN THROAT: ST. VITH

St. Vith had been the headquarters of the hapless 106th Division. By December 17 William Hoge's CCB/9th Armored Division had begun to arrive and was in the process of reinforcing the isolated 424th Infantry. The commander of CCB/7th Armored Division, Brigadier General Bruce Clarke, arrived in St. Vith at 1030hrs. Major General Alan Jones explained that he had lost contact with his two regiments on the Schnee Eifel, and that he wanted Clarke to attack towards the Losheim Gap to relieve them. With his armored columns having a difficult time moving from the Netherlands due to the congested roads, Clarke suggested that they contact both regiments and agree on a common meeting point. Clarke was disturbed to learn that the division had no firm radio communications with either regiment as all the field telephone lines had been cut and the division had not set up a proper radio net prior to the attack. During this discussion, Colonel Devine of the 14th Cavalry Group burst in, following the rout of his command along the Poteau–Recht road, in a state of near collapse. The divisional headquarters was in turmoil and paralyzed by confusion, yet at 1330hrs when Major General Middleton called Jones, he was told that "Clarke is here, he has troops coming. We are going to be all right." Clarke was disturbed that Jones would provide such a deceptive picture of the actual situation to the corps commander, but Jones remarked that "Middleton has enough problems already." By 1430hrs German troops were beginning to approach St. Vith from the east, and small arms fire could be heard on the approaches to the town. Jones turned to Clarke and said, "You take command, I'll give you all I have." Although inferior in rank to Jones and several of his divisional staff, Clarke was the only officer at the headquarters with any combat experience, and so took command of the rapidly disintegrating defense. The only organized force in the town was the divisional engineer battalion and an attached corps engineer battalion. Clarke ordered the division engineer, Lieutenant Colonel Tom Riggs, to take the troops along with the headquarters security platoon and to advance down the road to the east of the town, dig in, and stop any advancing German forces. There were a few bright spots. Lieutenant Colonel Roy Clay, commander of the 275th Armored Field Artillery Battalion, attached to the shattered 14th Cavalry Group, showed up at the headquarters and asked

Clarke if he wanted any fire support. His unit provided the only artillery support of the St. Vith defense until the 7th Armored Division arrived and remained a vital element of the defense.

By the afternoon some 7th Armored Division units began to arrive led by Troop B, 87th Cavalry Reconnaissance Squadron. They were hastily dispatched to create a defensive line north and east of the town. German

The Fortified Goose Egg: Rearguard Defense in St. Vith, December 21, 1944

General Bruce Clarke's approach to defending St. Vith was to use the mobility and firepower of his tank units to keep the Wehrmacht at bay as long as possible. US armored divisions were weak in infantry, only three battalions per division, and while they could be used for defense, the type of linear defense in depth practiced by infantry units was out of the question. So the tanks and other supporting troops held positions as long as possible, and then fell back to more defensible positions. Here we see a pair of M4 medium tanks conducting a rearguard action in the outskirts of St. Vith shortly before

Clarke was forced to abandon the town. The tank in the background has been hit and the crew can be seen baling out. One of the most common causes of US tank losses in the late 1944 fighting was the German Panzerfaust, a small disposable rocket launcher that fired a shaped-charge grenade. While not particularly accurate, if it did hit the M4, it stood a good chance of setting off an internal ammunition fire. It is largely a myth that the Sherman burned due to its use of a gasoline engine. (Artwork by Howard Gerrard) attacks were uncoordinated due to the rush to move westward. Elements of Kampfgruppe Hansen bumped into the western defenses near Poteau, while infantry forces from the 18th Volksgrenadier Division probed along the eastern edges of the town. The bitterest fighting on December 18 took place around Poteau as CCA/7th Armored Division attempted to seize the town, which was essential to keep open supply lines to the rear.

Manteuffel had expected his units to capture St. Vith on the first day of the offensive. However, the town posed a variety of problems, not the least of which was that it split the 5th Panzer Army in two. Furthermore, it controlled the best roads through the area between 6th Panzer Army and 5th Panzer Army, including the only decent east–west rail-line, vital to resupply the offensive once the Meuse was reached. On the night of December 17/18, Manteuffel discussed the problem with Model, who suggested that the Führer Begleit Brigade be committed to destroying the St. Vith pocket. This brigade was one of the best in 5th Panzer Army, its cadres having been taken from the "Grossdeutschland" Division. It was in army reserve, with an aim to use it as the main exploitation force after one of the Panzer corps succeeded in making a breakthrough. So reassigning it to deal with St. Vith meant giving up the opportunity to use it in the central role in the later phase of the campaign. This reassignment indicates how seriously both Model and Manteuffel viewed the threat posed by St. Vith. Manteuffel hoped that the injection of this unit into the St. Vith battle would result in a quick decision, permitting the brigade to revert back to its original mission. Moving the brigade through the congested area behind the Schnee Eifel proved to be a major problem and even though the brigade was underway on the morning of December 17, it was still tied up in the traffic

Command of the St. Vith sector fell to Brigadier General Bruce Clarke of CCB/7th Armored Division after the 106th Division's headquarters departed. Clarke had commanded the CCA/4th Armored Division in September 1944 when it repulsed an earlier German counteroffensive during the Lorraine campaign. (Military History Institute)

jams around Schönberg late the following night. The plan called for the Führer Begleit Brigade to attack the town from the north, the 18th Volksgrenadier Division from the east, and the 62nd Volksgrenadier Division from the south. Although the initial attack was scheduled for December 19, the continued delays in moving the Führer Begleit Brigade into position made this impossible.

The southern sector, held by CCB/9th Armored Division and the 424th Infantry, was precarious, so late in the day Hoge's combat command withdrew over the Our River. Hoge drove to St. Vith that night expecting to meet with General Jones, but encountered Bruce Clarke instead. Although nominally under the command of the 106th Division, Hoge agreed to remain in the salient with Clarke to protect the southern flank. Other units also gravitated to the St. Vith pocket including the 112th Infantry, separated from its 28th Division.

The first serious attack against St. Vith developed around midnight on December 19/20, when the Führer Begleit Brigade deployed the first units to arrive in the sector, an infantry battalion and two assault gun companies. This attack was quickly repulsed, but later in the day the lightly defended outposts in Ober- and Nieder-Emmels were taken. The attacks substantially intensified on December 21 as more of the Führer Begleit Brigade arrived. One battalion from the brigade managed temporarily to seize control of a portion of the road westward from St. Vith to Viesalm, but this force was pushed back by CCB/7th Armored Division. One of the most significant changes from the previous day's fighting was the more extensive use of German artillery, which had finally escaped from the traffic jams. An intense barrage of the town began at 1100hrs. Most of the German attacks were preceded by intense artillery fire, and the grenadiers attacked with little respite. The positions of the 38th Armored Infantry Battalion on the eastern

The CCB of 9th Armored Division was the first reinforcement to reach St. Vith, and was commanded by Brigadier General William Hoge. He commanded the Engineer Special Brigade at Normandy, and when posted to the 9th Armored Division the commander complained, arguing that he should have been given a divisional command. (NARA)

side, which included the remnants of Colonel Riggs' original engineer defense force, were hardest hit in five attacks that afternoon. More attacks followed with three more in the late afternoon and early evening, first along the Schönberg road, then down the Malmédy road, and finally up the Prum road. The defensive line of the CCB/7th Armored Division was penetrated in at least three places by evening, with few replacements available. By 2200hrs General Clarke realized that the current positions were not tenable and decided to pull his forces out of the town, to the high ground southwest of the town. The town was occupied by the 18th Volksgrenadier Division the night of December 21/22. Clarke estimated that he had lost almost half his strength in the day's fighting.

The American resistance in the St. Vith salient was substantially delaying the German advance westward since it prevented the 6th Panzer Army from supporting the rapid advance of the 5th Panzer Army further south. Model

M4 medium tanks of the 40th Tank Battalion, 7th Armored Division, in the fields outside St. Vith after the town was recaptured in January 1945. (NARA)

An 81mm mortar team from the 7th Armored Division performs fire missions from a trench on the outskirts of St. Vith in late January 1945 after the town was retaken. (NARA)

ordered the pocket crushed and directed Dietrich to commit elements of the 2nd SS-Panzer Corps to assist in the task. The early morning fighting of December 22 took place in the midst of a heavy snowfall, and began at 0200hrs with a major attack of the Führer Begleit Brigade against Rodt, to the west of St. Vith. This saw the heaviest use of Panzers in this sector to date, amounting to three companies with about 25 tanks. The Führer Begleit Brigade had great difficulty operating tanks due to the extremely muddy conditions in the area, and several Panzers became stuck in the mud before reaching the town. The fighting in Rodt was savage, with M4 tanks blasting away at Panzergrenadiers ensconced in the town's stone houses, but by late morning the US defenders were forced to withdraw. The fighting lasted for nine hours and separated Clarke's CCB from the rest of the 7th Armored Division. The 62nd Volksgrenadier Division also succeeded in pushing back the CCB/9th Armored Division, further compressing the St. Vith pocket.

On December 20, command of the northern sector of the Ardennes front was turned over to Bernard Montgomery. Reporting to him was Major General Matthew Ridgway of the XVIII Airborne Corps who took over the St. Vith sector from Middleton. Ridgway wanted the 7th Armored Division and other units around St. Vith to stay in place in "fortified goose eggs" behind German lines, a plan Monty vetoed after Clarke dubbed it "Custer's last stand." (NARA)

There had been a reorganization of the command structure in the sector that day, with the 7th Armored Division now falling under the XVIII Airborne Command, and the northern elements of the First US Army coming under the overall command of the British 21st Army Group and Field Marshal Bernard Montgomery. During the fighting Clarke was visited by his divisional commander, Major General Robert Hasbrouck, who had brought along the new plan for the sector from General Matthew Ridgway of the XVIII Airborne Corps. Ridgway proposed that 7th Armored Division remain in place, even though surrounded, in several "fortified goose-eggs" that would be supplied by air. Clarke remarked that it looked more like "Custer's last stand" and both officers were disturbed by the concept, which they thought reflected Ridgway's paratrooper mentality, inexperience with armored units, and lack of understanding of the precarious state of the units in the salient. Ridgway wanted Clarke to hold on to St. Vith and planned to eventually push forward with the 82nd Airborne Division. The British liaison officer at Hasbrouck's command post caught wind of the argument and informed Montgomery. Montgomery visited the 7th Armored Division to gain his own impressions, and later left for Ridgway's headquarters. After a heated discussion with Hodges at First US Army headquarters, Montgomery sent a message to the 7th Armored Division commander, Robert Hasbrouck, "You have accomplished your mission – a mission well-done – It is time to withdraw," having rejected Ridgway's unrealistic plan. The 82nd Airborne pushed forward to Vielsalm to create an escape corridor for the forces inside the St. Vith salient.

By the evening of December 22, CCB/7th Armored Division had been pushed back about half a mile (1km) along a ridge line stretching from the village of Hinderhausen to Neubruck, with CCB/9th Armored Division being pushed in behind it from the south. By this stage, the 82nd Airborne Division held the west bank of the Salm River near Vielsalm, but intense pressure from the 6th Panzer Army was making this defense increasingly difficult. The plan was to withdraw the CCB/9th Armored Division first but this proved impossible due to the intensity of the contact with the 62nd Volksgrenadier Division and the muddy condition of the roads. Hoge was seriously concerned that they would have to abandon all their vehicles and retreat on foot as the mud was so deep. Hasbrouck radioed Clarke and Hoge that "if you don't join them [the 82nd Airborne] soon, the opportunity will be gone." The withdrawal time was reset for 0600hrs on the morning of December 23. That evening Clarke instructed rear area troops to chop branches from pine trees along the escape route to provide some firm footing along the muddy road. Much to his relief, the temperature dropped abruptly on the night of December 22/23, freezing the ground rock hard along the one road out of the salient. The withdrawal was successfully executed, with German forces close on the heels of the retreating US forces. During the morning fighting, two Führer Begleit Brigade Panzers were knocked out, and a few of the US tanks were lost as well. The cost of the defense of St. Vith was 3,400 casualties, 59 M4 tanks, 29 M5A1 light tanks, and 25 armored cars.

An officer from the 87th Reconnaissance Squadron, 7th Armored Division, looks over the ruins of St. Vith on January 24, 1945 after the town was retaken. (NARA)

THE STRUGGLE FOR THE TAILLES PLATEAU

When the "Russian High" arrived on the night of December 22/23, the rain-soaked, muddy fields began to harden. This improved the prospects for German mobile operations since the Panzer columns were no longer trapped on the roads, and no longer obliged to fight for every village and road junction. While the cold weather restored some fluidity to the battle, it also led to clearer conditions that permitted Allied fighter-bombers to return to the fray, with frightful consequences for exposed German supply columns in the Eifel. The change in the weather had an immediate and dramatic impact on the fighting in the central sector of the Ardennes front, the battle for road junctions along the eastern edge of the Tailles plateau stretching towards Marche. This road net roughly paralleled the front line running from Trois Ponts in the north, west through Bra, Manhay, Grandmenil, Erezée, Hotton, and finally to

Marche. These road junctions were a German tactical objective since they controlled access to routes leading north and west towards the Meuse.

Krüger's 58th Panzer Corps had made the initial breakthrough in this sector, with the 116th Panzer Division pushing past Houfallize on December 19 and reaching Hotton on December 21 with the 560th Volksgrenadier Division to its right. Hotton was weakly defended by headquarters elements of the 3rd Armored Division, but the advance guard of the 116th Panzer Division was not strong enough to capture the town. Likewise, task forces of the 3rd Armored Division at Soy and Amonines stopped the 560th Volksgrenadier Division. Since December 20, Model had hoped to commit the 2nd SS-Panzer Corps into this sector to reinforce this breakthrough, but lack of fuel and the continued hold-out of US forces in the St. Vith salient blocked access from the northern sector of the Ardennes into the central area between the Salm and Meuse rivers. From the Allied perspective, the salient had been held far longer than expected, and, with the defenses on the verge of collapse, Montgomery authorized a withdrawal.

When the ground froze on the night of December 22/23, the trapped CCB, 7th Armored Division, and the other units in the St. Vith salient could finally pull back over the Salm. With the obstruction posed by the St. Vith

Although the 116th Panzer Division managed to break into Hotton, they were pushed out by headquarters elements of the 3rd Armored Division. This is a PzKpfw IV tank of 2/16th Panzer Regiment knocked out during the fighting on the afternoon of December 21. (NARA)

Two tanks helped buttress the US defense of Hotton on December 21 and this M4 of Co. G, 33rd Armored Regiment, was knocked out in the fighting. (NARA)

salient removed, Obergruppenführer Bittrich's 2nd SS-Panzer Corps began to flood into the vacuum created by the US withdrawal into the area from the Salm to the Ourthe River. The objective of the 2nd SS-Panzer Corps was to further rupture the US defensive lines in the La Gleize–Bra–Erezée–Marche area with a secondary, if somewhat hopeless, mission of relieving Kampfgruppe Peiper trapped in La Gleize. With the prospects for the 1st SS-Panzer Corps growing increasingly poor, it was becoming clear to Berlin that the failure of Dietrich's 6th Panzer Army was having a ripple effect by exposing the advances of Manteuffel's 5th Panzer Army, since their lines of communication were now vulnerable to US reinforcements pouring in from the north. Model and Rundstedt wanted the 2nd SS-Panzer Corps to gain control of the road net on the Tailles plateau to weaken US armored attacks against the 5th Panzer Army from the north.

The 2nd SS-Panzer Division "Das Reich" began moving over the Salm River on December 23 heading for the Baraque de Fraiture crossroads, while the neighboring 9th SS-Panzer Division "Hohenstaufen" moved to its right, against the withdrawing St. Vith garrison and the 82nd Airborne Division. The roadblock at Baraque de Fraiture was held by a small detachment from the 589th Field Artillery led by Major Arthur Parker, and reinforced by some tanks from Task Force Kane of CCB, 3rd Armored Division. The crossroads was at a key junction between the 3rd Armored Division and 82nd Airborne Division, but was weakly held due to a lack of resources. On the afternoon of December 23, "Parker's Crossroads" was pummeled by German artillery for 20 minutes and then assaulted by a Panzergrenadier regiment supported by two tank companies. As this position was overwhelmed after nightfall, it opened the door to Manhay, which controlled access to the road leading to Liège.

A tank patrol of the 3rd Armored Division scans for signs of the 116th Panzer Division near Houfallize on December 23. The tank to the left is an M4A1 (76mm) while the one to the right is an M4A3E2 assault tank. (NARA)

An armored dough of the 3rd Armored Division mans a roadblock with a bazooka near Manhay on December 23, hours before the 2nd SS-Panzer Division attack. (NARA)

The 560th Volksgrenadier Division, the easternmost element of the 5th Panzer Army, began the push against Manhay from the western side, attempting to seize villages on the approaches to the town. The 1160th Grenadier Regiment attempted a two-pronged attack on Freyneux, held by Task Force Kane. Although supported by assault guns, the attacks were beaten back by tank fire and the regiment suffered such heavy casualties that it was no longer effective. Further west, the 1129th Grenadier Regiment advanced towards Soy and Hotton, but the attack was held up by other elements of the 3rd Armored Division.

The American defenses around Manhay were in a confused state, with elements of the XVIII Airborne Corps, including the 7th Armored Division withdrawing from the St. Vith salient, intermingled with newly arrived and scattered task forces of the 3rd Armored Division under Collins' VII Corps. Field Marshal Montgomery was very unhappy about the weak and exposed defensive positions of the 82nd Airborne Division and on the morning of December 24 he instructed Ridgway's XVIII Airborne Corps to pull back the scattered paratrooper detachments to a more defensible perimeter along the road from Trois Ponts to Manhay that night. Likewise, the 3rd Armored Division reorganized its defenses, reassigning elements of the 7th Armored

A patrol by the 23rd Engineer Battalion on January 7 near the scene of the earlier fighting for "Parker's Crossroads" at Baraque de Fraiture. (Military History Institute)

Division to the defense of Manhay. Amidst this confusion, the 2nd SS-Panzer Division began its attack up the Manhay road.

SS-Oberführer Heinz Lammerding of "Das Reich" delayed the attack towards Manhay until a key bridge at Odeigne could be completed. With the new bridge in place, he waited until nightfall to begin the attack to avoid being pummeled by American Jabos. Christmas Eve in this sector was a clear, moonlit night with the ground frozen hard and covered by a thin layer of snow, in other words excellent for tank movement and well suited to night operations. The 3rd SS-Panzergrenadier Regiment "Deutschland" began moving up the road from Odeigne around 2100hrs towards a roadblock defended by CCA, 7th Armored Division, which was in the process of pulling back as part of the reorganization. One of the German columns was led by a captured Sherman tank, and in the dark, the American tanks thought the column was simply an American unit withdrawing as part of the shuffle. The Germans began firing flares, and quickly decimated the surprised American tanks at close range, overrunning the roadblock in the process. There was poor coordination between the 3rd Armored Division and CCA, 7th Armored Division, about the withdrawal around Manhay, and in the pre-dawn hours the 3rd SS-Panzergrenadier Regiment was able to exploit the confusion and push into Manhay itself.

A Panther Ausf. G of the 2nd SS-Panzer Division knocked out in a fork in the road between Manhay and Grandmenil during the fighting on December 23, 1944 with the 3rd Armored Division. (NARA)

Task Force Brewster, the most exposed of the US outposts, began to withdraw, not realizing that the area between them and the rest of the 3rd Armored Division had been flooded by advancing German troops. When the two lead tanks were knocked out and blocked the retreat route, Brewster ordered his troops to abandon their vehicles and infiltrate back to US lines as best they could. Task Force Kane pulled back more successfully, but was forced to give up Grandmenil due to the shortage of infantry. Fortunately, infantry reinforcements from 289th Infantry, 75th Division, arrived shortly afterwards and blocked the roads leading out of Grandmenil. When 2nd SS-Panzer Division "Das Reich" attempted to push out the west side of town, again using a captured Sherman tank in the lead, it was halted when a lone bazookaman knocked out the lead tank. The road was constricted on either side by steep slopes, so "Das Reich's" column was effectively stopped for the moment.

Although the "Das Reich" assault had managed to thoroughly disrupt the planned American reorganization around Manhay, it fell far short of its objectives of gaining the road exits out of Manhay and neighboring Grandmenil northward, which were still firmly in American hands. On Christmas Day, Obergruppenführer Bittrich received new orders. Instead of pushing up the road to Liège, he was to turn his corps westward, down along the road towards Erezée and Hotton, to strike the flank of Collins' VII Corps, which at the time was closing in on the spearhead of Manteuffel's 5th Panzer Army near the Meuse River. "Das Reich" spent most of Christmas Day attempting to gain room to maneuver in the Manhay–Grandmenil area prior to its new drive west, while the US forces attempted to re-establish a cohesive defense and push "Das Reich" out of Manhay and Grandmenil. An attempt to retake Grandmenil on Christmas afternoon by the 289th Infantry backed by tanks from Task Force McGeorge faltered when US aircraft accidentally bombed the US tanks. An attack into Manhay by CCA, 7th Armored Division, was stopped in the late afternoon after the lead tanks encountered road obstructions and were knocked out by German antitank guns. "Das Reich" had no more success in its efforts, as the hills overlooking the towns were peppered with US artillery observers who called in repeated howitzer strikes every time the Panzers attempted to move. When the artillery let up, the towns were hit by repeated US airstrikes, and Manhay and Grandmenil were turning into a killing ground. Plans to move the other main element of the corps, the 9th SS-Panzer Division "Hohenstaufen," to

An armored dough of the 36th Armored Infantry, 3rd Armored Division, mans an M1919A4 .30cal Browning light machine gun near Amonines while behind him is one of the division's M4 medium tanks. (NARA)

The fields around Amonines are littered with the wrecks of SdKfz 250 half-tracks of the 116th Panzer Division, destroyed during an encounter with Task Force Orr of the 3rd Armored Division. The vehicle to the left is an unusual variant with a 2cm cannon. (NARA)

the Manhay area to reinforce the planned drive on Erezée also failed. The fighting for the crossroads was turning into a bloody stalemate, but one that favored the Americans since they could move in more reinforcements. By Christmas, the US Army had 17 field artillery battalions in the area from the Aisne to the Lienne rivers, and much of this was within range of the stalled "Das Reich."

To the west, the battered 560th Volksgrenadier Division continued its attempts to win control of the road west of Erezée around Soy and Hotton from overextended elements of the 3rd Armored Division. Task Force Orr reported that on Christmas Eve, the German infantry had made 12 separate attacks to break through their defenses and that "if they'd have had three more riflemen, they'd probably have overrun our positions." The American defenses along the key road gradually began to solidify as the green 75th Division came into the line. Although the inexperienced troops took heavy casualties during their hasty introduction into combat, the added rifle strength considerably bolstered the American lines.

By December 26, "Das Reich" could not wait any longer for the arrival of the 9th SS-Panzer Division, and early that morning deployed the 4th SS-Panzergrenadier Regiment "Der Führer" against the 325th Glider Infantry Regiment to the east at Tri-le-Cheslaing. This attack was stopped cold. The main attack was a two-pronged effort emanating out of Grandmenil, one group straight down the main road towards Erezée and the other up a narrow path towards Mormont intended to outflank the American defenses if the first attack did not succeed. The German attack out of Grandmenil coincided with an effort by Task Force McGeorge to retake the town, and a head-on tank duel ensued. The M4 tanks of Task Force McGeorge stood little chance in a direct confrontation with the "Das Reich" Panthers, and all but two M4 tanks were lost in the brief encounter. However, the tank duel derailed the main German attack. The northern probe towards Mormont was stopped when a German tank was knocked out in a narrow gorge, blocking any further advance. Grandmenil was subjected to a barrage by three artillery battalions, and then assaulted again by 16 M4 tanks of Task Force McGeorge and 3/289th Infantry. The US

The crew of a dug-in M4 (105mm) assault gun of the 7th Armored Division maintain a roadblock position near Manhay during the fighting with 2nd SS-Panzer Division on December 27. (NARA)

infantry captured about half of Grandmenil and the access to the road to Manhay. The 7th Armored Division made a half-hearted attempt to reach the Grandmenil–Manhay road at the same time, but the badly battered unit could not put enough strength into the field, and the attack was halted by German tank fire. After Manhay was softened up with fighter-bomber strikes, the village was attacked by 3/517th Parachute Infantry Regiment in the evening, and by dawn the paratroopers had pushed "Das Reich" out. By this stage, Bittrich realized that any effort to force open the road through Grandmenil was futile, and on the morning of December 27 "Das Reich" was withdrawn. Furthermore, the operational objective of the attack, to relieve pressure on the 5th Panzer Army spearhead near the Meuse, had

A GI from the 3/289th Infantry, 75th Division, examines a Panther Ausf. G of the 2nd SS-Panzer Division in the ruins of Manhay on December 30. (NARA)

become pointless after the 2nd Panzer Division had been trapped and crushed in the days after Christmas by the US 2nd Armored Division. Further attacks were attempted, including an assault on Sadzot on December 28, but the 2nd SS-Panzer Corps had reached its high-water mark days before, and in early January Berlin began stripping SS-Panzer units out of the Ardennes to reinforce the threatened Russian front.

A GI of the 325th Glider Infantry armed with an M3 "grease gun" .45cal sub-machine gun takes cover near a German supply trailer during the fighting on January 3, 1945. (NARA)

BASTOGNE AND THE SOUTHERN SECTOR

Manteuffel's 5th Panzer Army contained three corps from north to south: the 66th Army Corps, and the 58th and 47th Panzer corps. As mentioned in the previous chapter, Lucht's 66th Army Corps managed to penetrate the American front line by encircling the hapless 106th Division. However, the center of gravity of Manteuffel's forces was his two Panzer corps, which were aimed at the Meuse River via the critical road junction of Bastogne. Standing in their way was the badly depleted 28th Division, covering the approaches to Bastogne and Houfallize.

5TH PANZER ARMY VERSUS 28TH DIVISION

The German attack began in the dark, at 0530hrs on Saturday, December 16, 1944, with a brief 20-minute barrage, 40 rounds per tube, intending to disrupt communication and transport. The barrage succeeded in downing many telephone lines, but could not interfere with radio communication. It was followed by a "fire waltz," a rolling barrage against deeper targets with 60 rounds per tube. The barrage was a mixed blessing for the advancing German infantry, as in many sectors it did not hit the forward US troop dispositions and merely alerted them to the start of the German attack.

In the pre-dawn hours, shock companies of the German infantry regiments had already begun moving over the front lines in the hopes of infiltrating past the forward American strongpoints before the initial artillery salvoes. These tactics had mixed results. The 116th Panzer Division pushed the shock companies of its two Panzergrenadier regiments forward. One was nearly

Opposite:
After the 14th Cavalry Group column was ambushed at the Poteau crossroads, a German camera team staged a number of scenes near the burning vehicles. These are some of the only surviving images of the Battle of the Bulge from the German perspective, as the film later fell into US hands. This shows an often photographed SS-Rottenfuhrer in a dramatic pose alongside a disabled M2A1 half-track. (Corbis)

wiped out by flanking fire from US infantry. The other managed to make its way past the command post of the 1/112th Infantry by dawn, but once the sun rose found itself out in the open, and most of its troops were captured. The initial advance of the 60th Panzer Regiment went little better, even after some flamethrower tanks were used to soften up the US infantry machine-gun nests. The 116th Panzer Division's only real success on the first day occurred at the boundary between the 112th and 110th Infantry when the 112th Panzergrenadier Regiment managed to seize a bridge over the Our River near Heinerscheid. Attempts to seize bridges near Ouren were repeatedly rebuffed by stiff US resistance. The 116th Panzer Division responded the next morning by dispatching 13 Panther tanks to reinforce the Panzergrenadiers. The Panthers advanced right up to the dug-in infantry foxholes, firing point blank. After a frantic radio call, a platoon of M18 76mm gun-motor carriages of the 811th Tank Destroyer Battalion arrived, and managed to knock out four Panzers at a cost of three of their four vehicles. Artillery support from the 229th Field Artillery Battalion proved instrumental in weakening the German attack. One of its forward batteries was brought under direct tank attack, but the accompanying Panzergrenadiers were cut down by a company of M16 antiaircraft half-tracks, each mounting quadruple .50cal machine guns. By the afternoon of December 17, the 116th Panzer Division had committed most of its armor to the fight for Ouren, gradually pushing back the US infantry.

A 105mm howitzer of Battery B, 229th Field Artillery Battalion of the 28th Division, near Welchenheusen shortly before the start of the Ardennes offensive. (NARA)

By late afternoon, the 112th Infantry was given permission to withdraw to the ridge line behind Ouren after dark. The 1/112th Infantry, which had been surrounded for most of the day, managed to make its way out by a ruse. On approaching a bridge manned by a few German infantry, the battalion officers lined up the troops in "German formation" and, shouting orders in German, marched them across the bridge. The vigorous defense of Ouren forced the 116th Panzer Division to turn its attention south. The 112th Infantry was gradually forced northward, eventually merging its efforts with the defenders of St. Vith. In conjunction with the 560th Volksgrenadier Division, the bridgehead at Heinerscheid was reinforced and expanded through December 17/18, exploiting the gap between the 112th and 110th Infantry.

5TH PANZER ARMY VS. 28TH DIVISION

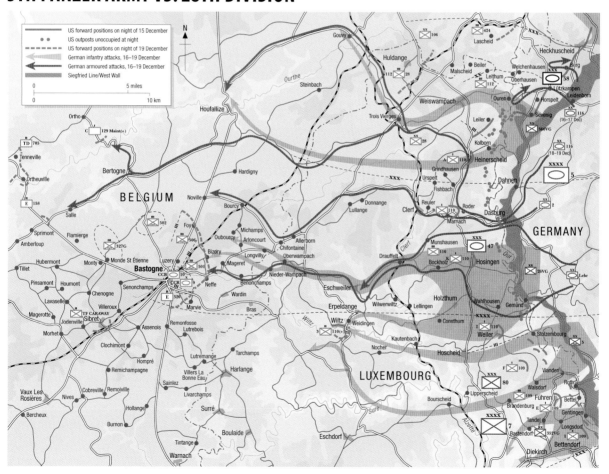

The hardest hit of the 28th Division's regiments was Colonel Hurley Fuller's 110th Infantry. At a reduced strength of only two battalions, the 110th Infantry was hit by elements of three Panzer divisions and two infantry divisions, roughly 2,000 Americans against 31,000 German troops. The 110th Infantry attempted to hold a string of small villages against the onslaught of the 2nd Panzer Division and Oberst Heinz Kokott's 26th Volksgrenadier Division on December 16. Kokott wanted to start the offensive with his forces over the Our River, so he moved two entire regiments over the river prior to the start of the attack. The defenses of the 110th Infantry were so thinly held that this premature deployment was hardly noticed. The west bank of the Our River was soon swarming with Kokott's infantry and Panzergrenadiers from the 2nd Panzer Division. The 110th Infantry clung tenaciously to their village defenses, forcing the Germans to use battalions against single companies, and in some cases, battalions against platoons. The use of Panzers in this sector was delayed by the need to erect a heavy bridge near Dasburg. By late afternoon, the situation in this sector had become so precarious that Cota committed his reserve, the 707th Tank Battalion, in an effort to clear away German infantry who had infiltrated up to the Skyline Drive. The tanks were instrumental in bolstering the infantry defenses and assisting in local counterattacks. By the end of the first day, the situation facing the two forward deployed battalions of the 110th Infantry was grim. They were running low on ammunition, and, as darkness fell, the German infantry was flowing past them in increasing numbers. Several companies called in artillery on their own positions as they were overrun in the darkness. Two heavy bridges at Dasburg were finished at twilight, and Panzers began moving forward after dark. Although the 48th Panzer Corps had failed to reach its first day objective of the Clerf River, American resistance was obviously weakening as the 110th Infantry was being overwhelmed by forces many times their size. General Cota radioed to the 110th Infantry that they were to hold "at all costs," knowing full well that the regiment guarded the only hard-surface road to Bastogne, the route through Clerf (Clervaux). Cota still had a very modest reserve on hand, 110th Infantry's 2nd Battalion and the light tank company of the 707th Tank Battalion. Before midnight, he ordered the battalion forward to reinforce the Marnach sector in the hope of keeping the key road through Clerf blocked to the Panzers.

By dawn on December 17, German forces were nearing Fuller's headquarters in Clerf. The attempted counterattack by the 2/110th Infantry on the morning of December 17 had hardly set off when it was brought under heavy fire by German infantry supported by Panzers and assault guns. By this stage, the regiment's artillery battalion was down to a single battery, and this unit was driven from its position that morning, losing half its howitzers in the process. The attack by D/707th Tank Battalion went awry when eight of its M5A1 light tanks were picked off by German antitank guns, and three more succumbed to antitank rockets. A company of infantry made its way into Marnach, only to find that the town had already been abandoned.

With defense of Marnach now impossible, the 110th Regiment attempted to halt the German advance at Clerf. The town was located in a narrow valley with access roads entering down a wooded, winding road. A spearhead from the 2nd Panzer Division, consisting of about a dozen PzKpfw IV tanks followed by 30 SdKfz 251 half-tracks full of Panzergrenadiers, approached the town around 0930hrs. A platoon of M4 tanks from A/707th

The town of Clerf remains littered with destroyed vehicles in the aftermath of the fighting. To the left is an M4 of the 707th Tank Battalion which was supporting the 110th Infantry, and to the right is a knocked-out German StuG III assault gun. (NARA)

Tank Battalion clanked out of town to meet them, and in the ensuing skirmish the Germans lost four tanks and the American platoon lost three. Diverted from the main road, the German column attempted to enter the town via an alternate road, but this approach was blocked when the lead Panzer was hit. In the meantime, further US reinforcements had arrived in the shape of B/2nd Tank Battalion from 9th Armored Division's CCR. This was not enough to stem the advance, and by nightfall Clerf was swarming with German tanks and Panzergrenadiers. Around 1825hrs, Fuller was forced to abandon his headquarters when a German tank stuck its barrel through a window into the command post. Fuller and his headquarters attempted to join up with Company G but were captured. Most of the remnants of the 110th in Clerf withdrew in the darkness, but some US infantry continued to hold out in the stone chateau in the town, sniping at German columns through December 18 as the Panzer columns raced on towards Bastogne.

The 3/110th Infantry had been gradually pushed back out of the border villages by the advance of the 26th Volksgrenadier Division, with the last remnants of the battalion finally congregating in the village of Consthum on December 18. An afternoon attack, supported by assault guns, penetrated into the town, but fog permitted the American survivors to withdraw out of town, with some 40mm Bofors guns providing a rearguard. The following day, the remnants of the battalion were ordered to withdraw to the divisional headquarters at Wiltz. By the second day of combat, the 110th Infantry had been overwhelmed in their unequal struggle. But their two-day battle had cost the Germans precious time. Middleton later wrote to Fuller, after he was released from a PoW camp, that "had not your boys done the job they did, the 101st Airborne could not have reached Bastogne in time."

The 28th Division's third regiment, the 109th Infantry, was in the attack sector of the German 7th Army. The 5th Fallschirmjäger Division assaulted its northernmost companies on December 17. The inexperienced Luftwaffe troops did not advance as quickly as their neighbors from 5th Panzer Army to the north, but by December 18 were on their way through the American defenses and approaching the divisional headquarters at Wiltz. By this time, the lead elements of the Panzer Lehr Division had gained access to the roads, and headed towards Wiltz along the northern route. On the morning of

A pair of survivors of the 110th Infantry, 28th Division, on December 19 after the regiment had been shattered by the German assault. (NARA)

December 19, General Cota transferred the headquarters of the 28th Division from Wiltz to Sibret, leaving behind a provisional battalion formed from the headquarters staff and divisional support personnel, and later reinforced by the 200 survivors of 3/110th Infantry. The commander of the 5th Fallschirmjäger Division, Oberst Heilmann, had planned to bypass Wiltz, but had lost control of his units in the field. In the event, an uncoordinated attack began against Wiltz as the town was near the boundary between the 5th Panzer Army and 7th Army. Units from the 26th Volksgrenadier Division began an attack from the north on the afternoon of December 19, while the 15th Fallschirmjäger Regiment from 5th Fallschirmjäger Division began attacking the town from the south, even though Heilmann had ordered it to attack Sibret. By nightfall, the US defenses had been compressed into the center of the town. The American commander, Colonel Daniel Strickler, decided to retreat, but the withdrawal was confused. The provisional battalion ran a gauntlet of German formations on the way to Bastogne, losing many troops in the process. But some troops did manage to reach Bastogne. The 687th Field Artillery Battalion was surrounded to the south of town, and had to fight off numerous German attacks before a small portion of the unit could withdraw. The 44th Combat Engineers served as the rearguard in Wiltz itself and was decimated in the process.

By December 20, the 5th Panzer Army had finally overcome the principal centers of resistance held by the 28th Division, and the roads towards Houfallize and Bastogne were open. But the determined defense by the badly outnumbered 28th Division had cost precious time, and by the time that Wiltz was finally taken, Bastogne had been reinforced. It is worth comparing the performance of the veteran 28th Division against that of the inexperienced regiments of the neighboring 106th Division. While the 106th Division was quickly surrounded and forced to surrender, the battered but experienced regiments of the 28th Division were able to hold off much larger German forces for two days before finally being overwhelmed.

A patrol of the 28th Division links up with the last GIs to have escaped from Wiltz on December 20 after the town was taken by a combined assault of units of the 5th Panzer Army and 7th Army. (NARA)

7TH ARMY ATTACKS ON THE SOUTHERN FRINGE

The third of the attacking German armies was Brandenberger's 7th Army, located on the far left, southern flank of the assault in the Luxembourg area. This army had the least ambitious objectives of the three attacking armies, but also had the most modest resources with which to achieve them, and some of the most difficult terrain. The initial artillery barrage that started the offensive was not particularly effective as the 7th Army had poor intelligence on US dispositions. The shock companies leading the attack were generally successful in infiltrating past the forward US outposts due to the huge gaps in the US lines. In Vianden, the 2/109th Infantry outposts in the ruins of the chateau were overrun, but many other outposts were simply bypassed in the early morning fog. Other German assault companies managed to get across the Our River without opposition in rubber boats. The mountainous terrain and the porous defenses permitted the initial German assault battalions to slip through the positions of the 109th Infantry for most of the morning with only sporadic contact with US platoons in the villages. The 915th Grenadier Regiment of the 352nd Volksgrenadier Division was able to move most of its forces between the 2nd and 3rd battalions, 109th Infantry, via the deep ravines in the 2,000-yard (1,829m) gap between the two battalions. By noon, the 352nd Volksgrenadier Division had scouts well behind the forward US positions, with assault companies not far behind. In contrast, the 916th Grenadier Regiment had few terrain advantages, and was quickly pinned down along the Our River by two US artillery battalions that had observers with the 3/109th Infantry on the heights above. By nightfall, the 109th Infantry commander, Colonel James Rudder, thought his situation was reasonably secure except for an encircled company at Führen, not realizing that his positions had been thoroughly penetrated. Around 0240hrs on December 17, Rudder was ordered by General Cota to use his reserve to stop an unexpected German penetration. The 14th Fallschirmjäger Regiment had managed to move some StuG III assault guns and other vehicles across a weir near Vianden, and was motoring down Skyline Drive deep behind American lines from Hosheid towards Ettelbruck. The US garrison in Hosheid was finally forced to withdraw, but its defense held up the paratrooper regiment.

A platoon of Co. B, 630th Tank Destroyer Battalion, in newly dug foxholes outside Wiltz on the road to Bastogne on December 20. By this stage, the company had lost all of its 3in towed antitank guns and was assigned by Middleton to defend the approaches to Bastogne. (NARA)

On December 17, the two German divisions on the right wing of the 7th Army attack continued to move units over the Our River, but their advance was frequently frustrated by small US garrisons, and by accurate artillery fire delivered against their columns from forward observers on the hills above. US attempts to relieve the surrounded company in Führen were frustrated. By late in the day, the vital artillery positions were coming under direct attack as small groups of German troops infiltrated deep behind the forward US positions. Several artillery batteries had to deploy their personnel as riflemen to fight off German infantry. German prospects improved dramatically after nightfall on December 17 when a long-delayed bridge over the Our was finally completed, permitting the transit of the corps' only armor unit, the 11th Assault Gun Brigade, plus the vehicles and divisional artillery of the 5th Fallschirmjäger Division. The 352nd Volksgrenadier Division's bridge at Gentingen was slow in being completed, but by December 18 enough artillery and heavy arms had been moved over the Our for its attack against the 3/109th Infantry to intensify considerably. The renewed vigor of the reinforced German attacks on December 18 undermined the 109th Infantry defenses. In the early afternoon, Colonel Rudder received permission to withdraw the regiment back towards the high ground around Diekirch. The 352nd Volksgrenadier Division reached the 109th Infantry defenses around Diekirch on the afternoon of December 19. The 352nd Volksgrenadier Division had lost so many of its experienced officers and NCOs that in the afternoon the attack was led by the divisional commander, Oberst Erich Schmidt, who was wounded in the process. By the morning of December 20, the 109th Infantry withdrew to Ettelbruck, destroyed the bridges there, and established defensive positions in the hills west of the town.

Further to the south, the 7th Army attacks had not progressed as well. The 276th Volksgrenadier Division had crossed the Sauer River opposite the defenses of the 60th Armored Infantry Battalion (AIB) of CCA, 9th Armored Division. Although the division was able to gain a foothold all along the western bank of the river, the three regiments had been unable to overcome the US positions on the high ground. On December 17, the

The 5th Fallschirmjäger Division captured six M4 tanks intact in Wiltz, and put them back into service after painting them prominently with German crosses. This one is seen abandoned a few weeks later in the center of Esch-sur-Sûre. (NARA)

German infantry managed to infiltrate into the 60th Armored Infantry Battalion's positions via a deep, wooded gorge. However, the CCA managed to fend off many of the attacks by counterattacking with armored cars of the reconnaissance squadron. After dark, the 1/988th Grenadier Regiment managed to infiltrate behind the 60th Armored Infantry Battalion and capture the town of Beaufort in spite of a determined stand by a cavalry troop. General Brandenberger was extremely unhappy with the poor performance of the division, and he relieved the commander, even though many of its problems could be traced to the success of American artillery in preventing the construction of a bridge over the Sauer at Wallendorf.

The 60th Armored Infantry Battalion attempted to rout out the main German incursion by launching a counterattack with the remaining light armored vehicles of the reconnaissance squadron. But when the attack was launched at dawn on December 18, it stumbled into a battalion of the 986th Grenadier Regiment that had been reinforced with an antitank company with several dozen Panzerschreck and Panzerfaust antitank rockets intended for a planned attack towards Medernach. Seven M5A1 light tanks were quickly put out of action, and the cavalry force did not have enough riflemen to contest the German defenses. By the end of the day, the 276th Volksgrenadier Division had made so many penetrations past the forward defenses of CCA, 9th Armored Division, that a new defensive line was established away from the Sauer River. However, the three line companies of the 60th Armored Infantry Battalion were cut off, and it took three days to extricate the survivors. German attacks slackened on December 19 as the new 276th Volksgrenadier Division commander, Oberst Dempwolff, attempted to reorganize his demoralized troops, and put off any further attacks until the delayed assault guns finally arrived. When three or four Jagdpanzer 38s finally appeared in the afternoon of December 20, the 988th Grenadier Regiment at Haller launched an attack against a forward US outpost near Waldbillig. The attack failed, but after dark the 987th Grenadier Regiment advanced through a gorge on the other side of Waldbillig, forcing the US tank destroyer and cavalry detachments to retreat. Although not apparent at the time, this represented the high-water mark for the division.

The attacks further south by the 212th Volksgrenadier Division against the 12th Infantry, 4th Division, were even less successful. German intelligence in this sector was better and most of the 12th Infantry positions had been accurately spotted. The terrain in this sector was very rugged, the area being known as "Little Switzerland." Two regiments led the German attack over the Sauer River using rubber boats. The main opposition to the crossing proved to be the river itself. Attempts to land the 320th Grenadier Regiment near the main objective of Echternach failed due to the swift current, and the regiment had to be landed 3 miles (5km) downstream, delaying the attack. Although radio warnings went out to the widely dispersed 12th Infantry outposts in the early morning, many US units did not receive them, and were unaware of the German attack until German patrols appeared mid-morning. US artillery was less effective in this sector than further north, even though an artillery observation plane reported that the "area was as full of targets as a pinball machine." Most of the forward US outposts pulled back to the company positions in the forward villages along the frontier, but by late in the day some of these had been isolated by German infiltration. The 12th Infantry headquarters responded by sending small task groups down the road consisting of a few tanks from the badly under-strength 70th Tank Battalion carrying a small number of infantry reinforcements.

By December 17, the 212th Volksgrenadier Division had managed to reinforce its forward regiments even though its new supply bridge had been knocked down before being completed. While the Germans had significantly more infantry than the 12th Infantry in this sector, the Americans held an advantage in tanks, which was further reinforced on December 17 with a company from the 19th Tank Battalion, 9th Armored Division. In addition, the US forces still had markedly better artillery support since the absence of a bridge had prevented the Germans from bringing any significant artillery across the Sauer. The 987th Grenadier Regiment made a deep penetration along the Schwarz Erntz Gorge, but was unable to fight its way out of the gorge after a pummeling by American artillery. Task Force Luckett was formed from some tanks and tank destroyers, and sent towards the gorge to prevent further penetration. The 320th Grenadier Regiment had more success by circling around Echternach, thereby penetrating between two rifle companies, but none of these was serious enough to threaten the US defense line.

BREAKTHROUGH TOWARDS BASTOGNE

By the morning of December 18, or X+2 according to the German schedule, the roads to Bastogne were open. The 5th Panzer Army had managed to blast a massive gap in the American lines by overwhelming the 110th Infantry Regiment and pushing back the other regiments of the 28th Division on either side. However, due to the stubborn defense of the 110th Infantry, Hitler's timetable was slipping behind schedule. The plans had called for 5th Panzer Army to take Bastogne on X+1 and reach the Meuse by X+3. The 7th Army's attacks had proceeded less well, particularly in the southernmost area. There were two principal road nets towards the Meuse available to Manteuffel's forces, so the 116th Panzer Division set out via Houfallize while the bulk of the 5th Panzer Army and some elements of the 7th Army headed towards Bastogne.

The delaying actions by the 28th Division gave Middleton some breathing space to prepare the defense of Bastogne. On the afternoon of December 16, Bradley began to commit his reserves to bolster the badly overextended Ardennes sector. The only reserves available to the 12th Army Group were the 82nd and 101st Airborne divisions that were refitting near Reims after two months of hard fighting in Holland. The 82nd was directed towards the northern sector around St. Vith, and the 101st to the southern sector around Bastogne. With no other reserves on hand, Bradley was forced to pilfer resources from the neighboring armies. Patton's Third Army had the 10th Armored Division in reserve for Operation *Tink* and Bradley ordered it be sent to Middleton. Patton complained, but when it became evident that the Ardennes attack was no mere spoiling attack, Patton told his staff to reinvigorate plans to reinforce the First Army in the Ardennes.

While waiting for these reinforcements to arrive, Middleton began to deploy the modest reserves he had on hand. Since Bastogne was the most vital initial objective in the corps' area, he was determined to hold it at all costs. Shortly before midnight on December 17, Middleton learned that Clerf had fallen, giving the 5th Panzer Army access to a good hard road into Bastogne. He planned to block the road using the CCR of the 9th Armored Division. This was reorganized into combined arms teams with mixed companies of infantry and tanks. The weaker of the two forces, Task Force

Rose, was assigned to block the road from Clerf, using a company of tanks and a company of infantry. Task Force Harper was placed behind them near Allerborn, and included fewer than two companies of tanks and an infantry company. The M7 self-propelled howitzers of the 73rd Armored Field Artillery Battalion (AFAB), near Buret, covered the two task forces. To defend Bastogne itself, Middleton ordered the three engineer battalions of the 1128th Engineer Group to draw weapons and revert to an infantry role, forming a semi-circular defense of Bastogne from Foy in the northeast to Marvie in the south.

The first contact between the advancing 5th Panzer Army and the Bastogne defenders occurred at 0830hrs, when reconnaissance elements of the 2nd Panzer Division encountered Task Force Rose at the Lullange roadblock. The remainder of the division was delayed due to continued sniper fire from Americans still holding out in Clerf. After inconclusive skirmishing early in the morning, the lead Kampfgruppe laid smoke in front of the American positions, and moved two companies of Panzers forward

When the VIII Corps headquarters was ordered to evacuate Bastogne, many corps support units withdrew. This is a column from the 54th Signal Battalion on the road between Bastogne and Marche on December 19, 1944. (Military History Institute)

under its cover. When the smoke lifted around 1100hrs, tank fighting ensued at ranges of around 800 yards (732m) with both sides losing three tanks. The Kampfgruppe deployed forces on all three sides of the roadblock and gradually whittled it away. Permission was requested to pull back Task Force Rose or reinforce it from Task Force Harper, but Middleton refused both requests. The situation deteriorated in the early afternoon when elements of the advancing 116th Panzer Division brushed up against the 73rd Armored Field Artillery Battalion in Buret, forcing them to redeploy. In the early evening, Task Force Rose was given permission to pull back a few miles to Wincrange, in part to deal with Panzers that had been leaking past the Lullange roadblock. By the time it had pulled back, it was completely surrounded by advancing elements of the 2nd Panzer Division and cut off from Task Force Harper.

The Task Force Harper roadblock at Allerborn was hit by artillery around 2000hrs followed closely by a Panzer attack. The 9th Armored Division accounts claim that the attack was so successful due to the German's use of infrared night-fighting equipment but there is no evidence that this was actually the case. By midnight, Task Force Harper had been shattered. The commander and assault gun platoon escaped northward towards Houfalize, and the other battalion vehicles southward towards Tintigny. This left only some token headquarters units, two self-propelled artillery battalions, and a platoon of light tanks along the road into Bastogne. With its forces destroyed or surrounded, the headquarters elements of the CCR, 9th Armored Division, began pulling back to Bastogne shortly after midnight.

Combat Command B, 10th Armored Division, drove from Arlon to Bastogne on December 18 and was instructed by Middleton to divide into three teams to cover Longvilly, Wardin, and Noville. Team Cherry arrived in Longvilly on the night of December 18, but was instructed to advance no further in spite of the predicament of Task Force Harper. The plans to use CCB, 10th Armored Division, to defend this corridor quickly went awry.

The unit assigned to take Bastogne was Generalleutnant Fritz Bayerlein's Panzer Lehr Division. On December 18, it was split into two Kampfgruppen based around its two Panzergrenadier regiments, Kampfgruppe Poschinger (902nd Panzergrenadier Regiment) on the road behind the southern wing of

2nd Panzer Division heading towards Oberwampach, and Kampfgruppe Hauser (901st Panzergrenadier Regiment), still engaged with the 3/110th Infantry at Consthum. With Panzer Lehr in action east of Bastogne, the 2nd Panzer Division Kampfgruppe that had attacked task forces Cherry and Harper veered off northward towards Noville in an effort to reach the Meuse

Spearhead to the Meuse

This illustration depicts Kampfgruppe Böhm's race to the Meuse in the days before Christmas 1944. This battlegroup was based around the 2nd Panzer Division's reconnaissance battalion, 2nd Panzer Aufklärungs Battalion, but its combat power was reinforced by a few Panther tanks from the division's Panzer regiment, 3rd Panzer Regiment. This was necessary as its reconnaissance battalion had been only partially refitted prior to the Ardennes operation. The armored patrol seen here is led by an SdKfz 234 Puma armored car. This was one of the most effective scout vehicles of World War II, armed with a 50mm gun. Following behind the Puma is a Panther Ausf. G tank. The 2nd Panzer Division started the offensive with 51 Panthers

and 29 PzKpfw IV tanks. Behind the Panther is the lead SdKfz 251 armored half-track. Although more commonly associated with the Panzergrenadier regiment, this jack-of-all-trades was also used by scout units and there were 13 of these on hand at the beginning of the offensive.

The vehicles seen here mostly lack any distinctive tactical unit insignia since the division was re-equipped so soon before the start of the offensive. The Panther and Puma lack the usual tactical numbers on the turret, and the division's distinctive trident emblem is nowhere to be seen. The use of foliage for camouflage was common in the Ardennes, especially after December 23 when the clear weather marked the return of the dreaded American Jabos (fighter-bombers). (Artwork by Peter Dennis)

River. Delayed by the muddy road conditions, Kampfgruppe Poschinger reached Oberwampach around 1830hrs on the evening of December 18, and penetrated into Mageret after midnight. But the Panzers were without infantry support since the Panzergrenadiers and their Steyr trucks were stuck in the muddy roads leading to the town. There, Bayerlein encountered a Belgian civilian who told him, erroneously, that at least 40 American tanks and many more vehicles, led by an American two-star general, had passed through Mageret that evening. At the time, Bayerlein had fewer than a dozen of his tanks with him, and was concerned that he had stumbled into a US armored division. He ordered a defensive deployment on the northeast side of Mageret and decided to wait until morning to launch his attack towards Bastogne.

The lead elements of the 101st Airborne Division arrived in Bastogne by truck on the night of December 18. The division was led by Brigadier General Anthony McAuliffe, the divisional artillery officer, as its commander, Maxwell Taylor, was back in the US. The division had little time to prepare for the move, and the troops left without adequate cold weather uniforms or ammunition. In view of the increasingly precarious situation around Bastogne, Bradley ordered Middleton to pull his corps headquarters out of the city on December 19 and leave command of Bastogne to McAuliffe. Julian Ewell's 501st Parachute Infantry Regiment (PIR) was the first into Bastogne, and deployed a combat team from its 3rd Battalion to try to determine the situation along the road to Mageret.

Increasingly skittish due to the sudden appearance of more and more new American units, Bayerlein ordered his advance guard, Kampfgruppe Fallois, to push through Neffe in the hope that a fast raid might gain a foothold in the outskirts of Bastogne. Neffe was held by the headquarters of Team Cherry and a few tanks. Although Kampfgruppe Fallois was able to push into Neffe by 0800hrs, it had not thoroughly cleared the town of American troops, and had overlooked American infantry in the stone chateau. On reaching the edge of the town and peering towards Bastogne they saw columns of American infantry advancing forward, a glimpse of Ewell's combat team. The paratroopers were supported by an air-portable 105mm light howitzer, the sound of which Bayerlein misinterpreted as tank fire. Instead of raiding into Bastogne, Bayerlein ordered his forces in this sector to prepare to repulse what he thought was a major American counterattack and not merely a local

Newly arrived paratroopers of Ewell's 501st Parachute Infantry Regiment, 101st Airborne Division, head out of Bastogne towards Mageret on the morning of December 19. It was the appearance of this column that dissuaded Bayerlein from launching a raid by Panzer Lehr Division into Bastogne that day. (NARA)

probe. The pugnacious sally by the paratroopers derailed Bayerlein's long delayed attack into Bastogne. Furthermore, Panzergrenadiers marching through Neffe were dispersed by sniper fire from US troops still in the castle, and even tank gun fire could not get them to budge.

Even though Team Cherry was surrounded in Longvilly, it posed a threat to the planned attack of the 26th Volksgrenadier Division towards Bizory, so Bayerlein decided to clean it out once and for all. In the meantime, the division's second Kampfgruppe had been freed of its assignment near Consthum, and lead elements including the divisional tank destroyer battalion, the 130th Panzerjäger Lehr Battalion, arrived that morning. The attack on Longvilly began hours late, in the early afternoon. As the tank destroyers crested the ridge of Hill 490, they encountered an enormous traffic jam of US vehicles consisting of advancing elements of CCB, 10th Armored Division, retreating elements of CCR, 9th Armored Division, and various and sundry other US units. Besides the Panzer Lehr Kampfgruppe, the 26th Volksgrenadier Division was also closing in on this area, and the 2nd Panzer Division had sent six 88mm tank destroyers to deal with 9th Armored Division self-propelled howitzers that had been shelling their

GERMAN FORCES

A Kampfgruppe Hauser, Panzer Lehr Division
B Kampfgruppe Poschinger, Panzer Lehr Division
C 26th Volksgrenadier Division (-)
D Tank destroyers from 2nd Panzer Division
E 2nd Panzer Division (-)
F Reconnaissance patrol, 116th Panzer Division
G Kampfgruppe Böhm, 2nd Panzer Division
H Grenadier Regiment 39, 26th Volksgrenadier Division
I Kampfgruppe Fallois, Panzer Lehr Division
   (21 December)
J Reconnaissance patrol, 26th Volksgrenadier Division
K Kampfgruppe Fallois, Panzer Lehr Division
   (19 December)

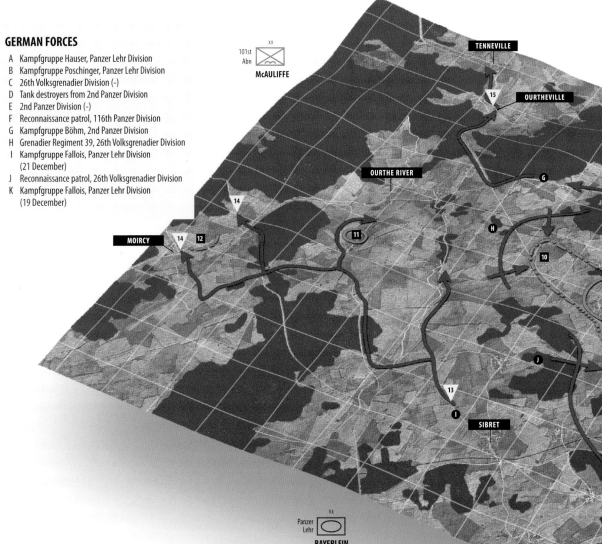

EVENTS

1.   December 18: General Middleton orders the corps engineer battalions to deploy as infantry in a belt along the southeastern side of Bastogne.

2.   December 18: CCB, 10th Armored Division arrives in Bastogne and divides into three teams to defend the eastern side of the town.

3.   Evening, December 18: 101st Airborne Division arrives in Bastogne and begins to deploy around the city.

4.   Night, December 18: Retreating elements of CCR, 9th Armored Division coalesce with Team Cherry outside Longvilly.

5.   1000hrs, December 19: Kampfgruppe Poschinger breaks into Mageret. Bayerlein declines to press into Bastogne until daybreak due to reports of US tank forces.

6.   0830hrs, December 19: Kampfgruppe Fallois pushes into Neffe, but spots an approaching patrol from the 3/501st Parachute Infantry Regiment.

7.   Early afternoon, December 19: A trapped column consisting of elements of the CCR, 9th Armored Division and Team Cherry, 10th Armored Division is attacked and destroyed by elements from three German divisions.

8.   Team O'Hara is attacked by Kampfgruppe Fallois, Panzer Lehr Division, which pushes them out of Wardin and back towards Marvie.

9.   December 19: The 26th Volksgrenadier Division attempts to break in to Bizory after dark, but the attack is stopped by paratroopers with heavy artillery support.

10. December 19: Kampfgruppe Poschinger attempts to take Neffe after dark but is stopped by the stubborn resistance of the paratroopers.

11. 0430hrs, December 20: 2nd Panzer Division, attempting to skirt around Bastogne on its way to the Meuse bridges, brushes up against Team Desobry in the dark. Intermittent fighting continues along the perimeter for the remainder of the day, intensifying with the arrival of the 1/506th PIR.

12. 0530hrs, December 20: Starting with a pre-dawn attack, 2nd Panzer Division pushes Team Desobry back from Noville and breaks into the paratrooper defenses in Foy.

13. December 21: As it becomes evident that the defense of Bastogne has hardened, Luttwitz gives Bayerlein permission to move the Panzer Lehr Division around the south side of Bastogne to continue its race for the Meuse bridges. With Kampfgruppe Fallois in the lead, this move will cut off Bastogne from the south and west.

14. December 21: Late in the day Kampfgruppe Fallois reaches the Ourthe River crossings.

15. December 20: Kampfgruppe Böhm, the reconnaissance element of the 2nd Panzer Division, seizes a bridge over the Ourthe River at Ourtheville. Kampfgruppe Cochenhausen follows, but the division is unable to quickly exploit the breakthrough due to a lack of fuel.

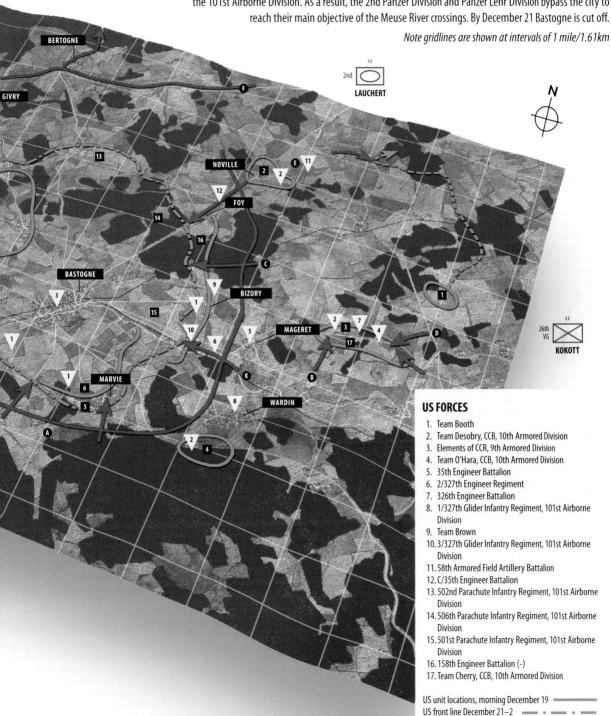

BASTOGNE ENCIRCLED

December 18–23, 1944, viewed from the southeast. Spearheads of the 5th Panzer Army reach the outskirts of Bastogne in the pre-dawn hours of December 19. They are thwarted in their attempts to capture the city on the run by the sacrifice of several armored task forces on the approach roads to the city, and by the timely arrival of the 101st Airborne Division. As a result, the 2nd Panzer Division and Panzer Lehr Division bypass the city to reach their main objective of the Meuse River crossings. By December 21 Bastogne is cut off.

Note gridlines are shown at intervals of 1 mile/1.61km

BERTOGNE

GIVRY

2nd
LAUCHERT

NOVILLE

FOY

BASTOGNE

BIZORY

MAGERET

MARVIE

WARDIN

26th
VG
KOKOTT

US FORCES

1. Team Booth
2. Team Desobry, CCB, 10th Armored Division
3. Elements of CCR, 9th Armored Division
4. Team O'Hara, CCB, 10th Armored Division
5. 35th Engineer Battalion
6. 2/327th Engineer Regiment
7. 326th Engineer Battalion
8. 1/327th Glider Infantry Regiment, 101st Airborne Division
9. Team Brown
10. 3/327th Glider Infantry Regiment, 101st Airborne Division
11. 58th Armored Field Artillery Battalion
12. C/35th Engineer Battalion
13. 502nd Parachute Infantry Regiment, 101st Airborne Division
14. 506th Parachute Infantry Regiment, 101st Airborne Division
15. 501st Parachute Infantry Regiment, 101st Airborne Division
16. 158th Engineer Battalion (-)
17. Team Cherry, CCB, 10th Armored Division

US unit locations, morning December 19 ——————
US front line December 21–2 — · — · — ·

When the advance guard of Panzer Lehr Division pushed into Neffe in the pre-dawn hours of December 19, the lead Panther tank of Feldwebel Dette struck a mine, blocking the road and ending the initial attack. This shows Dette's tank later in the month after it had been pushed off the road during subsequent attacks. (Military History Institute)

troops. Elements of these three German divisions began to descend on the trapped American column, systematically destroying it. Team Cherry tried to get off the road and defend the area, but lost all 14 of its medium and light tanks in the process. In all, about a hundred US vehicles were abandoned or destroyed, including 23 M5A1 and M4 tanks, 15 M7 105mm self-propelled howitzers, 14 armored cars, 30 jeeps, and 25 2½ ton trucks. The destruction of this trapped column distracted the lead elements of the Panzer Lehr Division from its main assignment of Bastogne.

The next element from the CCB, 10th Armored Division to encounter Panzer Lehr was Team O'Hara, located near Wardin, covering the southeastern approach to Bastogne. An attack by Kampfgruppe Fallois pushed them out of Wardin and back towards Marvie on the afternoon of December 19, but further German attacks were stymied.

On the afternoon of December 19, the corps commander, General Lüttwitz, visited Bayerlein to discuss the best approach to dealing with Bastogne. Lüttwitz was extremely agitated by the number of new US units showing up in Bastogne, and feared that if the corps did not race to the Meuse now and bypass Bastogne, then the Americans would soon receive more reinforcements. Bayerlein argued that Bastogne was indispensable to any future operations and that it would continue to pose a threat even if bypassed. Bayerlein ordered a night attack by Kampfgruppe Poschinger from Neffe starting at 1900hrs, which would coincide with a similar advance by the 26th Volksgrenadier Division towards Bizory. Neither attack proved fruitful and both encountered growing resistance. The outer defenses of Bastogne had been soft and relatively easy to penetrate; now they had hit a solid defense line.

While Panzer Lehr and the 26th Volksgrenadier Division were conducting their fruitless attacks on the southeastern edge of Bastogne, the 2nd Panzer Division had raced to the northeast outskirts with the intention of heading west. Around 0430hrs, reconnaissance units had discovered the outer perimeter of Team Desobry, the third of the CCB, 10th Armored Division, outposts. Lauchert radioed to Lüttwitz to get permission to bypass the roadblocks near Bourcy and Noville in order to head west to the Meuse River, and the corps commander agreed. The German armored columns advanced in the fog, one of the columns moving across a ridge southeast of Noville. The fog occasionally lifted, leading to sharp, close-range duels between the Panzers and the US tanks. Realizing he was seriously outgunned, Desobry asked for permission to withdraw. This was denied as the 101st Airborne needed time to get its rifle companies into the line. When

A view near Wardin along the main road into Bastogne from the south, with a knocked-out M4 medium tank of Task Force O'Hara, 10th Armored Division to the right. (Military History Institute)

paratroopers of the 1/506th Parachute Infantry Regiment arrived in the early afternoon, the aggressive paratroopers staged a counterattack, but it was quickly suppressed by tank fire. The 2nd Panzer Division responded with an infantry attack backed by two companies of tanks, but the German Panzers wisely decided to avoid tangling with the paratroopers and their bazookas in the ruins of Noville. The town could not be easily bypassed since the fields were too muddy to support the trucks following the lead Panzer columns. The attacks resumed at 0530hrs on the morning of December 20, cutting off Noville and pushing the paratroopers out of neighboring Foy. McAuliffe recognized that the Noville force stood no chance, and so gave permission for it to withdraw while other paratroopers tried to retake Foy. The column started to move out around dusk and, to its good fortune, fog settled, which hid its movement from surrounding German troops. The 2nd Panzer Division continued its race east, and captured a bridge over the Ourthe River near Ourtheville. But the lead columns were so short of fuel that they had to wait nearly a day for supplies to catch up.

Bayerlein resumed his attempts to crack through the Bastogne defenses near Bizory on the morning of December 20. Small arms fire and artillery put an end to the Panzer Lehr attack, forcing Bayerlein to look elsewhere. Kampfgruppe Poschinger and infantry from the 26th Volksgrenadier Division attempted to fight their way further south, near Neffe, but a strong response from US artillery broke up several attacks. By December 21, it was becoming obvious that Panzer Lehr Division was being wasted in costly attacks against the Bastogne defenses. The 2nd Panzer Division had already skirted around Bastogne to the north, and finally Lüttwitz gave Bayerlein permission to try the same to the south. But Kampfgruppe Hauser was left behind to reinforce the attacks by the 26th Volksgrenadier Division, thereby significantly weakening the division's attempt to reach the Meuse. The Panzer Lehr Division, with Kampfgruppe Fallois leading, set out for the Ourthe River near St Hubert on December 22. Combined with the 2nd Panzer Division's advance to the Ourthe the preceding day, this left Bastogne surrounded.

While Manteuffel focused most of his attention on the Bastogne sector, Krüger's 58th Panzer Corps had encountered prolonged delays in executing its breakthrough on the Tailles plateau. Although the 112th Infantry had been pushed northward after three days of fighting, the 116th Panzer

Division had been very slow to exploit the rupture in the American lines. Poor bridges, traffic jams, and the ensuing lack of fuel proved as mettlesome as the US Army. Manteuffel was so upset that on December 19 he told Krüger he was thinking of relieving the divisional commander. His attitude changed during the day as the fortunes of the division abruptly improved. US defenses in the area around Houfallize were extremely thin, as units were tending to coalesce around St. Vith to the north and Bastogne to the south. In the early morning, the divisional reconnaissance reported that Houfallize was not occupied by US forces and that the bridges were intact. The divisional commander, General von Waldenburg, decided to bypass Houfallize to the south, and the division reached Bertogne and the main road from Marche to Bastogne by evening. Indeed US resistance was so weak that even the unmotorized 560th Volksgrenadier Division was making good progress, passing by Houfallize to the north. Now the concern was no longer the corps' slow advance, but the open flank to the south as the 58th Panzer Corps outpaced its southern neighbor, Lüttwitz's 47th Panzer Corps around Bastogne. One of the unit officers recorded that "the Americans are completely surprised and in substantial turmoil. Long columns of prisoners march towards the east, many tanks were destroyed or captured. Our Landsers are loaded with cigarettes, chocolates, and canned food, and are smiling from ear to ear."

Paratroopers of the 1/506th Parachute Infantry Regiment, 101st Airborne Division, set off from Bastogne for Foy in the late morning of December 19 to reinforce Team Desobry near Noville. (NARA)

THE US ARMY COUNTERATTACKS

On December 18, Patton met with Bradley at his Luxembourg headquarters. When asked what the Third Army could do to help the First Army in the Ardennes, Patton asserted that he could have two more divisions on the move the following day and a third in 24 hours. Patton was not happy to give up Operation *Tink*, but he ruefully remarked, "What the hell, we'll still be killing Krauts." Unwilling to gloat in view of Bradley's anguish, Patton did not mention that his ability to shift a corps into the Ardennes was precisely because his staff had anticipated the German attack and had already prepared a set of contingency plans, while Bradley's had failed him. The following day, Eisenhower held a conference of all the senior US commanders in Verdun. The atmosphere was glum except for Patton who was his usual cocky self.

US Army doctrine suggested that the essential ingredient to countering an enemy offensive was to hold the shoulders. This objective seemed to be well in hand. Units on the northern shoulder on the Elsenborn Ridge had rebuffed every German assault, and the battered 4th Division was holding steady in the hills of Luxembourg. Eisenhower's short-term objective was to prevent the Germans from crossing the Meuse. Once forces were in place to hold the river line, Eisenhower wanted to begin a counteroffensive, and he turned to Patton asking him when he could start. Patton promptly replied that he could begin with a corps of three divisions within two days, on the morning of December 21, to which Eisenhower blurted, "Don't be fatuous, George," thinking that it was merely Patton's usual bluster. The other officers present were equally skeptical, recognizing the enormous difficulties of reorienting a corps 90 degrees, moving it in winter conditions, and keeping it supplied

Opposite:
A view inside Bastogne on January 20 as a truck column of the 90th Division passes through. (NARA)

along a tenuous supply line. In the ensuing discussion, Patton made it quite clear that his plans had been well considered. Eisenhower, who had just received his fifth star, quipped to Patton: "Funny thing, George, but every time I get a new star, I get attacked." Patton smiled and responded, "And every time you get attacked Ike, I pull you out," referring to his role in redeeming the US Army after the Kasserine Pass debacle in 1943.

Patton's actual dream for this campaign would have been to allow the Germans to penetrate 40 or 50 miles (60 or 80km), and then cut them off in an envelopment operation. But he realized that the senior US commanders were too cautious for such a bold plan, especially under the present confused circumstances. Curiously enough, Patton's notion of a deep envelopment battle was the worst nightmare of the senior Wehrmacht commanders. Model was concerned that the US Army would wait until after the Wehrmacht had reached or even crossed the Meuse before launching a major counteroffensive, trapping most of Army Group B and ending the war in the west.

As mentioned earlier, on December 20, under pressure from his senior aides, Eisenhower decided to temporarily shift control of the elements of the US Army in the northern sector, including First and Ninth Army, from Bradley's 12th Army Group to Montgomery's 21st Army Group. The ostensible reason was the fear that the Germans were about to capture a vital communications junction that would have severed the landlines between Bradley's headquarters in Luxembourg and the northern commands. But there were also concerns that the First Army staff was still in disarray and that Bradley had not been vigorous enough straightening out the problems. The switch caused enormous resentment due to past problems between Bradley and Montgomery in North Africa and Sicily, and Montgomery's persistent efforts to poach units from Bradley to reinforce his infantry-weak 21st Army Group. The short-term effects were beneficial, and Montgomery's take-charge style impressed American officers fighting in the St. Vith salient. In the long term, the switch in command would prove to be troublesome due to Montgomery's maladroit control of the US corps.

Montgomery arrived at First Army HQ in Chaudfontaine on the afternoon of December 20. After Hodges explained the current dispositions, Montgomery responded that he wanted to redeploy the forces, create a reserve, and use this reserve to counterattack once the German attack had run out of steam. The US officers strongly resisted giving up any ground, and wanted to begin counteroffensive operations immediately. Montgomery accepted the current dispositions, and ordered the transfer of Collins' VII Corps, which would form the northern counterattack force, from the idle Ninth Army sector. British officers on Montgomery's staff thought that Hodges looked like he had "been poleaxed" but when Montgomery tried to relieve him the following day, Eisenhower told him to be patient. The matter was dropped, but Hodges' performance over the next few weeks was underwhelming and the First Army staff depended heavily on his chief of staff, Major General William Kean.

The mobilization of the two heavy armored divisions, the 2nd and 3rd Armored, stationed north of the Ardennes was already under way, and these were assigned to Collins' corps. Since the 3rd Armored Division was more easily redeployed than the 2nd, on December 18 its CCA was detached and sent to V Corps, taking part in the fighting against the spearhead of the 1st SS-Panzer Division, Kampfgruppe Peiper, near La Gleize in the northern sector. The remainder of the division arrived around Hotton on December 20. The two heavy divisions followed the old 1942 tables of organization and had six tank battalions instead of the three found in all other US armored divisions. The divisions were tank-heavy and infantry-weak, so they were usually paired with infantry divisions for a more balanced force with an infantry regiment added to each of their three combat commands. Collins' VII Corps deployed two infantry divisions, the green 75th Division and the more experienced 84th Division, in this role.

On the evening of December 18, 1944, a series of telephone conversations were held between the senior Wehrmacht commanders. In separate conversations with Rundstedt and Jodl, Army Group B commander Walter Model told them that the offensive had failed due to the inability of the SS divisions to move forward, and the slow progress of Manteuffel's 5th Panzer Army. He indicated that not only were the "Grand Slam" objectives out of reach, but that he doubted that even "Little Slam" could be achieved since the Panzer spearheads were so far from the Meuse. This sentiment gradually permeated the various headquarters in Berlin, and on December 20, 1944, when Heinz Guderian visited Hitler's headquarters and the OB West (Oberbefelshaber West, Rundstedt's High Command) offices, he tried to pry away some of the prized Panzer divisions in the Ardennes to reinforce threatened sectors on the Russian front. Hitler would not hear of such a thing and scorned the generals for their pessimism. Due to the dissension in the high command as well as difficulties in moving reserve units forward, Model was slow to reorient the focus of the offensive. Even Dietrich and the 6th Panzer Army staff understood the problems, and on December 20 suggested to Model that either all the Panzer divisions be directed towards Dinant to exploit the breakthrough of the 2nd Panzer Division, or, alternately, their own attack be reoriented away from the stubborn Elsenborn Ridge, towards the central route being spearheaded by 116th Panzer Division, Houfallize–La Roche–Liège.

At noon on December 20, the 2nd SS-Panzer Corps was ordered to begin moving forward. Since there was still a slim hope that the 1st SS-Panzer Corps might secure a breakthrough in the northern sector, no decision was made whether its SS-Panzer divisions would be committed to the 6th Panzer Army as planned, or shifted to exploit the successes of Manteuffel's 5th Panzer Army. Manteuffel later argued that it was this indecision in these critical few days that prevented the success of "Little Slam," since an early commitment of the several Panzer divisions in reserve could have provided the added impetus needed to push to the Meuse. But Model recognized that until the American salient at St. Vith was eliminated, there was no maneuver room to shift the SS-Panzer divisions into the central sector. The German appreciation actually became more optimistic in the days before Christmas. The OB West intelligence briefing of December 22 asserted that a major Allied counterattack by the US Third or Seventh Army from the south was unlikely before the New Year, and that limited intervention along the flanks would probably not start for a week. In conjunction with the reduction of the American salient at St. Vith, the German high command began to take steps to redeploy the 2nd SS-Panzer Corps away from the northern sector and into the center where it could support the penetration by the 5th Panzer Army.

The stage was now set for some of the largest and most bitter battles of the Ardennes campaign. The fighting through Christmas in the southern sector was concentrated in three main areas: Bastogne, the approaches to the Meuse River near Dinant, and the road junctions along the Tailles plateau beyond Houfallize.

DEFENSE OF BASTOGNE

The decision to free Panzer Lehr Division to race for the Meuse reduced the strength of the German forces around Bastogne. Although Lüttwitz had ordered Bayerlein to leave Kampfgruppe Hauser behind to reinforce Kokott's 26th Volksgrenadier Division, this meant that the attack was only being conducted by a reinforced division. Even after two days of futile fighting to penetrate into Bastogne, Kokott had not lost hope. When he accompanied a reconnaissance battalion in a move towards Sibret, he continued to see evidence of US troops retreating out of the city towards the south, an area not yet firmly in German hands. If he could not break into Bastogne, at least he could choke it. From December 20 to 22, Kokott continued to draw the cordon around Bastogne with the 77th Grenadier Regiment on the north and east side, Kampfgruppe Hauser on the southeast and the 39th Grenadier Regiment on the southern flank around Sibret. Even though his forces did not yet firmly control the western side of Bastogne, word from the neighboring corps was that the 5th Fallschirmjäger Division was making good progress, and so would presumably take care of this sector.

When the road to Neufchateau was cut on the night of December 20, Bastogne was effectively surrounded, even if the Germans did not control the western sector in any force. Until that point, command within the city was disjointed, with Colonel Roberts controlling CCB, 10th Armored Division, and General McAuliffe commanding the 101st Airborne, with a number of separate corps units and groups of stragglers. Middleton decided that it was time to unify the command in Bastogne and so it was turned over to McAuliffe. The scattered stragglers were formed into Team SNAFU, a GI jibe against the fondness of the Army for acronyms, meaning "Situation Normal All F'ed Up." Team SNAFU was broken up into security patrols and used where needed around the city. The German repositioning on December 21/22 gave McAuliffe time to better organize the defenses.

At 1130hrs on December 22, two Panzer Lehr officers and their drivers walked up the road from Remonfosse under a white flag. Under Lüttwitz's direction, they were to offer the Bastogne defenders an honorable surrender. They encountered an outpost of the 327th Glider Infantry and the officers were taken to McAuliffe's HQ in blindfolds. When told of the surrender

Surviving troops of the 28th Division and stragglers from other units were used to form Team SNAFU to conduct security patrols around Bastogne like this 28th Division patrol on December 20. (NARA)

demands, McAuliffe laughed and said "Aw, nuts." The idea of surrendering seemed preposterous to him as the Germans had proven unable to break into the city after four days of fighting. McAuliffe was at a loss as to how to reply to the formal surrender demand, however, until one of his staff suggested that his first reaction was fine. So they typed out "Nuts" on some stationery, thereby creating one of the legends of the Ardennes campaign. When the response was handed over to the German officers before they returned to Lüttwitz, they expressed puzzlement at the answer, to which the 327th Glider Infantry commander, Colonel Harper, responded, "If you don't understand what 'Nuts' means in English, it is the same as 'go to hell,' and I'll tell you something else – if you continue to attack we will kill every goddam German that tries to break into this city."

The success of the Bastogne garrison in repulsing repeated German infantry attacks was closely tied to the field artillery battalions that had accumulated within the Bastogne perimeter. But ammunition reserves were becoming dangerously low by the evening of December 22. This led to restrictive instructions on the use of the howitzers, frustrating the paratroopers and infantry along the front line who would often see the Germans moving about in the open without any response. The situation

Christmas in Bastogne

In the early morning of Christmas Day Kampfgruppe Maucke of the newly arrived 15th Panzergrenadier Division launched an attack against the positions of the 502nd Parachute Infantry and the 327th Glider Infantry on the northern side of the Bastogne perimeter. The attack was beaten decisively, smashed in a series of savage skirmishes in the woods and villages outside the city. This scene shows the aftermath of the skirmish as the paratroopers attempt to reinforce their positions for a possible renewed German onslaught.

The paratroopers seen here could easily be mistaken for any other US Army infantry unit in the Ardennes. The 101st Airborne Division was hastily deployed to the Ardennes after months of fighting in the Netherlands. By this stage, their distinctive paratrooper garb had given way to the same types of uniforms worn by other US infantry. This was especially true of new replacements and the glider infantry. While some of the veteran paratroopers might still have the M1943 paratrooper battledress with its more extensive pockets, the winter coats largely obscured this.

In the background is a pair of burning PzKpfw IV tanks. Although overshadowed by the larger Panther tank, the PzKpfw IV was still the workhorse of the Wehrmacht, and the most common German tank type in the Ardennes fighting. Hidden in the tree line is an M18 76mm gun motor carriage. This tank destroyer was the fastest tracked combat vehicle of World War II, designed to fulfill the Tank Destroyer Command's motto of "Seek, strike, destroy." In fact, by the time it entered service, its effectiveness was undermined by the inadequate performance of its gun against the new generation of German armored vehicles such as the Panther and the Jagdpanzer IV/70. The more powerful M36 tank destroyer with its 90mm gun was the preferred choice in the winter of 1944–45. (Artwork by Peter Dennis)

Trench foot was a significant cause of US casualties in the Ardennes fighting that could be prevented by proper foot care. This corporal of the 327th Glider Infantry is drying his feet while serving along the Bastogne perimeter. (NARA)

became so bad that one regimental commander pleaded with McAuliffe for artillery support only to be told: "If you see 400 Germans in a 100-yard [90m] area and they have their heads up, you can fire artillery at them, but only two rounds!" McAuliffe's primary concern was that ammunition would run out before Patton's Third Army arrived.

After two days of skirmishing, significant German attacks resumed on December 23. In the late afternoon, Kampfgruppe Hauser made another attempt to push into Marvie on the southern side of the city, supported by the 39th Grenadier Regiment to the west. German infantry attempted to stealthily probe past the scattered US outposts and once in position, a pair of assault guns came clanking up the road but were halted by a wrecked half-track that blocked the approach. A platoon from G/327th Glider Infantry was overwhelmed on Hill 500 after dark, and the attack penetrated into Marvie. Two M4 tanks from Team O'Hara discouraged any further advance into the village, but German attacks continued in earnest until midnight, and controlled the southern fringe of the village through the following day in spite of US efforts. Kampfgruppe Hauser had a hard time reinforcing the operation with any armor, as the area was heavily wooded with only a single road into the village.

On the night of December 22/23, the Russian high-pressure front bringing cold weather and clearing skies arrived and changed the fortunes of war. The next morning, a wave of 16 C-47 transports appeared over Bastogne, dropping the first batch of supplies. By dusk, 241 aircraft had flown to Bastogne, dropping 441 tons of supplies. Drops by 160 aircraft the following day added another 100 tons of supplies.

Kokott was convinced that any further assaults into the southern sector of Bastogne would be futile, so he proposed to Manteuffel that the next attack would be conducted where he suspected the Americans were weakest, in the northwest. He hoped that he would be able to use whatever armor was available, since the terrain in the northwest was much more favorable for tanks, and the cold weather was hardening the ground. In fact, the US defenses were probably best in this sector. Impressed by Kokott's determination, Manteuffel promised that the 15th Panzergrenadier Division would be put at his disposal for this attack. The 15th Panzergrenadier Division had recently arrived from the Italian front, and was both experienced and well equipped. The attack was scheduled for Christmas Day and Manteuffel grimly relayed Hitler's message that "Bastogne must be taken at all costs." The lead elements of the 15th Panzergrenadier Division arrived on the northern side of Bastogne shortly before midnight on Christmas Eve. The reinforcements included Kampfgruppe Maucke with two battalions of infantry, a tank battalion with about 30 tanks and tank destroyers, and two artillery battalions. Kokott decided to launch the attack in the pre-dawn hours since otherwise the armor would attract the attention of American fighter-bombers that were now swarming over the battlefield in the clear skies. With so little

Air resupply was critical to the defense of Bastogne. Here, a C-47 of the 73rd Troop Carrier Squadron, 434th Troop Carrier Group, drops para-crates near Bastogne. (NARA)

time to deploy, many of the troops of the 115th Panzergrenadier Regiment rode the Panzers into the attack zone.

McAuliffe received first news of the attack at 0330hrs on Christmas Day, when A/502nd Parachute Infantry Regiment in Rolle reported that the Germans were on top of them and then the line went dead. The regimental headquarters alerted the rest of the companies with orders to send reinforcements to Rolle. The battalion HQ hesitated to rush another company into the fight in the dark until it became clearer where the Germans were actually attacking and in what numbers. At dawn, this became evident when tanks of Kampfgruppe Maucke were spotted moving near the junction of the 502nd Parachute Infantry and the 327th Glider Infantry regiments. There were three principal thrusts, the 15th Panzergrenadier Division attack furthest west between Champs and Hemroulle, an initial 77th Grenadier Regiment attack in the center coming down the road into Champs, and a smaller attack by the 77th Grenadier Regiment that began around 0500hrs when Germany infantry infiltrated

The catastrophic effects of an ammunition fire and explosion are all too evident from the shattered hulk of this PzKpfw IV of Kampfgruppe Maucke, 15th Panzergrenadier Division, knocked out north of Bastogne during the engagement with the 101st Airborne Division on Christmas Day. (NARA)

through some woods between Champs and Longchamps. The most serious threat came from the Panzer attack which rolled right over A/327th Glider Infantry Regiment. However, the Panzergrenadiers did not drive out the infantry, and when the next wave of Panzergrenadiers approached the Co A positions on foot, they were greeted with intense rifle fire. The 15th Panzergrenadier Division tank attack split up, some tanks heading towards Hemroulle and others to the rear of the B/502nd Parachute Infantry Regiment. Two M18s from 705th Tank Destroyer Battalion knocked out a few of the advancing Panzers but were in turn knocked out when they tried to withdraw. Before reaching the woods where C/502nd Parachute Infantry Regiment was deployed, the tanks veered northward towards Champs, exposing their flanks to rifle fire from the woods and to a pair

Another PzKpfw IV named *Lustmolch* (Happy Salamander) of Kampfgruppe Maucke, 15th Panzergrenadier Division, abandoned in Champs during the fighting with the 502nd Parachute Infantry Regiment on Christmas Day. (NARA)

A view inside Bastogne on December 26 shortly before the relief column from the 4th Armored Division arrived. In the background is an M4A3 tank, probably of the 10th Armored Division. (NARA)

of M18s from 705th Tank Destroyer Battalion. The Panzergrenadiers on the tanks took the worst beating from intense small arms fire, while three PzKpfw IVs were knocked out by gunfire and two more by bazookas at close range. A single PzKpfw IV broke into Champs but was stopped by 57mm antitank gunfire and bazookas.

The group of tanks and Panzergrenadiers that had split off earlier towards the 327th Glider Infantry Regiment received a far hotter reception. Four tank destroyers were located between Cos A and B, and Co C received support from a pair of M4 tanks that arrived shortly before the German attack. None of the German tanks survived the encounter, two being hit point-blank by 105mm howitzers, and the rest being knocked out by tank destroyers and bazookas. Not one of the 18 PzKpfw IVs that started the attack survived, and most of the Panzergrenadiers were either killed or captured. The Christmas attack was the last major assault until Patton's relief column arrived.

Paratroopers of the 101st Airborne Division recover supplies after the air-drop of December 27 along the Bastogne perimeter. (NARA)

THE AIR CAMPAIGN

The weather for the first week was too poor for the Luftwaffe to have any significant impact on the battle and only 170 sorties were conducted on the first day of the offensive. On December 17, 600 daylight sorties were flown including some strafing missions, and these were followed after dark by over 250 ground-attack missions by night-fighters striking at major communication centers such as Liège. The plan was to keep at least 150 fighters in the air at all times during daylight to provide an aerial umbrella for the Panzer divisions, but this was seldom achieved and the number of sorties continued to decline. The US Ninth Air Force also had its close-support operations hampered by the weather as well, and it was distracted by the unusually large numbers of German fighters active over the battlefield. Its two tactical air commands (TAC) flew about 450 tactical sorties daily for the first week of the offensive, mainly fighter sweeps with few ground-attack missions. When the weather finally cleared on December 23, both the IX and XXIX tactical air commands turned out in force, making 669 fighter-bomber sorties. Medium bombers from IX Bomber Command conducted interdiction missions against German supply lines, but were met by furious resistance from German fighters, losing 35 bombers and suffering damage to 182 more out of the 624 that took part. As a result, on Christmas Eve, the Eighth Air Force conducted 1,400 bomber sorties against 12 Luftwaffe airfields over the Rhine to dampen down Luftwaffe activity. Four of the airfields suffered little damage, but the other eight were shut down on average for eight days. On Christmas Day, American air activity reached levels not seen since the August missions against the Falaise Gap, totaling 6,194 tactical sorties including 4,281 fighter sorties. Oberst Ludwig Heilmann of the 5th Fallschirmjäger Division grimly recalled that by nightfall, the attacking Jabos had left "an uninterrupted trail of burning vehicles extending like a torchlight procession from Bastogne all the way back to the Westwall … in my opinion, the Ardennes offensive was irretrievably lost when the Allies sent their air forces into action on December 25, a fact that even the simplest soldier realized."

The Luftwaffe was powerless to stop this, as their inadequately trained fighter pilots suffered disproportionate losses in encounters with the more numerous US fighters. Allied fighters claimed to have shot down 718 German aircraft from December 17 to 27, while losing 111 aircraft to German fighters and 307 more to other causes. A post-war RAF history of the Luftwaffe pungently noted that "bad servicing of the Luftwaffe's aircraft was becoming more widespread, and the pilots were all too ready to seize on the slightest excuse for returning early from their missions. Many pilots, insufficiently trained as they were, had no zest for facing the heavy Allied air onslaught which was carried out during the four days of good weather, December 24–27." A total of 346 fighter pilots were lost between December 23 and 27, including 106 on Christmas Eve, the worst losses during a very costly month for the Luftwaffe fighter force. By the beginning of January, the Allied air forces had conducted about 34,100 missions including 16,600 tactical sorties over the Ardennes compared to 7,500 for the Luftwaffe. The Wehrmacht received little solace from the heightened Luftwaffe activity since so few of the missions were ground-attack.

The last great Luftwaffe operation in the west was conducted on New Year's Day when the 2nd Jagd Corps finally staged Operation *Bodenplatte* two weeks late. The attack included every serviceable fighter in the west, totaling about 1,035 aircraft including pathfinders. The attack caught the

Allied airbases in Belgium and Holland napping, and 144 American and British aircraft were destroyed on the ground, 62 damaged, and a further 70 lost in aerial combat. But it was a Pyrrhic victory for the Luftwaffe. Over a third of the attack force was lost, some 304 aircraft, including 85 shot down by their own flak. A total of 214 aircrew were killed or captured, including

Operation *Bodenplatte*, New Year's Day 1945

At 0930hrs on New Year's Day, the Luftwaffe staged its long-delayed attack on Allied airfields, codenamed *Bodenplatte* (Base Plate). Among the participants were the Me-262A-2a fighter-bombers of KG51, one of Hitler's new wonder weapons. A total of 21 of these aircraft took part in attacks on RAF airfields at Eindhoven and Heesch in the Netherlands. The Eindhoven strike was conducted in conjunction with Bf-109 and FW-190 fighters of Jagdgeschwader 3 and was the more successful of the two missions, destroying or damaging about 50 of the Typhoons and Spitfires stationed with the three wings there. The attack on Heesch with Jagdgeschwader 6 had little effect and one Me-262 was lost to ground fire.

Kampfgeschwader 51 was the principal Luftwaffe unit operating the fighter-bomber version of the Me-262 at the time, and it was responsible for the majority of Me-262 sorties in late 1944. The I Gruppe flew from the Rheine and Hopsten airbases while II Gruppe flew from Hesepe. These fighter-bombers were used repeatedly in ground attack missions in the Ardennes, though there is little evidence to suggest they were very effective in this role given the difficulty of delivering unguided bombs at high speed and at low altitude. KG 51 lost a total of five aircraft during the Ardennes missions in December, four to fighters and one to flak. (Artwork by Howard Gerrard)

On December 19, the 353rd Fighter Squadron attempted to bomb the headquarters of the 116th Panzer Division but was bounced by about 40 Luftwaffe fighters. In the ensuing melee, the outnumbered but more experienced squadron downed nine German fighters while losing three Thunderbolts. This is "Big Jake," the P-47D of Lieutenant Lloyd Overfield, credited with two fighters that day, and seen here taxiing at Rosières during the Battle of the Bulge. (NARA)

three Geschwader commanders, all six Gruppe commanders, and 11 Staffel commanders – an irreplaceable loss. *Bodenplatte* had a crippling effect on subsequent Luftwaffe operations in the west; in contrast Allied losses were replaced quickly from depots and few aircrew had been lost.

PATTON STRIKES BACK

The Third Army began moving its III Corps towards Arlon on December 19. The spearhead of the northern attack was Patton's favorite, the 4th Armored Division. Muscle came from the 26th and 80th divisions, reinforced by three field artillery groups. The attack was launched in the late afternoon of December 21 by all three divisions, with the corps advancing from 3 to 5 miles (5 to 8km). The following day, the 4th Armored Division reached Martelange 13 miles (21km) south of Bastogne, the 26th Division moved up alongside it to the east and the 80th Division took Heiderscheid. As the III Corps approached Bastogne, German

PATTON'S RELIEF OF BASTOGNE

resistance intensified. By December 23, elements from Brandenberger's 7th Army were finally approaching the southern outskirts of Bastogne, and the 5th Fallschirmjäger Division was assigned to cover the main road from Arlon through Marvie into Bastogne. Combat Command A took this route, but was halted by determined German resistance around Livarchamps. Recognizing that this route was the one most likely to be contested, the two other combat commands were sent up alternate routes. CCB went across country from Habay-la-Neuve but was stopped near Hompré. CCR was redeployed on Christmas Day, and after a 30-mile (50km) road march to the west, resumed its attack along the narrow Cobreville–Assenois road into southwestern Bastogne.

By the morning of December 26, CCR was the closest of the three combat commands to Bastogne, and by mid-afternoon fought its way to

The first US tank into Bastogne was this M4A3E2 assault tank named *Cobra King* of Lieutenant Charles Boggess from Co C, 37th Tank Battalion, 4th Armored Division. (Patton Museum)

within a short distance of the Bastogne defense. A task force was formed under Captain William Dwight consisting of Co C, 37th Tank Battalion, and Co C, 53rd Armored Infantry Battalion, which set off for Assenois at 1610hrs after a preliminary artillery strike. The tanks proceeded into the village even before the artillery fire had lifted, avoiding much German resistance. Once the artillery lifted, the German defenders tried to disable the armored infantry column by throwing Teller mines underneath their half-tracks, blowing up one with mines, and knocking out three more with Panzerfaust antitank rockets. But the American infantry drove out the defenders in bitter house-to-house fighting and 428 prisoners were taken. By late afternoon, Captain Dwight was greeted by the commander of the 101st Airborne Division, General McAuliffe, in the outskirts of Bastogne. Shortly after midnight, the task force attacked the woods north of Assenois and by 0300hrs the road was clear for vehicular traffic. The light tanks of Co D, 37th Tank Battalion, escorted a relief column into Bastogne consisting of 40 supply trucks and 70 ambulances later in the day. While CCR had managed to break into Bastogne, it would take several more days of hard fighting to secure and widen the corridor. However, German forces in this

Patton's initial assault against the 7th Army by the 80th Division led to a series of sharp battles along the Luxembourg border with the 352nd Volksgrenadier Division, supported on December 23 by Panzers of the Führer Grenadier Brigade. This StuG III assault gun is inspected by GIs of 2/319th Infantry in Heiderscheid a few days later. (NARA)

A Kampfgruppe of the Führer Grenadier Brigade attacked Patton's 80th Division in Heiderscheid on Christmas Eve and amongst its losses were the StuG III to the left and this SdKfz 251 half-track, one of the rare SdKfz 251/17 variants with a turreted 2cm autocannon. (NARA)

sector were the weakest of the siege force, and the corridor was never seriously threatened. While this was not the end to the fighting for Bastogne, clearly the momentum was shifting in favor of the US Army.

THE HIGH-WATER MARK

Late on the evening of December 23, the reconnaissance battalion of the 2nd Panzer Division reported that it had approached to within 5½ miles (9km) of the Meuse River near Dinant. This would prove to be the high-water mark of the Ardennes offensive. The reconnaissance battalion of 2nd Panzer Division had reached and crossed the Ourthe River at Ourtheville on December 21, followed by Panzergrenadiers later in the day. The advance beyond was slowed for more than a day by a lack of fuel. By December 23, the division was again on the march in two columns, the main one along Route N4 to Marche and a smaller column en route to Hargimont. Present with the division was the impatient corps commander General Lüttwitz, who relieved one of the regimental commanders when the pace of the advance was slowed by a weak American roadblock. While Hargimont was captured, Marche was stoutly defended by arriving elements of the 84th Division. Lüttwitz ordered Lauchert to turn the bulk of his division west towards

A group of prisoners from the 1/914th Grenadier Regiment, 352nd Volksgrenadier Division, captured near Mertzig on December 24 by the 319th Infantry, 80th Division, during Patton's drive to relieve Bastogne. (Military History Institute)

Dinant and the Meuse, and to leave only a blocking force towards Marche. He hoped to deploy the 9th Panzer Division near Marche once it arrived. The division was preceded by Kampfgruppe Böhm consisting of its reconnaissance battalion reinforced with a few Panzers. On the night of December 23/24, Kampfgruppe Böhm raced up the highway towards Dinant, finally reaching the woods near Foy-Notre Dame. It was followed on December 24 by the advance guard of the division, Kampfgruppe Cochenhausen, consisting of the 304th Panzergrenadier Regiment and 1/3rd Panzer Regiment.

Radio reports of the advance caused jubilation in Berlin. Hitler personally congratulated Rundstedt and Model, and freed up the 9th Panzer and 15th Panzergrenadier divisions to reinforce the 5th Panzer Army. Model was under few illusions about reaching the "Grand Slam" or "Little Slam" objectives, but Panzers reaching the Meuse was enough of an accomplishment that it would help the Wehrmacht save face from all the disappointments of the campaign. Model immediately directed the 9th Panzer Division to follow the 2nd Panzer Division and protect its right flank from advancing American forces. As noted earlier, he ordered the entire 15th Panzergrenadier Division into the area north of Bastogne to finally crush the resistance there.

But by this late date, the advance of the 2nd Panzer Division no longer had any strategic significance. There was no operational value in reaching the Meuse at Dinant, as the town was backed by high cliffs and could be easily defended by the Allies. Namur was even less attractive and its fortifications posed a substantial hurdle for any attacker. The spearhead Panzer divisions were exhausted, short of functional tanks and dangerously short of fuel. This was not immediately apparent to Hitler or the Allied commanders.

The threat of German units crossing the Meuse prompted Field Marshal Montgomery to begin redeploying his reserve, the British XXX Corps, on December 19 to cover the exits over the river. This took time, but by December 23, the major river crossings at Givet, Dinant, and Namur were

Lieutenant Robert Boscawen, commander of 2 Troop, the Coldstream Guards, sits in a Sherman (17-pdr) guarding one of the bridges over the Meuse at Namur on Christmas Day. British armored units were deployed along the Meuse River in the days before Christmas to prevent a possible German crossing. (NARA)

each covered by tank battalions from the 29th Armored Brigade, each reinforced by a rifle company.

By the time that Kampfgruppe Cochenhausen approached the Meuse, Allied reinforcements were becoming a growing threat. Its attack was constantly diluted by the need to detach units to fight off flank attacks by American units appearing in the area. One of its Panzer columns was wiped out in the pre-dawn hours when it stumbled into an advancing column from CCA, 2nd Armored Division, along the Ciney–Rochefort road. To make matters worse, the division was threatened from the rear when the 335th Infantry of the 84th Division began an attack near Marche that at one point captured the main supply road. Although elements of the 2nd Panzer Division managed to hold the road open, American pressure was increasing as more reinforcements arrived.

On the night of December 23/24, a single captured jeep with a scout party of three German soldiers approached the bridge at Dinant, but was blown up when it ran over a mine planted by the British defenders. The advance of Kampfgruppe Böhm was finally brought to an end on the morning of December 24. As one of its columns began probing towards the river crossing, their lead PzKpfw IV tank was destroyed by a Sherman 17-pdr of the British 3rd Royal Tank Regiment which had taken up defensive positions on the east bank of the river the day before. Later in the morning, two more Panthers were knocked out, and the 3rd Royal Tank Regiment roadblocks established the farthest advance point of the Wehrmacht during the Ardennes offensive. CCA, 2nd Armored Division, advanced down the Ciney–Rochefort road for most of Christmas Eve, joined up with the British tankers, and pushed on to Buissonville in the afternoon, threatening to isolate Kampfgruppe Cochenhausen.

By late on Christmas Eve, it had become clear to Lüttwitz that the advance had come to an end. By now he recognized that he was facing major opposition in the 2nd Armored Division and 84th Division. Instead of ordering the long-delayed Panzer Lehr Division to Celles to join with the 2nd Panzer Division to race for the Meuse, Lüttwitz realized he would need to block any further advance of the Americans to buy time for the vulnerable 2nd Panzer Division to return to the corps bridgehead at Rochefort. He hoped to take Humain and Buissonville, thereby relieving pressure on the beleaguered 2nd Panzer Division. The desperately needed and long-delayed 9th Panzer Division was still behind schedule and lost another day when fuel could not be provided.

General Ernest Harmon of the 2nd Armored Division was itching to attack Kampfgruppe Cochenhausen after it was spotted by aerial reconnaissance. US units had intercepted German radio messages that made it very clear that the German units were seriously short of fuel. The opportunity to crush the Wehrmacht spearhead was almost thrown away. Montgomery was still concerned that the Germans were planning to throw their weight through the center and continue the advance towards Liège. Hodges had visited Collins on December 23 and knew that he wanted to attack the 2nd Panzer Division spearhead with the 2nd Armored Division. Yet in the wake of the fighting around Manhay, precipitated by the confused withdrawal on December 23, Montgomery talked to Hodges about withdrawing VII Corps back to the Andenne–Hotton–Manhay line, not pushing forward. Montgomery's preoccupation with "tidying-up" the northern sector of the front so alarmed Bradley that he sent a note to Hodges that warned that while he was "no longer in my command, I would view with serious misgivings the surrender of any more ground." The following

The prospects for any breakthrough over the Meuse were doubtful after the British XXX Corps moved forces into this sector. Here on December 27, 1944, some GIs chat with British paratroopers in Givet, France, on the Meuse River near the Belgian border. (NARA)

day, Montgomery reiterated his intent for the VII Corps to go over to the defensive. Hodges and the First Army staff were not enthusiastic to rein in Collins. A senior staff officer was sent to VII Corps headquarters with Montgomery's instructions, but First Army consciously neglected to forbid an attack, anticipating that the aggressive Collins would use his discretion to destroy the German spearhead. As Hodges' staff hoped, Collins ordered an attack. This decision proved timely as it allowed the 2nd Armored Division to beat up the weakened Panzer divisions of Lüttwitz's corps piecemeal rather than having to confront them simultaneously.

The 2nd Armored Division's main thrust on Christmas Day was conducted by CCB against Kampfgruppe Böhm and Kampfgruppe Cochenhausen, while CCA and the 4th Cavalry Group blocked Panzer Lehr Division and the newly arrived 9th Panzer Division further east. CCB launched an enveloping attack out from Ciney in two task forces joining at Celles in the mid-afternoon and clearing the town. This trapped two large concentrations of 2nd Panzer Division units in the woods north of the town. Panzer Lehr Division attempted to push CCA out of Buissonville with an early morning attack at 0750hrs, but was repulsed with the loss of eight tanks, an assault gun, and numerous infantry. A Panzergrenadier attack 40

A pair of GIs from the 207th Engineer Combat Battalion prepare a bazooka by fitting a battery into the launcher during the fighting near Buissonville on December 29. (NARA)

minutes later was also hit hard, putting an end to attacks that day. Another battalion from Panzer Lehr was more successful at Humain, pushing a troop from the 4th Cavalry Group out of the village early on Christmas Day, and holding it against further attacks.

Lauchert formed Kampfgruppe Holtmayer from remaining elements of 2nd Panzer Division near Marche in the hope of relieving the Celles pocket, and it departed Rochefort on the night of December 25/26. It reached to within half a mile (1km) of the Celles pocket but, without significant armored support, it was shattered by artillery and then roughly brushed off by CCB, 2nd Armored Division. To further seal off the pocket, on December 27 elements of the 4th Cavalry Group established a blocking position near Ciergnon and CCA, 2nd Armored Division, pushed south from Buissonville, reaching the 2nd Panzer Division's main assembly area in Rochefort. CCB, 2nd Armored Division, spent December 26/27 reducing the Celles pocket. At 1530hrs on December 26, the 2nd Panzer Division headquarters radioed survivors in the pocket to destroy any remaining heavy equipment and attempt to fight their way out. The trapped German units made two major breakout attempts on December 26, but on December 27 the pocket began

After nearly reaching the Meuse River, the vanguard of the 2nd Panzer Division became trapped in a pocket near Celles, Belgium, where it was overwhelmed by the US 2nd Armored Division. Here, the US Army retrieves an abandoned PzKpfw IV and Panther Ausf. G. (NARA)

An M4A1 (76mm) of Task Force B, CCA, 2nd Armored Division, carries infantry into an assault near Frandeux on December 27, during the attempts to contain the Panzer Lehr Division near Rochefort. (NARA)

to collapse and about 150 tanks and vehicles were found destroyed or abandoned and 448 prisoners were taken. About 600 soldiers escaped from the woods on the nights of December 26 and 27. By the end of December, the 2nd Panzer Division had been reduced in strength from about 120 tanks and assault guns to only about 20 and was no longer combat effective.

Panzer Lehr Division, reinforced by elements of the 9th Panzer Division, continued attempts to hold back the VII Corps attack. Harmon committed both CCA and CCR against Humain on December 27, finally retaking the town from the 9th Panzer Division shortly before midnight. The neighboring 335th Infantry pushed down out of Marche, further sealing off the main highway onto the Marche plateau. Manteuffel by now realized that any further attempts to reach the Meuse would be futile, and his two best Panzer divisions were too weak for further offensive operations, with only about 50 operational Panzers.

This Panther Ausf. G from the Panzer Lehr Division was knocked out during the attacks on Buissonville in the days after Christmas in the fighting with the 2nd Armored Division on the approaches to the Meuse. (NARA)

SECURING BASTOGNE

The corridor between Patton's Third Army and Bastogne was precarious for the first few days, and was initially located on poor secondary roads. The last week of December was spent trying to gain control of the main roads, while at the same time both Manteuffel's 5th Panzer Army and Brandenberger's 7th Army desperately tried to sever the corridor. Manteuffel still held out hope that the "Little Slam" objectives might be reached, by first eliminating American resistance in Bastogne, then swinging back northwest towards Dinant. Model and Rundstedt agreed, adding a new 39th Panzer Corps headquarters under Generalleutnant Karl Decker to manage the units scraped together from elsewhere in the Ardennes. The Führer Begleit Brigade was assigned to the attack south of Bastogne, and other units moved into the area, included the badly decimated 1st SS-Panzer Division "Leibstandarte," the 3rd Panzergrenadier Division and the Führer Grenadier Brigade. The first attempt by Remer's Führer Begleit Brigade was aborted after the unit was pounded by American fighter-bombers. On the US side, the CCA, 9th Armored Division, began a push out of Bastogne on the morning of December 27 to clear the western side of Bastogne, and spent three days grinding into the German defenses.

There were several strategic options for eliminating the "Bulge" in the Ardennes. Patton proposed the most ambitious, an attack by his Third Army from the area of Luxembourg City with a corresponding First Army lunge from the northern shoulder, joining at St. Vith and entrapping as much of the 5th and 6th Panzer armies as possible. This operation was never seriously entertained by Bradley or Eisenhower as there were serious doubts that such a mobile operation could be supported in the winter months over the restricted road network in Luxembourg and in the Elsenborn Ridge/Hohes Venn area as well as the recognition that the Germans could withdraw faster than the US Army could advance. Both Collins and Ridgway were anxious to start offensive operations after Christmas, but Montgomery remained fearful that the Germans might still break through somewhere along the First Army's extended defensive perimeter. The First Army corps commanders doubted that the Germans had the resources and held a more realistic appreciation of the solidity of the First Army defenses. When pressed by Collins about a possible attack from the Tailles plateau towards St. Vith to cut off the German

A patrol from the 101st Airborne Division moves out of Bastogne during the fighting on December 29. (NARA)

offensive at its base, Montgomery said, "Joe, you can't supply a corps along a single road," to which Collins "in disrespectful exasperation" replied, "Well Monty, maybe you British can't, but we can." Montgomery's stalling of offensive operations by the First Army made Eisenhower rue the day he had turned over command of the First Army to him. Collins offered Hodges three options for closing the Bulge, the least ambitious of which was a push by VII Corps to coincide with Patton's offensive, meeting forces near Houfallize. While it would cut off any German forces in the deepest pockets of the Bulge to the northwest of Bastogne, most senior commanders realized it would trap few German forces. Eisenhower approved the plan on December 27 with Patton's Third Army to jump off on December 30 and First Army to start counterattacks on January 3. This approach meant pushing the Germans out of the Bulge, rather than trapping them within and counted on attrition rather than envelopment to destroy Wehrmacht units.

After several days of inconclusive skirmishing around the Bastogne perimeter, and considerable repositioning of forces, both sides planned major attacks on December 30. Middleton's VIII Corps had been reinforced and consisted of the 87th Division to the west, the newly arrived and green 11th Armored Division in the center, and the 9th Armored Division at the base of the corridor. The aim of this attack was to begin to push the German forces away from the western side of Bastogne. At the same time, Manteuffel planned a three-phase assault, beginning with an attack by the 47th Panzer Corps against the corridor from the northwest and the new 39th Panzer Corps from the southeast.

Both sides exchanged heavy artillery fire in anticipation of the attacks, and both the 11th Armored Division and 87th Division made modest gains. Remer's Führer Begleit Brigade hardly got past its start point and the neighboring 3rd Panzergrenadier Division was tied down in defensive operations for most of the day. The attack by the 39th Panzer Corps with a Kampfgruppe of the 1st SS-Panzer Division and the newly arrived 167th Volksgrenadier Division struck the US 35th Division around Lutrebois. The US infantry defended tenaciously, and were backed by divisional artillery, the artillery of the 4th Armored Division and significant close air support. General Höcker of the 167th Volksgrenadier Division reported that his lead battalion was "cut to pieces … by tree smasher shells," the new and secret

US Army proximity fuzes debuted at Bastogne that detonated at predetermined altitudes over the ground, substantially improving their lethality against exposed infantry. When the main Panzer column of the 1st SS-Panzer Division Kampfgruppe moved into action around noon, it was pummeled by air attack along the Lutremange–Lutrebois road. A Panzer company that escaped the Jabos stumbled into an ambush of the 4th Armored Division and was stopped after losing about a dozen tanks and three assault guns. By the end of the day, the German attacks had completely failed and the momentum was clearly shifting to the American side.

A planned 6th Armored Division attack on December 31 from the eastern side of the corridor became trapped by icy roads and the congested road network. The attack began in earnest on New Year's Day, making good progress with the capture of Bizory and Mageret, and progress was even better on January 2. The division's neighbor, the 35th Division, was slow in joining the attack due to the need to clear out remaining pockets of German resistance from the attack the preceding day. The VIII Corps continued to push up along the right side of Bastogne, with the tanks of the 11th Armored Division slugging it out in a series of skirmishes with Remer's Führer Begleit Brigade. In four days of fighting, the 11th Armored Division advanced only 6 miles (10km) at a cost of 660 casualties, 42 M4, and 12 M5A1 tanks. Nevertheless, the VIII Corps had stopped the 47th Panzer Corps attack cold,

An M4 medium tank of the 4th Armored Division takes part in operations to push out of Bastogne on January 3, 1945 with a .30cal machine gun team in the foreground. (NARA)

and its capture of the road junction at Mande-St Etienne threatened to cut off the German forces on the northwest side of Bastogne.

With his own prospects for offensive action now gone, Manteuffel was so worried that the American advances on the west side of Bastogne might trap the 47th Panzer Corps that he recommended a general pull-back to the line Odeigne–La Roche–St Hubert. While Model agreed, he knew that Hitler would countenance no retreat. In later years, Manteuffel pointed to the January 3, 1945 fighting as the final turning point in the Ardennes when the strategic initiative passed entirely to the US side. After this date, the Wehrmacht was never again able to stage a significant attack in the Ardennes and for the most part endured a series of grinding defensive battles.

ELIMINATING THE BULGE

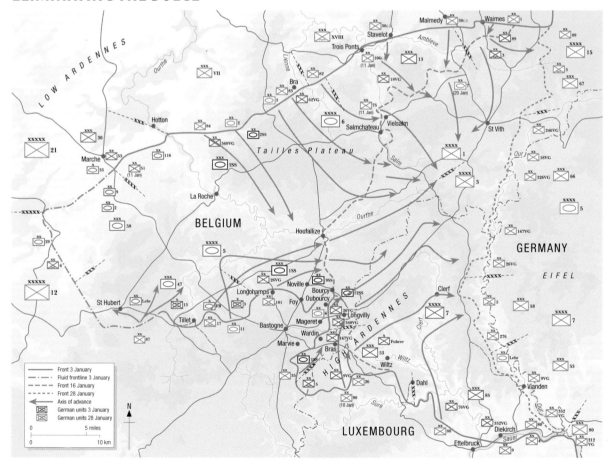

ERASING THE BULGE

By late December, even Hitler had given up hope of victory in the Ardennes. On December 27, the 6th Panzer Army was ordered to go over to the defensive. Hitler's enthusiasms turned in another direction, to Alsace, hoping to exploit the overextended defensive lines of the US 6th Army Group there, which had been stretched to cover part of the line formerly held by Patton's Third Army. Operation *Nordwind* was launched on January 1, 1945, gaining some initial successes. But it had no strategic consequences, and little impact in the Ardennes beyond placing even more stringent limits on German reinforcements and supplies. Manteuffel asked Model on January 2 to authorize a general withdrawal from the Bastogne vicinity to a more defensible line hinged on Houfallize, but Model knew of Hitler's opposition to any withdrawal and so refused. Hitler instead ordered another attack on Bastogne for January 4, which fizzled after only minor gains. The US First Army began its offensive operations to join up with Patton's Third Army on January 3, 1945. On January 5, Model was forced to pull out two of the

During the clean-up phase of the campaign, the British XXX Corps deployed forces on the Marche plateau to clear out German forces there. These are troops of the Parachute Battalion, 1st Canadian Division, serving with the 51st Highland Division passing through Marche on January 9, 1945. (NARA)

A .30cal machine gun team of the 3/289th Infantry, 75th Division, has set up in a house in Salmchateau on January 16 during the fighting to link up with Patton's Third Army. (NARA)

Panzer divisions from the Bastogne sector to reinforce the badly pressed 6th Panzer Army, ending any further attempts against Bastogne.

From the American perspective, the early January fighting was as much against the weather as against the Germans. The snowy conditions grew progressively worse, and the struggles for the many small road junctions between Bastogne and Houfallize were bitter and costly for both sides. On January 8, Hitler recognized the obvious, and authorized a withdrawal to prevent German units from being trapped by the slow but steady American advance. But the withdrawal did not proceed as planned, and La Roche was captured sooner than anticipated. Hitler planned to gradually have the 5th Panzer Army take over the 6th Panzer Army sector, with the 6th Panzer Army

US ARMY SELF-PROPELLED TANK DESTROYER STRENGTH AND LOSSES IN THE ETO, 1944–45

	M10 strength	M36 strength	M18 strength	Total strength	M10 losses	M36 losses	M18 losses	Total losses
November 1944	573	183	252	1,008	45	5	7	57
December 1944	790	236	306	1,332	62	21	44	127
January 1945	760	365	312	1,437	69	26	27	122
February 1945	686	826	448	1,960	106	18	16	140

US ARMY M4 MEDIUM TANK LOSSES IN THE ETO, NOVEMBER 1944–FEBRUARY 1945

	November	December	January	February
Losses	257	495	585	319
Unit strength	2,832	4,076	4,561	5,297
% of strength	9.1	11.7	12.8	6.0

serving as a reserve to counter an anticipated Allied attack at the base of the Bulge, the type of operation proposed by Patton that was not in fact in the works. However, other events intervened. The fighting in the Ardennes became irrelevant on January 12, 1945 when the Red Army launched its long-expected winter offensive. With the Red Army on Germany's doorstep, there were no longer any resources for Hitler's foolish gambles in the west.

On January 14, Rundstedt himself pleaded with Hitler to permit a withdrawal in stages all the way to the Rhine, but Hitler would only countenance a withdrawal to the Westwall. On January 16, the US Third and First armies met at Houfallize, marking the end of the first phase of erasing the Bulge. It would take until January 28 to recapture all of the territory lost to the German offensive.

CONCLUSION

Hitler's final gamble in the west had failed within its first week when the 6th Panzer Army was unable to secure the Meuse River bridges at Liège. Although the 5th Panzer Army had far greater success in penetrating the American defenses in the central and southern sector, this was a race to nowhere that was operationally irrelevant as it neither destroyed any significant US forces nor secured any vital terrain. At best, the Ardennes attack disrupted the pace of Allied offensives into western Germany, but even this is debatable since the attrition of the Wehrmacht in the Ardennes weakened later defensive efforts in 1945. The most significant strategic effect of the Ardennes offensive was to distract German attention from the growing threat of Soviet offensive actions. The drain of resources to the west prevented the creation of viable reserves to counter the predictable Red Army assault into central Germany in mid-January 1945, helping to ensure the disaster that followed.

The most impressive German accomplishment was the ability of the Wehrmacht to achieve operational surprise against the US Army in spite of the obvious US advantages in aerial reconnaissance and signals intelligence. This was accomplished both by rigorous signals security and by careful movement plans which minimized the visibility of Wehrmacht units in transit. While the weather helped this process, it still took considerable skill in execution.

From a tactical perspective, the performance of Manteuffel's 5th Panzer Army clearly outshone Dietrich's 6th Panzer Army. When the US Army in 1995 used historical data from the Ardennes offensive to test one of their

Opposite:
January 30, 1945. US Army Pfc DC Cox of Company M, 26th Infantry, 1st Division, searching for German snipers among the ruins in a Belgian town near Muringen, after the Battle of the Bulge. (Topfoto)

For months after the battle, the Belgian countryside was littered with wrecked armored vehicles. This is a knocked-out German SdKfz 251/9 (7.5cm) "Stummel" used to provide fire support for Panzergrenadier units and photographed by the US Army Howell mission. (NARA)

computer war game simulations, the war game concluded that the 5th Panzer Army had performed better than expected, and the 6th Panzer Army more poorly than its resources would have suggested. The Waffen-SS continued to suffer from mediocre leadership at senior levels, which was particularly evident in offensive operations such as the Ardennes. In contrast, the regular army continued to display a high level of tactical excellence even under the trying circumstances of the Ardennes operation, epitomized by Manteuffel's superior leadership in preparing and executing the badly flawed Ardennes plan.

Nevertheless, the emaciated Wehrmacht of late 1944 did not have the combat effectiveness in offensive operations of years past. The combat effectiveness of the infantry divisions had been fatally compromised by the manpower losses in the summer of 1944. The head of Rundstedt's staff later wrote that the Ardennes had "broken the backbone of the Wehrmacht on the western front." A meeting at Model's headquarters after the fighting concluded that morale had plummeted since the defeat, and "the German soldier is in general fed up." The head of the Luftwaffe fighter force, Adolf Galland, later wrote that the Luftwaffe was "decimated in the large air battles, especially during Christmas and finally destroyed" during the Ardennes campaign. As the diarist of the Wehrmacht high command, P. E. Schramm later noted, "The abortive (Ardennes) offensive had made it clear not only the aerial but the armored superiority of the enemy."

Losses in the Ardennes fighting were heavy on both sides. US casualties totaled 75,482 of which there were 8,407 killed, 46,170 wounded, and 20,905 missing through the end of January. The British XXX Corps lost 1,408 including 200 killed, 239 wounded, and 969 missing. Estimates of German losses vary from about 67,200 to 98,025 casualties depending on the parameters. In the case of the lower of the figures, this included 11,171 killed, 34,439 wounded, and 23,150 missing. The Wehrmacht lost about 610 tanks and assault guns in the Ardennes, or about 45 percent of their original strength, compared to about 730 US tanks and tank destroyers.

Although the US Army suffered from some serious mistakes by senior commanders at the outset of the offensive, at the tactical level, its units performed well. The only division to be completely overwhelmed, the 106th Division near St. Vith, was a green unit in an exposed and badly overextended position, overwhelmed by more numerous enemy forces. The American response to the German offensive was timely and effective, exploiting the US advantage in battlefield mobility to quickly shift units to block the German advance. The stalwart defense by US infantry, armor, and engineer units, backed by ample artillery support, stopped the German offensive.

Kampfgruppe Peiper's rampage in Belgium led to post-war criminal proceedings for war crimes. Here, Joachim Peiper is seen on trial in Dachau after the war. (NARA)

From an operational perspective, the Allied response after Christmas was lackluster with the exception of Patton's prompt relief of Bastogne. Bradley and Eisenhower suffered a blow to their confidence by failing to anticipate the German offensive. Combined with the unfortunate decision to allow Montgomery to control the US forces in the northern sector of the front, the Allied counterattack was timid and failed to exploit the potential either to trap significant German forces or at least to force a less organized withdrawal. In spite of these problems, the US Army's defeat of the Wehrmacht in the Ardennes crippled the German Army in the west and facilitated the offensive operations into northwestern Germany in February and March 1945.

Many Belgian towns lay in ruins after the fighting. This is Houfallize in early 1945. The Panther sitting in the river is probably the same one later recovered and put on display in the town square. (NARA)

The Ardennes campaign precipitated a crisis in Allied command after Montgomery made a number of tactless remarks that exaggerated his own role in the victory. Montgomery had been campaigning for months to be named the supreme land forces commander as part of a broader effort to shift Allied strategic planning towards his view that the offensive against Germany should be conducted on a narrow front by his own 21st Army Group. Eisenhower considered asking for his resignation as the best solution to this nagging problem and Montgomery backed down, largely ending the Allied debate about the strategic conduct of the war in northwest Europe in Eisenhower's favor.

Although it was not immediately apparent, the Ardennes campaign also led to the final collapse of the German war industry. The German attack led to a shift in Allied strategic bombing missions to isolate the battlefield by striking at German railways that were supplying the attacking armies. These missions happened to coincide with many of Germany's most critical industrial feeder lines into crucial industrial regions. Coal delivery was paralyzed and German energy production fell by more than half. The second catastrophe occurred further east when the Red Army overran Upper Silesia after the start of its January 1945 offensive. Next to the Ruhr, Silesia was Germany's principal source of coal and other industrial resources.

ALTERNATIVE SCENARIOS

One way to gain a better overview of the conduct of a campaign is to examine alternative scenarios in order to appreciate better how the campaign was actually conducted. Four of these seem especially pertinent: an early Rhine crossing, an early Patton offensive in the Saar, reversal of the Allied intelligence failure, and advantageous weather for the German attack.

Eisenhower and SHAEF focused their attention on the northern wing of the Allied armies, in no small measure due to Montgomery's vocal insistence that priority be afforded to the 21st Army Group. In contrast, Eisenhower tended to ignore the southern flank of the Allied advance being managed by General Jacob Devers' Franco-American 6th Army Group. One of the few Allied successes in the autumn of 1944 was the spectacular performance of the 6th Army Group in overcoming the substantial geographic barriers that blocked access to the Rhine plains. While Hodges' First US Army was beating itself bloody in futile attacks in the Hürtgen forest, Patch's Seventh US Army overcame the High Vosges mountains. This feat had not been accomplished by any other army in modern times, and as a result, the Seventh Army gained access to the Rhine plains. Simultaneously, de Lattre's First French Army overcame substantial German defenses, and gained access to the southern Rhine plains via the Belfort Gap. As a result of these successes, in late November, Devers wanted to stage a crossing of the Rhine near Rastatt with an aim to send forces up the east bank. Eisenhower turned Devers down, and sent the Seventh US Army into the Low Vosges to support Patton's drive on the Saar. This cautious approach was due to Eisenhower's conviction that Alsace provided a poor springboard for operations into Germany. Alsace faced the Black Forest, a hilly and wooded area not ideal for mechanized operations. But Devers was not interested in the Black Forest, but in a northern drive up the Rhine valley. While this did not have any operational significance in itself in terms of either gaining a major industrial region or trapping a large German force, it had intriguing possibilities for the conduct of operations into the Saar. An advance by Seventh Army would have unhinged German defenses in Lorraine and the Saar facing Patton, and thereby facilitated Patton's drive on Frankfurt. Such a scheme was too bold for Eisenhower, who feared that US columns on the east bank of the Rhine would be too vulnerable to German attack.

Such a bold attack into Germany would have inevitably forced a Wehrmacht response. A drive northward along the Rhine plains would have circumvented the Westwall defensive line the Saar and trapped much of the German 1st Army on the west bank of the Rhine between Patton's Third Army and Patch's Seventh Army. Patch's Seventh Army on the east bank of the Rhine would have offered a tempting target for a German envelopment operation. Such a temptation might have proven irresistible to Hitler, and it might have led to a diversion of the reserves being hoarded for the Ardennes attack a few weeks later. Under this scenario, the Ardennes offensive would not have occurred, and a major campaign might have emerged along the Rhine and in the Saar instead.

The second alternative scenario involves a minor schedule change. Patton's Operation *Tink*, an assault in the Saar towards Frankfurt, was scheduled to begin on December 19, three days after the start of the German Ardennes offensive. What would have happened if it had occurred before the German offensive started? This scenario was actually anticipated by Patton and Oscar Koch, the head of his G-2 intelligence section. Koch was following the build-up of German forces in the Ardennes sector, since it abutted the Third Army sector and might constitute a flank threat once Operation *Tink* was launched. Indeed, the most likely outcome of an early launch of Operation *Tink* would be precisely what Koch feared, that the left flank of the German attack force, especially the 5th Panzer Army, might turn its attention southward towards Patton's Third Army instead of northward against the weak First Army defenses in the Ardennes. This is by no means certain as there were significant terrain issues involved. Patton's operational sector in the Saar was separated from the Ardennes by some particularly formidable mountain areas in Luxembourg that created a geographical dead zone between the two combat arenas. A case can be made that the Wehrmacht would have simply ignored Patton's attack for the time being, and launched their own assault, realizing that Patton's forces would just become tied up in the Saar-Palatinate defenses as they had been in Lorraine for October–December 1944. Nevertheless, the Operation *Tink* scenario offers more dramatic possibilities if Patton had managed to conduct another "Rhine Rat Race" comparable to the March 1945 attack into this areas that destroyed the German 1st Army. This was not at all guaranteed, since the March 1945 offensive occurred in the wake of

Operation *Nordwind* which substantially weakened the German forces in the Saar. Nevertheless, a Patton attack days before a planned German Ardennes offensive would have created a very different environment in which the campaign would have taken place. It might have completely derailed the German offensive and shifted its focus southward, or it might have led to a more complex battle, spread from the Ardennes down to the Saar.

A third scenario revolves around the Allied intelligence mistake which failed to anticipate the Ardennes offensive. It is not even necessary to suggest that the Germans might have blundered and broadcast a radio message that was intercepted and decoded by the Ultra system. A perfectly plausible scenario would have been that Hodges' G-2, Benjamin Dickson, concurred with Patton's G-2, Oscar Koch, that the evidence pointed to a near-term German action. In one of the sadder bits of intelligence history, Dickson had been right about German intentions at Kasserine Pass in February 1943 but had been ignored, while he was wrong about the Ardennes in December 1944 but widely believed. Two likely outcomes can be sketched on the presumption of Allied anticipation of the Ardennes offensive. Operation *Nordwind* provides a model for the passive option. Under this scenario, First Army would have scraped together reserves from other sectors and reinforced the weakest portions of the Ardennes front. While the sheer size of the German attack force probably would have resulted in some local penetrations of the front, the main attacks would have been blunted, and US reserves would have been in place to counterattack the penetrations. Under this scenario, the German attack would have fizzled out. Yet was this an ideal outcome for the US Army? Taking this scenario one step further, it can certainly be argued that a quick failure of the Ardennes offensive would have left the Wehrmacht in the west in a stronger position to resist Allied offensive operations in February–March 1945. The decimation of the Wehrmacht in the Ardennes was a major factor in the rapidity of the Allied advance in 1945.

A possible variation on this scenario is a combination of the Operation *Tink*/intelligence success alternatives. Instead of a passive response to the anticipated German Ardennes offensive, what about an offensive response in the form of a spoiling attack? Under this scenario, Patton's Third Army is held in check until the Wehrmacht stages its Ardennes attack, and then

Patton's Third Army is unleashed in its Operation *Tink* offensive, pushing behind Army Group B. If the commanders had been reversed, and the more experienced German Russian front veterans were in charge of the US Army, this seems like a very plausible operational alternative. This particular scenario was a major concern for German planners and reflected their own preference for operational boldness. It was not very plausible given Eisenhower and Bradley's cautious operational style.

Finally, are there any scenarios that would have enhanced the German chances for success? The German options were quite limited due to the shortage of resources, so some other alternative would have been needed. The most plausible would have been a fortuitous change in weather. The main problem facing the Wehrmacht in the critical first few days of the attack was the soggy ground. The autumn of 1944 had been unusually rainy, and hard winter had not yet arrived. As a result, German Panzer columns were obliged to stick to the roads, and small villages along the frontier such as Krinkelt-Rocherath and St. Vith became fortified roadblocks. What was needed was a premature frost that would have hardened the ground in the first few days as occurred later on December 22.

The arrival of the Russian high-pressure weather system on December 22 hardened the roads, but it also brought along clear weather. Clear weather made the Panzer columns more vulnerable to Allied air attack. So a shift of weather patterns by a few days would not have guaranteed any tactical advantage. The only way the Panzer columns would have been given an advantage would have been a premature winter in the Ardennes with a hard frost early in December followed by weeks of overcast weather to keep away the dreaded Allied fighter-bombers. Unfortunately for the Wehrmacht, weather cannot be ordered from the heavens. Furthermore, the Allied disruption of German forward weather reporting stations in the Atlantic undermined the Wehrmacht's ability to do accurate weather forecasting. This scenario highlights the fragility of the German planning and its dependence on a concurrence of several lucky events to increase its chance of success.

THE BATTLEFIELD TODAY

The Battle of the Bulge devastated the small towns in the Ardennes, and much has been rebuilt since the war. Nevertheless, rural communities such as these do not change quickly, and though the roads are much better than they were in 1944, the terrain features are much the same. Some of the wooded areas have changed little, and there is still evidence of the trenches and dugouts from the fighting. A set of good road maps is an absolute must, as it is easy to get lost in the maze of small roads.

The National Military History Museum in Diekirch, Luxembourg has an excellent collection of artifacts of the Battle of the Bulge including this RSO Raupenschlepper Ost tractor, typically used to tow artillery such as the 105mm field howitzer. (Author)

The town of Bastogne is ringed with the turrets of US Sherman tanks knocked out during the fighting which indicate the perimeter of the American defenses. This is a turret from an M4A3(76mm) of the 10th Armored Division. (Author)

A road trip from Lanzerath to La Gleize takes only a few hours, and highlights why Kampfgruppe Peiper had such a hard time reaching the Meuse. There are numerous monuments to the fighting scattered around the Ardennes, notably the Malmédy massacre memorial at the Baugnez crossroads, and many museums catering to the tourist trade. The December 1944 Historical Museum located near the church in La Gleize is one of the best in the area, with a very good selection of artifacts and historical photos and it is located in the midst of the battlefield where Kampfgruppe Peiper made its last stand. One of the more intriguing museums is the Ardennen Poteau '44 Collection of Jacqueline and Rob de Ruyter, which is located on the site where many of the famous German wartime photos were taken. This museum includes a vehicle collection, and tours of the battlefield are offered from the back of an OT-810 half-track modified to resemble its wartime antecedent, the German SdKfz 251 Ausf. D.

Having been made famous by the battle, Bastogne commemorates the fighting with many memorials and several museums. The city is ringed with US Sherman turrets destroyed during the fighting, and placed on stone pedestals to mark the outer boundaries of the defenses in 1944. In McAuliffe Square in the center of town sits an M4 tank, *Barracuda*, of the 41st Tank

Sitting in McAuliffe Square in Bastogne is this M4 tank. Although it carries the markings of the 4th Armored Division, the hull is actually that of an 11th Armored Division tank knocked out during the fighting, mated with a turret from another knocked-out Sherman. (Author)

Battalion, 11th Armored Division, knocked out on December 30, 1944 near Rechimont, and recovered after the war. The Bastogne Historical Center outside town is one of the best of the many Battle of the Bulge museums and has an exceptional collection of uniforms and equipment. There are many tanks and other items of equipment scattered around this section of Belgium, in mute testimony to the battle. A trip to neighboring Luxembourg is also highly recommended, although its present-day scenic beauty belies the difficulties faced by the soldiers fighting there in the winter of 1944–45. The National Military History Museum in Diekirch is devoted to the Battle of the Bulge, and has an excellent collection of vehicles, equipment, and uniforms.

GLOSSARY

6th Army Group	Devers' field command including Seventh US Army and First French Army
12th Army Group	Bradley's field command including First, Third, and Ninth US armies
21st Army Group	Montgomery's field command including Second British and First Canadian armies
AFV	Armored fighting vehicle
Army	Formation consisting of several corps; also called field army
Army group	Formation consisting of several armies
Army Group B	Model's army group including the 5th and 6th Panzer armies and 7th Army
Assault gun	Armored vehicle used to provide fire support
CC	Combat command of a US armored division; CCA, CCB, or CCR
Co.	Company
Corps	Formation consisting of several divisions
ETO	European Theater of Operations
G-2	Intelligence section in a higher US headquarters
GMC	Gun motor carriage; most often a US tank destroyer
HMC	Howitzer motor carriage: US self-propelled howitzer
Jabo	American fighter-bomber
Jagdpanzer	German tank destroyer

Kampfgruppe	Battle Group
OKW	Oberkommando Wehrmacht; German Armed Force High Command
PzKpfw	Panzerkampfwagen, German tank
Panzerjäger	German tank destroyer
RAF	Royal Air Force
SdKfz	Sonderkraftfahrzeug; Special (military) vehicle
SHAEF	Supreme Headquarters Allied Expeditionary Force; Eisenhower's HQ
SPzSpWg	Schwere panzerspahwagen (heavy armored car)
StuG	Sturmgeschütz, German assault gun
TAC	Tactical Air Command
TAF	Tactical Air Force
Task Force	Sub-formation of a US combat command
USAAF	US Army Air Force
VGD	Volksgrenadier Division

For brevity, the traditional conventions have been used when referring to units. In the case of US units, 1/179th Infantry refers to the 1st Battalion, 179th Infantry Regiment. D/37th Tank Battalion refers to Company D, 37th Tank Battalion. The US Army traditionally uses Arabic numerals for divisions and smaller independent formations (70th Division, 781st Tank Battalion), Roman numerals for corps (VI Corps), spelled numbers for field armies (Seventh Army) and Arabic numerals for army groups (12th Army Group).

In the case of German units, the abbreviated regimental numbering system differs from US/British practise in appearing as a suffix rather than prefix, so GR.77 is the 77th Grenadier Regiment; however, for purposes of consistency, German units have been presented in the same style as US units.

FURTHER READING

Due to its importance, the Battle of the Bulge has been the subject of hundreds of books, especially from the American perspective. In spite of its importance in the early failure of the German offensive, the northern sector has received far less treatment than Bastogne and the southern sector. The defense of Bastogne has been the focus of a disproportionate share of the books, not only because of the drama of the story, but also owing to the tendency of official histories to pay special attention to the units remaining under Bradley's control and less to those units under Montgomery. There are numerous divisional histories of the units fighting in the Ardennes, and Battery Press has reprinted many of the best of the US division histories including the superb 101st Airborne history *Rendezvous with Destiny* and other useful accounts such as the 28th Division history. These are not listed here due to their sheer number.

This book was heavily based on unpublished material as well. The best perspective on the German side is provided by the scores of interviews conducted with nearly all the senior German commanders by the US Army after the war as part of the Foreign Military Studies effort. Copies of these are available at several locations including the US Army Military History Institute at Carlisle Barracks, Pennsylvania, and the US National Archives and Records Administration (NARA) in College Park, Maryland. Some of these have been reprinted in two books edited by Danny Parker listed below, as well as the Steinhardt compilation on the Panzer Lehr Division. The FMS studies vary considerably in length; the earlier ETHINT series generally are brief transcripts of interrogations while the later A, B, and C series are more detailed. The Schramm account is particularly worthy of note since it is essentially the OKW war diary. US unit after-action reports are located at NARA in Record Group 407 and a variety of these were consulted for this book. The US Army Military History Institute has an extensive collection of interviews with senior US commanders, and the several interviews conducted after the war with General Bruce Clarke are particularly illuminating about the fighting for St. Vith.

Aside from data in the various studies, statistical data on the battle comes from a number of sources including *Ardennes Campaign Statistics: 16 December 1944–19 January 1945* prepared by Royce Thompson (Office of the Chief of Military History, 1952). In addition, during the early 1990s, the US Army Concept Analysis Agency commissioned the creation of a very large statistical database on the campaign to test its computerized Stochastic Concepts Evaluation Model, a computer war simulation program. This database was based on extensive archival research and provides day-by-day data on personnel, casualties, and weapons strength on both sides.

ARMY REPORTS AND STUDIES

n/a, *The Seventh Armored Division in the Battle of St. Vith* (7th AD Association: 1946)

n/a, *After Action Report of the 14th Cavalry Group (Mecz): Ardennes 16–24 Dec 1944*

Armored School, *Armor at Bastogne* (May 1949)

Armored School, *Armor under Adverse Conditions: 2nd and 3rd Armored Divisions in the Ardennes Campaign* (1949)

Armored School, *The Defense of St. Vith, Belgium 17–23 December 1944, A Historical Example of Armor in the Defense* (1948)

Armored School, *2nd Armored Division in the Ardennes* (1948)

Army Concepts Analysis Agency, *Ardennes Campaign Data Base* (1995)

Canadian Army Headquarters Historical Section, *The Campaign in North-West Europe: Information from German Sources, Higher Direction of Operations from Falaise Debacle to Ardennes Offensive 20 August–16 December 1944* (March 1958)

Cole, Hugh M., *The Ardennes: Battle of the Bulge* (OCMH: 1965)

Combat Studies Institute, *The Battle of St. Vith* (Battlebook 4-A, 1984)

First US Army, *After-Action Report: First US Army* (1945)

V Corps, *V Corps Operations in the ETO: 6 January 1942–9 May 1945* (1945)

Fontenot, Gregory, *The Lucky Seventh in the Bulge: A Case Study for the Airland Battle* (Command and General Staff School: 1985)

HQ ETO AFV & W Section, *Daily Tank Status June 1944–May 1945*

Third US Army, *After-Action Report: Third US Army, 1 August 1944–9 May 1945* (2 volumes, 1945)

Thompson, Royce, *Tank Fight of Rocherath-Krinkelt 17–19 December 1944* (OCMH: 1952)

Thompson, Royce, *Dom Bütgenbach Action, 26th Inf. (1st Div.) 19–22 December 44* (OCMH: 1952)

12th Army Group, *Report of Operations (final after action report) 12th Army Group (1945)*

US ARMY FOREIGN MILITARY STUDIES, OFFICE CHIEF OF MILITARY HISTORY

Bayerlein, Fritz, *Panzer Lehr Division: 1 Dec 44–26 Jan 45* (A-941)

Bayerlein, Fritz, *Pz Lehr Div and 26 Volks Gren Div in the Ardennes* (ETHINT 68)

Denkert, Walter, *Commitment of the 3rd Panzer Grenadier Division during the Ardennes Offensive* (A-978)

Diebig, Wilhelm, *277 Volks Grenadier Division Nov 44–Jan 45* (B-273)

Dingler, Hans-Jürgen, *LVIII Panzer Corps: Ardennes Offensive* (A-955)

Engel, Gerhard, *12th Volks Grenadier Division: 3–29 Dec 1944* (B-733)

Kokott, Heinz, *Breakthrough to Bastogne* (ETHINT 44)

Kraas, Hugo, *12th SS Panzer Division: 15 November–15 December 1944* (B-522)

Krüger, Walter, *Offensive in the Ardennes from 16 December to 2 February 1945* (B-321)

Lehmann, Rudolf, *I SS Panzer Corps: Ardennes, Special Questions* (A-926)

Lehmann, Rudolf, *The I SS Panzer Corps during the Ardennes Offensive* (B-779)

Lüttwitz, Heinrich, *The Assignment of the XLVII Panzer Corps in the Ardennes 1944–45* (A-939, A-940)

Peiper, Joachim, *1 SS Pz Regt (11–24 Dec 1944)* (ETHINT 10)

Peiper, Joachim, *Kampfgruppe Peiper: 15–26 December 1944* (C-004)

Preiss, Hermann, *Commitment of the I SS Panzer Corps during the Ardennes Offensive: 16 Dec 1944–25 Jan 1945* (A-877)

Remer, Otto, *Führer Begleit Brigade: Nov 44–12 Jan 45* (B-592)

Remer, Otto, *Führer Begleit Brigade in the Ardennes* (ETHINT 80)

Schramm, Percy, *The German Wehrmacht in the Last Days of the War: 1 January–1 May 1945* (C-020)

Skorzeny, Otto, *Ardennes Offensive* (ETHINT 12)

Staudinger, Walter, *Sixth Panzer Army Artillery in the Ardennes Offensive* (ETHINT 62)

Stumpff, Horst, *Tank Maintenance in the Ardennes Offensive* (ETHINT 61)

Von der Heydte, Karl, *German Paratroops in the Ardennes* (ETHINT 75)

Von Manteuffel, Hasso, *Fifth Panzer Army: Ardennes Offensive Preparations* (B-151)

Von Manteuffel, Hasso, *Fifth Panzer Army: Ardennes Offensive 16 Dec–25 Feb 45* (B-151a)

Von Waldenburg, Siegfried, *Commitment of the 116th Panzer Division in the Ardennes: 16–26 December 1944* (A-873)

Wagener, Carl, *The Main Reasons for the Failure of the Ardennes Offensive* (A-963)

Weiz, Rüdiger, *The 2nd Panzer Division in the Ardennes Offensive: Thrust on Dinant 21–26 Dec 1944* (B-456)

Westphal, Siegfried, *Planning the Ardennes Offensive* (ETHINT 79)

BOOKS

Breuer, William, *Bloody Clash at Sadzot: Hitler's Final Strike for Antwerp* (Zeus: 1981)

Castor, Henri, *La route des massacres* (De Krijger: 1999)

Cavanagh, William, *The Battle East of Elsenborn & the Twin Villages* (Pen & Sword: 2004)

Cavanagh, William, *Krinkelt-Rocherath: The Battle for the Twin Villages* (Christopher Publishing: 1986)

Cavanagh, William, *A Tour of the Bulge Battlefield* (Leo Cooper: 2001)

Cooke, David and Evans, Wayne, *Kampfgruppe Peiper: The Race for the Meuse* (Pen & Sword: 2005)

Craven, W. F. and Cate, J. L., *The Army Air Forces in World War II, Vol. III: Europe – Argument to V-E Day January 1944–May 1945* (University of Chicago: 1951)

De Meyer, Stefan, et al., *Duel in the Mist: The Leibstandarte during the Ardennes Offensive, Vol. 1* (AFV Publications: 2007)

Degive, Jacques, et al., *La véritable histoire du "Sherman" de place McAuliffe à Bastogne* (Cercle d'histoire de Bastogne: 1999)

Delvaux, Jean-Michel, *La bataille des Ardennes autour de Celles* (Self-published: 2003)

Doherty, J. C., *The Shock of War* (Vert Milon: 1997)

Dugdale, J., *Panzer Divisions, Panzer Grenadier Divisions, Panzer Brigades of the Army and Waffen SS in the West: Ardennes and Nordwind, Their Detailed and Precise Strengths and Organizations (Vol. I, Part 1: September 1944; Part 2: October 1944; Part 3: November 1944; Part 4A, 4B, 4C: December 1944)* (Military Press: 2000–05)

Dupuy, Ernest, *St. Vith: Lion in the Way* (Infantry Journal: 1949; also Battery Press reprint).

Eisenhower, John S., *The Bitter Woods: The Battle of the Bulge* (G. P. Putnam: 1969)

English, John, *Patton's Peers: The Forgotten Allied Field Army Commanders of the Western Front 1944–45* (Stackpole: 2009)

Forty, George, *The Reich's Last Gamble: The Ardennes Offensive, December 1944* (Cassell: 2000)

Gaul, Roland, *The Battle of the Bulge in Luxembourg* (Schiffer: 1995)

Grégoire, Gérard, *Les Panzers de Peiper face à l'US Army* (Chauveheid: 1986)

Guderian, Heinz Gunther, *From Normandy to the Ruhr* (Aberjona: 2001)

Hinsley, F. H., et al., *British Intelligence in the Second World War, Vol. 3, Part 2* (HMSO: 1988)

Hogan, David, *A Command Post at War: First Army HQ in Europe 1943–45* (CMH: 2000)

Jung, Hermann, *Die Ardennen-Offensive 1944/45* (Musterschmidt: 1971)

Kershaw, Alex, *The Longest Winter: The Battle of the Bulge and the Epic Story of WWII's Most Decorated Platoon* (De Capo: 2004)

Koch, Oscar, *G-2: Intelligence for Patton* (Schiffer: 1999)

Koskimaki, George, *The Battered Bastards of Bastogne* (Casemate: 2003)

McDonald, Robert, *The Hotton Report* (Finbar: 2006)

McManus, John, *Alamo in the Ardennes* (Wiley & Sons: 2007)

Macdonald, Charles, *Company Commander* (Burford Books: 1947, 1999)

Manrho, John and Putz, Ron, *Bodenplatte: The Luftwaffe's Last Hope* (Hikoki: 2004)

Marshall, S. L. A., *Bastogne: The First Eight Days* (Infantry Journal 1946, 1988 GPO reprint)

Meyer, Hubert, *The History of the 12.SS-Panzerdivison Hitlerjugend* (Federowicz: 1994)

Mierzejewski, Alfred, *The Collapse of the German War Economy 1944–1945: Allied Air Power and the German National Railway* (University of North Carolina: 1988)

Morelock, J. D., *Generals of the Ardennes: American Leadership in the Battle of the Bulge* (National Defense University: 1994)

Neill, George, *Infantry Soldier: Holding the Line in the Battle of the Bulge* (University of Oklahoma: 2000)

Nollomont, Charles, *Ardennes '44–'45: Résumé des opérations militaires dans la région de La Roche-en-Ardenne* (Commune de La Roche-en-Ardenne: 1995)

Pallud, Jean Paul, *Battle of the Bulge: Then and Now* (After the Battle: 1984)

Parker, Danny (ed.), *The Battle of the Bulge: The German View, Perspectives from Hitler's High Command* (Greenhill: 1999)

Parker, Danny (ed.), *Hitler's Ardennes Offensive: The German View of the Battle of the Bulge* (Greenhill: 1997)

Parker, Danny, *To Win the Winter Sky* (Combined Publishing: 1994)

Pergrin, David, *Engineering the Victory: The Battle of the Bulge* (Schiffer: 1996)

Phillips, Robert, *To Save Bastogne* (Stein and Day: 1983)

Quarrie, Bruce, *The Ardennes Offensive: VI Panzer Armee*, Order of Battle 4 (Osprey: 1999)

Quarrie, Bruce, *The Ardennes Offensive: V Corps & XVIII US Airborne Corps*, Order of Battle 5 (Osprey: 1999)

Quarrie, Bruce, *The Ardennes Offensive: V Panzer Armee*, Order of Battle 8 (Osprey: 2000)

Quarrie, Bruce, *The Ardennes Offensive: US VII & VIII Corps and British 30 Corps*, Order of Battle 9 (Osprey: 2000)

Quarrie, Bruce, *The Ardennes Offensive: I Armée & VII Armee*, Order of Battle 12 (Osprey: 2001)

Quarrie, Bruce, *The Ardennes Offensive: US III & XII Corps*, Order of Battle 13 (Osprey: 2001)

Reynolds, Michael, *The Devil's Adjutant* (Sarpendon: 1995)

Reynolds, Michael, *Men of Steel: I SS Panzer Corps* (Sarpendon: 1999)
This presents a German perspective on the fighting.

Reynolds, Michael, *Sons of the Reich: II SS Panzer Corps* (Casemate: 2002)

Ritgen, Helmut, *The Western Front 1944: Memoirs of a Panzer Lehr Officer* (Federowicz: 1995)

Rush, Robert, *Hell in the Hürtgen* (University of Kansas: 2001)

Rusiecki, Stephen, *The Key to the Bulge: The Battle for Losheimergraben* (Praeger: 1996)

de la Saulx, Christian, *La bataille des Ardennes* (CRIBA: 2001)

Steinhardt, Frederick (ed.), *Panzer Lehr Division 1944–45* (Helion: 2008)

Taghon, Peter, et al., *La bataille d'Ardenne: L'ultime blitzkrieg de Hitler* (Racine: 1994)

Tiemann, Ralf, *The Leibstandarte Volume IV/2* (Federowicz: 1998)

Vannoy, A. and Karamales, J., *Against the Panzers: US Infantry vs. German Tanks 1944–45* (McFarland: 1996)

Westemeier, Jens, *Joachim Peiper: A Biography of Himmler's SS Command* (Schiffer: 2007)

Wijers, Hans, *The Battle of the Bulge: The Losheim Gap – Doorway to the Meuse* (Brummen: 2001)

Wijers, Hans, *Hell at Bütgenbach: "We fight and die here"* (Self-published: 2004)

Wijers, Hans, *Holding the Line: V Corps Stops the 1st SS Panzer Corps* (Self-published: 2003)

Winter, George, *Freineux and Lamormenil – The Ardennes* (Federowicz: 1990)

Winter, George, *Manhay, The Ardennes: Christmas 1944* (Federowicz: 1990)

Winton, Harold, *Corps Commanders of the Bulge* (University Press of Kansas: 2007)

INDEX

BELGIUM

Bertogne
Hardigny
Moville
Bourcy
Foy
Michamps
Adoncourt
Ombourcy
Sallo
Longvilly
Oberwampach
Hardigny
Moinet
Monty
Monaville St. Menne
Lucery
Niederwampach
Houffaze
Bastogne
Senonchamps
Nette
Benonchamps
Wardin
Chenogne
Villeroux
Brus
SITE CARAWAY
Morhet
Assenois
Remoiville
Lutrebois
Clochimont
Forchamps
Hompré
Hubermont
Harlange
Remichampagne
Villers La
Bonne Eau
Cobreville Remoiville
Sainlez
Livarchamps
Hollange
Sure
Bavigne
Boulaide
Tintange